THE LIMOUSINE LIBERAL

THE LIMOUSINE LIBERAL

HOW AN INCENDIARY IMAGE UNITED
THE RIGHT AND FRACTURED AMERICA

STEVE FRASER

BASIC BOOKS
A Member of the Perseus Books Group
New York

Published by Basic Books,
A Member of the Perseus Books Group

Books published by Basic Books are available at special discounts for bulk purchases in the United States by corporations, institutions, and other organizations. For more information, please contact the Special Markets Department at the Perseus Books Group, 2300 Chestnut Street, Suite 200, Philadelphia, PA 19103, or call (800) 810-4145, ext. 5000, or e-mail special.markets@perseusbooks.com.

Designed by Trish Wilkinson
Set in 10.5-point Sabon LT Std

Library of Congress Cataloging-in-Publication Data

Names: Fraser, Steve, 1945– author.
Title: The limousine liberal : how an incendiary image united the right and
    fractured America / Steve Fraser.
Description: New York : Basic Books, 2016.
Identifiers: LCCN 2015045391 (print) | LCCN 2015047652 (ebook) |
    ISBN 9780465055661 (hardback) | ISBN 9780465097661 (ebook)
Subjects: LCSH: Liberalism—United States—History. | Political culture—
    United States—History. | Right and left (Political science—United
    States—History. | BISAC: POLITICAL SCIENCE / Political Ideologies /
    Conservatism & Liberalism.
Classification: LCC JC574.2.U6 F73 2016 (print) | LCC JC574.2.U6
    (ebook) |
DDC 320.51/30973—dc23
LC record available at http://lccn.loc.gov/2015045391

10 9 8 7 6 5 4 3 2 1

To Jill, Max, Emma, Elena, Jon, and Marco

Contents

Introduction

Limousine liberalism is the specter haunting American politics. That has been true and getting truer for the last half century. Nowadays, Hillary Clinton serves as "exhibit A" of this menace.

She's an odd choice in some ways. As the metaphor vividly suggests, a thoroughbred limousine liberal should be to the manner born, a patrician of outsized wealth, socially connected, credentialed by the toniest prep schools and the Ivy League, raised to rule, who for reasons sometimes sinister and sometimes of excessive credulity has gone over to the dark side: a limousine liberal is history's oxymoron, an elitist for revolution, working to undermine the ancient regime—or at least pretending to do so. Hillary Clinton was bred instead in far more modest circumstances. Her father owned a small fabric store outside Chicago. He ran a conservative home, demanding strict devotion to the frugality and work ethic of the respectable middle class. His daughter was politically precocious and had views congruent with her upbringing. Already by age thirteen she was out canvassing for Richard Nixon's election in 1960. Four years later she volunteered for the Goldwater campaign, inspired by the fervent anticommunism of her favorite high school history teacher.

Then everything changed. She went off to Wellesley College and there encountered the civil rights movement, antiwar outrage, and the iconoclasm of the counterculture. The rest is history. While immersed in the antiestablishment upheaval of that era, however, she kept her eye fixed on the political mainstream. Now she and her husband preside over the Democratic Party, cultivate their connections to leading centers of global business and finance, and are worth multiple millions. Yet well before she announced her latest run for the presidency, she was being vilified for crying crocodile tears on behalf of the poor while pocketing mega-sums for her State Department memoirs. She might claim to like beer with a booze chaser, but she really prefers zinfandel. She flirts with rural folk, but she actually thinks of them as hicks, rubes, and rednecks.

Hillary Clinton has become, in the eyes of right-wing populists, the quintessential limousine liberal hypocrite. All the Tea Party favorite sons—Ted Cruz, Marco Rubio, Rick Santorum, Rand Paul, Scott Walker—are long practiced in the art of limousine-liberal baiting. Tea Party bloggers tirelessly point out that Clinton might talk about sharing prosperity, make impassioned pleas for greater equality, but really means "that she will share YOUR prosperity and shared responsibility. . . . [T]hose of [you] who work hard will bear the burden of responsibility." They calculate that husband Bill is worth $80 million and that Hillary controls $20 million, and note that their daughter Chelsea wedded a hedge fund operator who once worked for Goldman Sachs. "Money. Power. That's what the Clintons are about. . . . You'll notice that it's always the super-rich who rage on about the need to share wealth, but they never, ever do. We've had enough hypocrisy over the last five years to last a lifetime."

When Clinton finally ended the nonsuspense surrounding her 2016 presidential candidacy, the indictment grew fiercer. Right-wing pundit Charles Krauthammer noted that "there's something surreal about Hillary Clinton's Marie Antoinette tour of sampling cakes and commons." Along with many others, Krauthammer found her so stage-managed and packaged, even beyond the normal artificial confections that pass for politicians these days, that he asked, "Who can really believe she suddenly has been seized with a new passion to champion, as she put it in Iowa, 'the truckers I saw on I-80 as I was driving here'?" Trying to position herself as a "champion of the little guy" was no easy sell "when you and your husband have for the last 25 years made a limo-liberal-Davos-world your home."

While Tea Party partisans and conservative journalists have most aggressively deployed the limousine liberal stigma, others find it apt as well. Mainstream media outlet Bloomberg Politics reported that "Hillary Clinton the Populist Begins Courting the Plutocrats." In a cynical age like the current one, everyone acknowledges the hypocrisy but most accept it as a form of realpolitik. Some are more put off. A left-wing journalist greeted the candidate's newly discovered antipathy toward Wall Street with a gimlet eye. He observed that the Donald Trump "zeitgeist" had become infectious; that Hillary was pumping for money and with great success from the financial sector; that the Clinton Foundation had harvested $5 million from nine financial institutions that avoided prosecution for financial transgressions; and that a key campaign aide was an ex–Goldman Sachs executive.

From the other shore, Republicans who might otherwise shy away from too close an association with Tea Party zealots nevertheless are on guard against this loathsome enemy from the elite left. So, for example, when Bernie Sanders, the Vermont via Brooklyn socialist senator and rival of Hillary's for the 2016 presidential nomination, spoke in Arlington, Virginia, in July 2015, the Young Republicans rallied in opposition. Observing that Sanders was speaking to "one of the most affluent liberal communities in the nation," these ideologues of the free market and limited government caustically advised: "We certainly hope he encourages Arlington limousine liberals and 'Mercedes Marxists' to practice what they preach by pulling out their checkbooks and writing checks to Uncle Sam during his presentation."[1]

That neither Clinton nor Sanders hail from pedigreed zip codes is suggestive. Especially over the last half century you need not have grown up on the Upper East Side of New York, graduated Harvard Law, run a major corporation or bank, captained a leading metropolitan newspaper or national magazine, architected American foreign policy, and at the same time made common cause with those determined to overturn the country's economic and racial status quo to get certified as a limousine liberal. How and why the social boundaries of that tribe have become so elastic is a story about the political and moral gridlock, the paralyzing cultural and ideological wars that have left Washington so dysfunctional. That drama unfolds in the pages that follow. Here it is worth noting that had there been a Bloomberg Politics in 1936 commenting on FDR's re-election campaign, its headline might have reversed the one about Clinton and said instead, "Franklin Roosevelt Plutocrat Begins Courting the Populists."

Nowadays, the limousine liberal congregation is more promiscuous. It embraces insiders and outliers. When Al Gore hopscotches the globe in his private jet, stopping off here and there to declaim against global warming, or when he comes home to his Tennessee mansion with its outsized carbon footprint, he exposes himself as a limousine liberal, a hypocritical, "dyed-in-the-wool elitist" who can talk the talk but not walk the walk. Or so his critics say. Gore is "old money" compared to the consummately ambitious and nouveau riche liability lawyer John Edwards, whose sins were picturesque, more about lifestyle than abuse of power. Before Edwards descended into his own private purgatory, when he still was imagining himself a populist president, his notorious $400 haircut marked him as someone who "lectures about poverty while living in gated opulence," a bona fide limousine liberal.

During the 2010 campaign for the Senate in Massachusetts, the incumbent Republican Mike Scott, seen everywhere in his pickup truck, tried to discredit his challenger Elizabeth Warren, the alleged scourge of Wall Street, by noting that she would likely feel more comfortable in a limousine. She could afford it, the senator suggested, thanks to her legal defense of consumer predators like Travelers Insurance seeking immunity from asbestos-related lawsuits or like LTV Steel in its attempt to shed liability for its retired coal miners' health fund. In this particular race, the pickup truck lost out to the limousine. But pinioning Warren for living in a $5 million home and compiling a stock portfolio worth $8 million while lecturing her fellow members of Congress that they ought to make it against the law for elected officials to own stock remains a Tea Party pastime. Master of the ad hominem generalization, Rush Limbaugh, channeling the late senator Joseph McCarthy, tirelessly evinces his contempt for the "striped pants crowd up in Foggy Bottom." Even newly elected mayor of New York City Bill de Blasio had barely assumed office when he was scorched for being one of those political fakers because his police entourage was caught speeding, ignoring His Honor's widely reported pledge to reduce traffic mayhem in the city.[2]

Nor is the epithet confined to politicians. Over the course of its strange career, *limousine liberalism* has become a signifier about lifestyle, about the affectations and disingenuousness of worlds orbiting light years away from the center of the political solar system. Here know-it-all moral superiority communes with a tone-deaf social isolation. Ben Affleck is but one among a horde of Hollywood celebrities accused of "feel-good limousine liberalism." In Affleck's case, he opened himself to this ridicule when he announced he was enlisting in the war on poverty in eastern Congo by living on $1.50 a day for a short while. A popular right-wing website made fun of actress Gwyneth Paltrow for her moral grandstanding when she announced she would spend a week living on a food stamp budget. Describing her as the "wealthy Obama-adoring member of the holier-than-thou Hollywood left," the site included a picture of packaged vegetables and beans that can be bought through the Supplemental Nutrition Assistance Program (SNAP) and suggested that the real "SNAP challenge" should "instead be focused on how to get people away from needing government assistance in the first place." Oprah, Bono, Stephen Spielberg, Martin Sheen, Barbra Streisand, and George Clooney, among other high visibility multimillionaire (in Oprah's case multibillionaire) entertainers are excoriated for the same conspicuously empty moralizing and self-righteous gesturing. Arianna Huffington, who perhaps best captures the sense of that neologism "the glitterati," was characterized early in the new millennium as the "queen bee" of the West Coast's branch of the limousine liberal tree. According to her detractors she decries great wealth while zoning out in her multimillion dollar Brentwood home, which she drives to in her Toyota hybrid (having ditched the fossil fuel guzzling SUV Lincoln Navigator she used to travel around in). For one critic, she epitomizes La Rochefoucauld's famous bon mot, "Hypocrisy is the homage vice pays to virtue."[3]

Far less likely suspects also get caught up in the limousine liberal dragnet. Jamie Dimon, who runs JPMorgan Chase, and Lloyd Blankfein, who does the same for Goldman Sachs, poured a lot of money into Barack Obama's first campaign for president. When later on they were affronted by the president's occasional unkind words directed at "the Street" and by the threat of more rigorous regulation of the financial system, they were reminded that they (and others in the banking and hedge fund community) were getting what they deserved for indulging their "limousine liberal dream." Even before the Obama era, a leading conservative pundit made fun of Goldman Sachs's claim that it was in the forefront of the environmental movement because it sent its bankers home at night in hybrid limousines, something this writer characterized as the "eco-pretensions of the rich and the stupefying gullibility with which they are received." Son of a postal clerk, Blankfein has gone on the record against inequality, observing that "too much of the gross domestic product over the last generation has gone to too few of the people." He ought to know. But he may also worry about the looming threat to social peace and economic growth this grotesque maldistribution may eventually entail. Others belonging to the same high-rent precincts as the Goldman chairman are less ambivalent about their reformist inclinations. Billionaire currency speculator George Soros, champion of all things liberal from income redistribution to same sex marriage, for years has exemplified the case that capitalism breeds its own renegades.

Whole counties sometimes come in for censure, as did Westchester, New York. An article in Salon.com reported on how this nesting ground for the two-faced liberal had defied for years a federal court order to desegregate its housing. Towns like Scarsdale, Larchmont, Bedford, and Rye—where people like Soros, Martha Stewart, and Ralph Lauren, along with less well-known Wall Street bankers and hedge fund operators, have residences—kept putting off plans to desegregate, maintained exclusionary zoning protocols, and when compelled to act slotted low-income housing for neighborhoods that were overwhelmingly nonwhite.

Enclaves like Westchester crop up all over the country, but the homeland of the limousine liberal, according to those who track this elite's whereabouts, is concentrated on both coasts. They hail from Wall Street, Silicon Valley, and Hollywood. There supremely wealthy "feel-good" bicoastal liberals, who care nothing about "fly-over

America," who secretly hope the middling classes who populate the country's midsection would simply go away, live sheltered from the real world in gated houses, their kids in private schools. Meanwhile, they nourish a patronizing regard for the poorest of the poor, or as one commentator waggishly observed, they occupy James Cameron's polarized universe of "evil rich white people and noble blue poor people." Awash in white guilt, they genuflect before impassioned journalists like Ta-Nehisi Coates. He reminds them ceaselessly of their undeserved privileges and offers a kind of absolution because his work promises to "radicalize the establishment."

When it comes to matters of sex and marriage, orthodox social liberals are ready to overturn immemorial customs and institutions. They have no regard for constitutional principles, so they encourage discriminatory policies like affirmative action, violations of the second amendment right to bear arms, and trespasses of private property in their misguided zeal to rein in greenhouse gases and other pollutants. Some call them "gentry liberals" and "affluent winners in the era of globalization and the beneficiaries of the 'financialization' of the economy." Favored people they most certainly are. But in part for just that reason they are also the object of intense loathing.[4]

No political metaphor in recent American history—not even potent ones like *silent majority*—has enjoyed the longevity of *limousine liberal*. It remains part of the lingua franca of our political debates today. It has managed to mobilize an enduring politics of resentment directed against most of the major reforms of the last seventy-five years, everything from civil rights to women's liberation, from urban renewal to the war on poverty, from gay rights to the welfare state, from affirmative action to environmental regulation. It remains at the heart of an aggrieved sense felt by millions that they have been passed over—their material needs ignored, their cultural preferences treated with contempt—by a cluster of elites that run the country.

As an epithet, *limousine liberalism* has displayed a remarkable elasticity and richness. It mixes together hostility to the New Deal political and economic reforms of the 1930s with animosity aimed at the countercultural and racial reformations of the 1960s. That has proven to be a catalytic formula for inciting discontent. The social reach of the stigma associated with the limousine liberal has gradually expanded from upper class patricians like Franklin Delano Roosevelt to self-righteous middle class urban sophisticates. As a battle cry, "limousine liberalism" has mobilized the armies of a double counter-revolution, as if attempting to erase from the public record the two most tumultuous decades of the last century.

To have unhorsed liberalism as the country's regnant political practice and ideology is no mean accomplishment. A half century ago few would have thought that possible. There was opposition to that liberal consensus to be sure. But it was fragmented. An enterprising milieu of Sunbelt nouveau riche business people and professionals intensely disliked the all-too-liberal leadership of the Republican Party to which they nonetheless belonged. Barry Goldwater was their champion. In a social galaxy far, far away, the ethnic white working and lower middle classes of the urban Northeast, loyal Democrats, raged against the leadership of their own party, convinced it had betrayed their racial and economic well-being.

But family capitalism and racial populism did not inhabit the same political space, nor did they pursue the same objectives. Family capitalism, rooted in the proprietary pride, old-fashioned morality, and provincial customs of its patriarchs, chafed at the preeminence and political agnosticism of those faceless managerial bureaucrats running the nation's Fortune 500 and wielding so much influence over both major political parties. Yet middling sorts from the ethnic barrios of metropolitan America cared less about that than they did about how liberal elites dismissed every grievance voiced by the white working class as a form of disguised racism. No common language linked these two worlds of the discontented.

Limousine liberalism served as that bilingual translator. It is impossible to understand the perseverance and passion of right-wing populist politics in America without coming to grips with this metaphor, where it originated, how it evolved, why it persists, and where it may be taking us.

Limousine liberal is also a surpassingly bizarre metaphor. It turns all previously recorded history upside down.

Conventional wisdom has it that ruling elites are inherently conservative. There is a ton of historical evidence to support that supposition going back millennia. Why wouldn't there be? Aristocracies, oligarchies, and monarchies; feudal lords, slave owners, and sheiks; imperial overlords, Brahmin castes, and dynastic families; robber barons and Wall Street bankers—all spend their time defending the existing order of things, fending off angry insurgencies, building fortresses to preserve their ways of life and the social order over which they preside. That is to be expected. Yet in the face of what would seem to be a self-evident instinct to ward off serious social upheaval, to defend the status quo, the metaphor of the limousine liberal suggests just the opposite.

What do Glenn Beck, Henry Ford, Father Coughlin, Joseph McCarthy, Barry Goldwater, George Wallace, Spiro Agnew, Pat Buchanan, Louise Day Hicks, Phyllis Schlafly, and Sarah Palin have in common? They are or were all warriors in a peculiarly American version of the class struggle. A motley crew otherwise—a TV and radio shock jock, a Midwestern carmaker, a Detroit priest, an alcoholic senator from Wisconsin, a "maverick" senator from Arizona, a Southern demagogue, a dishonored and deposed vice president, a renegade presidential adviser, a lace-curtain Irish rabble-rouser from Boston, a champion of traditional housewifery from the heartland Midwest, and a moose-hunting ex-governor of Alaska—each in his or her own way took up arms against the ruling class composed of limousine liberals. For nearly a century now, a strain in American politics that has grown stronger and stronger with the passage of time has blamed a shifting array of elites with fostering profound transformations in the country's race and gender relations, in its moral values and religious life, in its attitudes about work and sexual behavior, in the role of government in everyday life, and in how the nation deals with the rest of the world. The limousine liberals are, in effect, charged with being covert subversives. They have put at risk the country's birthright as the homeland of liberty. And, as a matter of historical fact—or so their enemies would have it—they have largely succeeded, finding allies among the disaffected and deluded, sometimes among the most deprived, who have supplied the popular muscle for this revolution from above.

One reason the metaphor endures is that the limousine liberal is not pure paranoid fantasy, but has roots in economic, political, and cultural reality. The country's economic, social, and racial institutions have indeed undergone profound upheaval and reform, especially since the advent of the New Deal. The moral "certainties" that once were taken for granted have for a long time now been subject to serious amendment, some even overturned entirely. And there is no question that elite circles have played a decisive if not the sole role in making all this happen. The limousine liberal metaphor is compelling in helping to depict what's gone awry.

Limousine liberalism has described first this and then that elite. It provides a peculiarly configured map of the shifting terrain of power in twentieth- and twenty-first-century America. And, not surprisingly, it made its public debut during an especially fiery moment in our public life.

1

In the Beginning Was the Word

Most, if not all, limousine liberals are Democrats. Limousine liberalism functions as a political lightning rod, as a metaphor bearing such emotional force it polarizes the political universe. It freezes the system, locking it in place, rendering it inert. It defines beyond any doubt what is Republican and what is Democrat. So it is noteworthy that the original limousine liberal—the person to first suffer from the wound of that epithet—was a Republican. The metaphor—perhaps the most vivid one in the nation's political lexicon over the past half century—turns out to be nonpartisan.

Victorious in war and prosperous once again, postwar America seemed firmly committed to the New Deal political order that had rescued the country from the trauma of the Great Depression. That the government had an essential role to play in regulating the economy and assuring a modicum of social welfare was broadly accepted. Because it had given birth to that new way of organizing society, the Democratic Party enjoyed what seemed at the time to be an enduring legitimacy. Its life expectancy, however, turned out to be greatly exaggerated.

When the New Deal Order first began to fall apart at the seams during the political and social upheavals of the 1960s, a New York City political apparatchik from the Bronx named Mario Procaccino won the Democratic Party's nomination for mayor in 1969 after a nasty primary campaign. His foe, running on the Liberal Party line, was the sitting mayor, John Lindsay, once upon a time a Republican congressman representing the "silk-stocking district" (the wealthiest district in the nation, whose name derived from Teddy Roosevelt's day) on Manhattan's Upper East Side. In 1965 Lindsay had become the city's first Republican mayor since Fiorello LaGuardia. Procaccino coined the term *limousine liberal* to characterize what he and his largely white ethnic following from the "outer boroughs" considered the repellent hypocrisy of elitists like Lindsay: well-heeled types who championed the cause of the poor, especially the black poor, but who had no intention of bearing the costs of doing anything about their plight. They were, according to Procaccino, who was then the city's comptroller, insulated from any real contact with poverty, crime, and the everyday struggle to get by, living in their exclusive neighborhoods, sending their children to private prep schools, sheltering their capital gains and dividends from the tax man, and getting around town in limousines, not subway cars. Not about to change the way they lived, they wanted everybody else to change, to have their kids bused to school far from home, to shoulder the tax burden of an expanding welfare system, to watch the racial and social makeup of their neighborhoods turned upside down. These self-righteous folk couldn't care less, Procaccino proclaimed, about the "small shopkeeper, the homeowner. . . . They preach the politics of confrontation and condone violent upheaval."[1]

John Vliet Lindsay was in every way a perfect specimen of this odd political subspecies: to the manner born, but prepared to overturn the ancient regime. To begin with Lindsay looked the part; he was a lean, strikingly handsome six-foot-three WASP who could have modeled for a publication like *Gentlemen's Quarterly* or *Esquire*. Then there were his bloodlines: son of an international investment banker father who served as the president of the American Swiss Corporation, which was itself affiliated with Credit Suisse in Zurich. Lindsay's mother hailed from the higher reaches of seventeenth-century Anglo-Dutch New York. They were a Social Register household living on Park Avenue.

Their son was bred accordingly, attending the Buckley School in New York, then on from there to St. Paul's, the exclusive preparatory school in Concord, New Hampshire, which prepared him for Yale. There he rowed crew and was elected to Scroll and Key, not quite Skull and Bones, but nonetheless a young gentlemen's club of considerable social prestige. After a stint in the US Navy as a commissioned officer in World War II, where he saw action in Sicily and the Pacific, he resumed the life he was fated to lead: law school at Yale, which in turn launched him into adulthood at a white-shoe law firm (Webster, Sheffield, Fleishman, Hitchcock, and Chrystie). And he married well to a Vassar graduate (and distant relation of two presidents—William Henry and Benjamin Harrison) whom he met in Greenwich, Connecticut, at the wedding of the daughter of Senator Prescott Bush. The Lindsays settled down in New York, began a family, and attended St. James's Episcopal Church on Madison Avenue.

Credentials like those qualified Lindsay for an equally distinctive place in public life when that turned out to be what the young lawyer decided he wanted. From the outset, he displayed sympathies that past generations of men from his social station would usually have eschewed. He went to work for the Justice Department in the Eisenhower administration, where he helped craft the Civil Rights Act of 1957, a toothless piece of legislation but nonetheless a straw in the way the wind had begun to blow. Next he ran for Congress from the seventeenth district, the same silk-stocking district he grew up in, known for its genteel, patrician politics: conventional when it came to economic policy, leery of the messiness of urban mass politics, but in other ways quite forward-looking, favoring civil rights, civil liberties, and an internationalist foreign policy. This was the neighborhood of Nelson Rockefeller, Herbert Claiborne Pell, Jacob Javits, and Thomas Dewey, lions of what back then was the dominant wing of the Republican Party.

Lindsay was a younger iteration of this patrician type. He was even more open to the unorthodox political and cultural currents that had begun to course through the country when he defeated William vanden Heuvel, a Democrat but otherwise an exemplar of the same elite liberalism, to become the district's congressman in 1960. In office he endorsed all the reforms associated with Lyndon Johnson's "Great Society," including Medicare and the war on poverty, federal aid to education, the creation of a Department of Urban Affairs and the National Endowment for the Arts, immigration reform, and above all the dismantling of American apartheid. The latter included vigorous efforts to promote school desegregation, abolish the poll tax, decertify unions guilty of racial discrimination, and promote anti-lynching legislation and the Civil Rights and Voting Rights Acts of 1964 and 1965, respectively. The congressman even opposed the seating of the all-white Mississippi delegation to the 1964 Democratic Party convention in Atlantic City, a gesture without force since he was a Republican, but of some symbolic significance.

In that same fateful year and despite considerable pressure from Republican Party leaders, Lindsay refused to endorse Barry Goldwater for president. He was repelled by what the *New York Times* referred to as "Bastille Day in Reverse" led by "Cactus Jacobins" from the Republican Sunbelt, who had so rudely dismissed the presumptive limousine liberal favorite Nelson Rockefeller at the party's convention in San Francisco. Later, when ghetto riots and rebellions turned city after city into bloody theaters of racial mayhem, Lindsay was appointed vice chairman of the National Advisory Commission on Civil Disorders (generally known as the Kerner Commission after its chairman Otto Kerner, the governor of Illinois). Lindsay became its most vocal spokesman. The commission's investigations into what was happening and why concluded that white racism was to blame, a verdict that seemed at one and the same time both self-evident and an evasion.[2]

What really earned him Mario Procaccino's memorable bon mot, however, was the architecture of Lindsay's political ascension in New York and what he did with power once he had it. Lindsay constructed an odd coalition of those with too much and those with far too little. His Republicanism notwithstanding his appeal to the normally Democratic African American and Puerto Rican communities was substantial. He made plain his sympathies for civil rights activism and, once in office, deliberately circumvented the black political establishment, sometimes appointing street insurgents instead to positions in his administration. He championed, sometimes at great political risk, controversial reforms including a civilian police review board, low-income scatter-site housing, school decentralization, community control, and New York's version of the "Philadelphia Plan" to compel the construction unions to open their ranks to minority workers.[3]

"Power to the People" turned out to be strangely appealing to the people who already had power, or rather to a distinct subset of the privileged and especially the children of privilege who completed the circle of the mayor's limousine liberalism. On the night of Lindsay's first victory in 1965, the journalist Jack Newfield reported that the crowd celebrating at the candidate's headquarters had "Princeton and Radcliffe etched in their Scott Fitzgerald faces." Newfield had a point. From the outset, Lindsay was the favorite of a New York establishment that included John Hay (Jock) Whitney of the Whitney dynasty and owner of the *Herald Tribune,* David Rockefeller, John Loeb, Walter Thayer, Mrs. Winthrop Aldrich, Mrs. Vincent Astor, William Paley, Paul Warburg, Mrs. August Belmont, Harold Vanderbilt, Henry Ford II, Mr. and Mrs. Nicholas Biddle, General Lucius Clay, Christian Herter, and cultural celebrities like Sammy Davis Jr., Bennett Cerf, Liza Minnelli, James Earl Jones, Richard Rodgers, and Harold Prince, as well as top-draw, politically active philanthropies like the Ford Foundation. The chairman of the finance committee for Lindsay's reelection campaign in 1969 was Gustave Levy, who as the head of Goldman Sachs was ideally positioned to pull in Wall Street money.[4]

For its more senior figures, this was a world of genteel, cosmopolitan sophistication that honored a commitment to formal equality before the law and cultivated a sense of noblesse social responsibility for those less privileged, less gifted, less able. However, the passions unleashed by the social upheaval and mass mobilizations of the 1960s altered the valence of these political emotions. Appalled by the viciousness of the American racial order, whose ugliness became more and more intolerable with each new shooting, church burning, lynching, beating, and police riot, a younger cohort—some of them, like Lindsay, offspring of what by then was widely known as the establishment—had come to romanticize the ghetto activist as a liberator from the nation's peculiar form of domestic colonialism, just as it cheered on the guerrilla armies warring against Western imperialism around the world. The barrio might be dirt poor, but for just that reason it bred an outlier purity of moral purpose. A certain degree of patronizing was at work that the New York Times called "elegant slumming" and that Tom Wolfe skewered in New York magazine as "radical chic" in his description of a fund-raiser for the Black Panther Party hosted by Leonard Bernstein in his midtown Manhattan penthouse and attended by the city's "beautiful people." Whether condescending or self-deluded, this same milieu was far more comfortable with the politics of the barricades and with the currents of sexual liberation than were their more lawfully minded and morally conventional elders.[5]

Granting "power to the people," however, had its limits. It was not meant to apply to those among the hoi polloi who already had access to their own instruments of power. Both Lindsay administrations were marked by fierce confrontations with the city's muscular labor movement. Protracted strikes involving transit and sanitation workers, public school teachers, and bridge tenders, among others, heightened the general sense that no one was in control. This was especially so during the mayor's first administration, though less so during the second, by which time an uneasy peace prevailed. Lindsay's liberalism accepted organized labor as a fact of modern life, but treated it with none of the sympathy it exhibited for the marginalized poor. Nor did it feel at home having to share power; it preferred to bestow it with all the sense of dependency and gratitude such a gift implicitly entailed.

If the workplace was in chronic turmoil, so were the neighborhoods, or rather those outer borough habitats of the ethnically diverse, white working and lower middle classes. Here the impact of the limousine liberal penchant for social engineering, especially over matters of racial integration, was profoundly disruptive. Here the distinctive character of this strange new elitism was strikingly apparent: it sought to overturn not defend the old order of things. Indeed, Time noted that the mayor was the "self-righteous, abrasive enemy of the way things are."

Consequently, in the outer boroughs all the comforting familiarities of school, kinship, and residential customs were placed in jeopardy. Procaccino's run for mayor in 1969 was preceded by years of protest that promised to transform the racial makeup of lower-middle-class and working class neighborhoods like Ridgewood in Queens or Canarsie in Brooklyn by desegregating schools and breaking up ethnic job monopolies run by various craft unions. Urban renewal projects subsidized by the state and local governments paid little attention to established neighborhood configurations of parks, schools, commercial thoroughfares, and residential arrangements. Countermobilizations by community groups resisted these attempts to undermine the status quo. Conservative politicians and intellectuals, including the indubitably elitist William Buckley (founder of the *National Review* and himself a onetime candidate for mayor), had begun drawing support early in the decade from white lower-middle-class precincts that had traditionally leaned Democratic. Here accountants and clerks and teachers and shopkeepers clung to their vulnerable achievements as upwardly mobile, second generation immigrants. Moreover, the precariousness of their everyday lives grew more worrisome as the economy faltered, unemployment rose, and stagflation threatened the well-being and aspirations of working people who already felt threatened.[6]

None of this registered in the land of limousine liberalism. What limousine liberals conveyed instead was disdain for the parochialism, prejudice, and uncouthness of a world they found alien and unattractive. This grand canyon of class and cultural division kept widening. Whitney Young of the National Urban League called the people who gathered around the Procaccino campaign "affluent peasants," by which he meant they had some money but not much in the way of civilization. Lindsay's hostility to labor union types—the Police Benevolent Association, for example—often seemed about his feeling ill at ease among the Irish and Italians who policed the streets, put out the fires, ran the subways, and picked up the garbage.[7]

Caricatures of Procaccino and his *paesani* showed up everywhere during the 1969 race. The *New York Post* (then a decidedly liberal newspaper) mocked him as a stereotypical "ward heeler, so much so that many who demand a degree of dignity in a public figure find it hard to take him seriously." Reporters seemed obsessed with his "pencil thin mustache" (the telltale mark of an Italian wannabe). *Time* magazine ran a cover story that included a cartoon of the candidate leading an assault on the Bastille, which made sure to note the mustache plus his "electric blue suits and watermelon pink shirts." And the magazine informed its readers that the world where it was all right to dress and shave like that could be found in "the dreary reaches of the boroughs." A profile in *The New Yorker,* practically the house organ of limousine liberalism, derided the comptroller's mustache, his speech, the vulgarity of his supporters, and the sweat that poured off him at campaign stops. And it got nastier than that. According to one paper, "If you put Mario Procaccino in a white apron he could be hawking mackerel at the Fulton Fish Market." That market was widely thought of as Mafia controlled, which was the point, as was a comparison of the candidate's apparel to "George Raft suits."

Not so long before this these same white, lower class borough dwellers—Irish and Italian and German and even Jewish—modest in dress and demeanor, had been regarded as cultural heroes standing up to the fat cats, applauded for their everyman insouciance. Now they had become culturally disreputable, reactionary outlaws, decidedly unstylish in what they wore and drank and in how they played; they were looked on as lesser beings. Limousine liberalism in one scholar's view had "hardened into an orthodoxy of the privileged classes."

Mercilessly, the media took delight in Procaccino's penchant for malapropisms. Perhaps his most painfully embarrassing one also revealed the social deafness of the new liberalism. It signaled as well that right-wing populists like Procaccino and politicians in other cities were prepared to give as good as they were receiving when it came to social putdowns. In front of an African American audience, the candidate declared that "my heart is as black as yours." For some that was merely a lurid confirmation of his racism. (There is no evidence at all that he was a racist, and he had risen in rather ordinary fashion through the Democratic Party machine in the Bronx until elected comptroller.) Procaccino not only protested against being labeled a racist. He went on to explain what he was thinking: namely, that as the son of shoemaker from a small town near Naples in southern Italy, he was all too familiar with the insults and discriminations an

Anglo elite could direct toward anyone of the "wrong" ethnic background or complexion. Living in a racial twilight zone, called "guinea" and "wop," southern Italian immigrants were reminded again and again of their inferiority by Brahmin Americans like Senator Henry Cabot Lodge, who at the turn of the century welcomed northern Italians, or what he called "Teutonic Italians," because they were fair-skinned and industrious. But the senator had no use for "dark-skinned southerners," who were in his view lazy, emotionally volatile, and criminally minded.[8]

"My heart is as black as yours" was a clumsy attempt to connect. It failed miserably among African Americans. But it resonated in many of the white ethnic communities of the city that chafed at the stereotypes used by their social superiors to denigrate them. Italians were fed up with being depicted as swarthy garbage men with plastic pink flamingoes on their lawns or as barbers with a Madonna on the dashboard and plastic slipcovers on the living room furniture. Procaccino's campaign came to be defined largely by this class resentment.

Naturally he described himself as the "little guy for the little guy." This had always been a standard trope in the American political lexicon. But his barbs could be much more pointed than that. Addressing a gathering of cab drivers, he promised that "the day is coming when the working people will run this city again," alluding to the era of New Deal liberalism, which had won the hearts of working class New Yorkers. Now, however, this populist appeal emphasized the failure of governing elites to carry out their defining responsibility to ensure respect for law and the moral order. So the first item of business was to depose that peculiar new breed of liberal like Lindsay who was "a swinger in the city," that is to say an upper class, sexual libertine at odds with the moral and religious convictions of working class New Yorkers. A Procaccino campaign memo recommended an attack on the owners of the city's mainstream media, who were backing Lindsay because they were "rich super-assimilated people who live on Fifth Avenue and maintain some choice mansions outside the city and have no feeling for the small middle class shopkeeper, homeowner, etc. They preach the politics of confrontation and condone violent upheaval in society because they are not touched by it and are protected by their courtiers, doormen, and private police guards." Pursuing that strategy, the candidate drew an indelible line between his workaday following and what he called "the Manhattan arrangement," an alliance composed of intellectuals, editors, broadcasters, and big business. In addition to his frequent promises to re-establish "law and order," the comptroller campaigned for what today we would call a "stock transfer tax" to help fund the city's ballooning costs. Lindsay, the liberal with Wall Street connections, opposed it. A graduate of City College (and later Fordham Law School), Procaccino praised his alma mater, where he was president of the graduating class of 1935, and defended it against a plan to open up admissions (at all the city's municipal colleges) to all city residents without recourse to qualifying exams and grades. Open admissions, Procaccino and the plan's opponents claimed, would damage the integrity of an institution that for generations had functioned as the pathway to economic opportunity and social mobility for New York's working classes. It was one vital arena where a subordinate class could stand up against the pretensions of its betters: "City College is what New York is all about. It always had more heart than Harvard. It has always been more real than Yale. It has always had more purpose than Princeton. That school is the soul of our city." Inverting the scorn his enemies sent his way at every opportunity, Procaccino never tired of reminding people that "I am not one of the select few. I am not one of the Beautiful People." Not shy about drawing cultural comparisons with Lindsay and his world, he vented feelings felt by many of his constituents: "Yes, we have different cultures; yes, we have different customs . . . we aren't sick, we don't have to be remade in Lindsay's image." On the contrary, Procaccino and his constituents were entirely ordinary people trying to get by: "I'll tell you who the average man is. He's the guy who works hard all day and maybe comes home at night too tired to move, but he has to moonlight anyway to pay his bills. . . . He doesn't have a doorman. His kids go to public schools. He rides the subway and the buses. He never burned his draft card or a flag and he never will. He tries to play the game by the rules, and for all that he's getting pushed into a corner. That's who the average man is."

All of this registered emotionally in the ethnic working and lower-middle-class enclaves outside of Manhattan. "The rich liberals, they look down on my little piece of the American dream, my little back yard with the barbeque here," said one Procaccino supporter, voicing a widely shared sense of the way things had evolved under Lindsay. An ironworker told the journalist Pete Hamill, "What the hell does Lindsay care about me? . . . None of these politicians give a good goddamn. All they worry about is the niggers." A Brooklyn storekeeper called out the social and cultural stupidity of the limousine liberal: "Lindsay doesn't know what our life is like. Look at the WASP—what could he know?" At a campaign stop in a heavily Irish American neighborhood in Queens, hecklers called Lindsay a fake and a traitor and a communist. In Bay Ridge he was known as "Lefty Lindy," a label that traveled into the German and Irish precincts of Ridgewood as well.

Lindsay won, barely. He picked up black and Latino votes that normally went Democratic, triumphed in white liberal Manhattan, and lost legions of Republicans in the other boroughs. That gave him a plurality in a three-man race. But his victory changed nothing; if anything the vitriol got worse. Just months after the November election hundreds of construction workers in lower Manhattan (some building the World Trade Center) rampaged through an anti–Vietnam War rally on Wall Street, violently dispersing the demonstrators. Similar "hard hat" rolling rallies continued over the next couple of weeks. And when the mayor ordered the flag at City Hall to fly at half-mast in memory of the students slain at Kent State, construction workers marched there to demand the flag be hoisted back up and carried placards reading "Bury the Red Mayor." Others denounced Lindsay as a "faggot."[9]

Faggot was a peculiarly telling epithet. It signaled just how profound the estrangement had become. More than economic power and privilege was at stake. This was also a war against cultural imperialism. Bedrock beliefs about masculinity, the family, sexual behavior, religious conviction, and moral integrity were under siege, along with the dignity of hard work and an equally hard-won sense of social accomplishment. *Faggot* and *nigger* rose out of these depths to the surface of public debate to capture the existential danger represented by limousine liberalism.

Lindsay was the enemy not merely because he hailed from the upper classes and was clueless if not hostile when it came to sympathizing with the plight of working people. That was elite politics as usual. Lindsay and his ilk were different. Unlike their predecessors, who defended the old order of things against insurgencies from below, limousine liberals incited rebellion, wanted to overturn the racial status quo; they were ready to jettison traditional rules governing the family such as how women were to behave and the way children were to be raised; for them conventional sexual relations were boring and inhibiting; pious on public occasions that demanded it, they were committed secularists who turned to the social sciences, not scripture, for guidance in resolving social dilemmas. They were immoralists—hence "faggots"—and also moral tyrants eager to impose their own self-righteous preferences on others.

John Lindsay enjoys the dubious distinction of being the first to bear the stigma that would facilitate the decline of liberalism for the rest of the twentieth century and that continues to shadow it today. His "victory" in 1969 was also a reveille for the massing of a right-wing populism that would transform American politics over the next half century and turn limousine liberals into an endangered species. However, Lindsay was far from the first elitist to be pilloried in this peculiar way—that is, as someone who by all rights ought to have spent his legacy defending the status quo but who instead chose to subvert it. The political anxieties, social suspicions, and moral disquiet that ultimately produced Mario Procaccino's inspired aperçu were already simmering at the surface of public life when his father was still cobbling shoes outside Naples at the turn of the twentieth century.

2

Bankers, Bolsheviks, and Jews

The Prehistory of the Limousine Liberal

For those seeking to exorcize it from our public life, limousine liberalism seems to engage in a diabolical masquerade. One of the foundational presumptions about limousine liberals is that while they feign commitment to social justice and egalitarian reform in public, in private they engage in clandestine behavior to increase their own wealth and power. Today, Tea Party partisans often work to unearth the hidden machinations of elites. The Clintons, for example, are depicted as running a secretive and global network of political and economic power brokers. A successful GOP candidate for the Senate from Montana, Ryan Zinke, went so far as to describe Hillary as that arch–secret agent, the Antichrist (although later he said he was joking). A Texas-based radio host, Alex Jones, was not the only one to claim that Obama's candidacy was a plot by leaders of the New World Order to "con the American people into accepting global slavery." 2016 presidential hopeful Ted Cruz, who has been called "the Glenn Beck of the Senate," has characterized a UN resolution on the environment as a masked scheme devised by George Soros "to abolish 'unsustainable' environments including golf courses, grazing pastures, and paved roads." Cruz, who graduated Harvard Law himself, describes the faculty as infested with communists: "There was one Republican. But there were twelve who would say that they were Marxists who believe in the Communists overthrowing the U.S. government." This way of looking at the world has been characteristic of rebellious movements long before the Tea Party came along. Moreover, while this outlook sometimes descends into the inky realms of pure paranoia, it cannot be dismissed as entirely delusional.[1]

No one has articulated more notoriously this odd amalgam of fact and fiction than Glenn Beck. Fancying himself an amateur historian, Beck has taken us back to the prehistory of the limousine liberal during the turn-of-the-century Progressive Era. That's when one of Beck's bête noires, the Federal Reserve, was created.

Although quick to distance himself from conspiracy mongers, in describing this original iteration of the limousine liberal (long before the phrase itself was invented) Beck felt compelled to acknowledge that "there's a point when conspiracy is not a conspiracy; it's just true." And these founding generation conspirators were not, according to the polemicist, the usual suspects: furtive, faintly demented members of a clandestine revolutionary cell, bohemian vagabonds skulking about in some shadowy underground, hatching plots to overthrow their masters. Instead, they were the masters. They operated in broad daylight, occupied positions of great economic and political power, were showered with honorifics, and spent their days presiding over the dawn of the "American century." In a word, these conspirators were, at one and the same time, also America's ruling class, men like Morgan, Rockefeller, and homegrown agents of the Rothschild's.

Strange indeed! Here in the homeland we don't easily resort to the language of class struggle. Normally, it offends "true" Americans like Beck, who think of class warfare, if they think of it at all, as alien, something they have in Europe or had in Russia—but not here certainly, not in the New World, where classes were providentially banned from the beginning. Still, Beck does talk this talk (as did his forebears), gets his hackles up over an upper-crust claque that's been running the country off the rails for nearly a century. He pillories presumptuous elites, warning of "the inevitable rise of a tyranny from the greed and gluttony of a ruling class."[2]

Glenn Beck is more a fabulist than a historian; he makes up stories, omits what's inconvenient, tells half-truths, and specializes in a kind of lachrymose vitriol. Nevertheless he's onto something.

Momentous doings were under way as the nineteenth century turned into the twentieth; Beck fixates on the creation of the Federal Reserve Bank in 1913. In this inside-out story of revolution from above, the Bank was allegedly designed to concentrate control of the nation's credit and capital resources in the hands of a tiny group of government bureaucrats and eastern bankers. On Beck's Fox network show back in March of 2011 (a month later he was fired), he made his case: that in "great secrecy" a tiny gathering of the country's elite bankers on a small, privately owned island (Jekyll Island off the Georgia coast) in "partnership with government," functioning in ways analogous to a "Mexican drug cartel," connived successfully to establish a closely held, publicly sanctioned central bank. Its purpose was to quash competition from newly emerging banks; create money out of nothing for favored financial institutions; control all bank reserves to quell the panics that had frequently turned the marketplace into a hellish chaos; and shift all possible future losses from the banks' "owners" to the nation's taxpayers. Beck called it a "money cartel," privately owned by "no one knows," "a mysterious magic money dispenser." Democracy and economic opportunity were the losers.[3]

Fantasy and fact comingle in this origins story. A group of immensely powerful bankers did indeed meet at a millionaire's secluded retreat on Jekyll Island in 1910. They came there costumed like hunters, but they were after bigger game than any of the wildlife likely to show up in the island's fields and forests. They included Senator Nelson Aldrich from Rhode Island (considered to be John D. Rockefeller's factotum in the upper chamber and dubbed "the boss of the Senate" by Lincoln Steffens), Henry P. Davison of Morgan Bank, Frank A. Vanderlip of Rockefeller's National City Bank, Paul Warburg of Kuhn, Loeb, and Co., and Harvard economist A. Piatt Andrew.

There never has been an "executive committee of the ruling class." But this group came close. They met with a sense of urgency, worried about the periodic panics, booms, and busts that had been characteristic of the American economy for well over a half century. These disturbances not only ravaged businesses large and small. They also aggravated already abrasive social tensions between "the classes and the masses"; raised the temperature of political life, encouraging breakaway parties and movements like the populists, the "Wobblies," and the socialists; incited muckraking journalists to undress business and political kleptocrats; and prompted a general hullabaloo about the unchecked power of the Money Trust.

In the aftermath of the most recent near financial catastrophe—the panic of 1907—it had become customary for Morgan to work with his friendly rivals, George F. Baker of the First National Bank and James Stillman of National City Bank, to watch over the country's liquidity and money supply and steer its major banking institutions. They came to be known as the "Trio," carrying out, in effect, the work of a private central bank.

Monitoring such a vital artery of national well-being could not forever remain a strictly private affair, however. The economy had become too complex, too intricately reticulated to be directed by even someone as Olympian as Morgan and his conferees. In fact, agitation in and outside the halls of Congress demanding that something be done to rein in the power of the Money Trust and trusts in general had become a chronic feature of public life well before the turn of the century. Moreover, the white-shoe investment banking community and the new, publicly traded corporations it had recently helped to bring into being and helped direct had their own reasons for looking to the government to play a role in regulating and stabilizing the economy. The "duck hunters" had come to Jekyll Island as draftsmen, determined to put together legislation that would answer the call for public oversight of the nation's monetary system while preserving the prerogatives of Wall Street's trusteeship.

In the end, the Federal Reserve System emerged as a hybrid concoction reflecting more than the views of the Jekyll Island conspirators. It allowed for a greater degree of public control over monetary affairs than they might have wished. Nevertheless, it marked a definitive moment in the evolution of the investment elite's career as a ruling class, translating their economic and social power into formal political authority, albeit imperfectly. But it was not a provincial and selfish piece of legislation. Rather, it was conceived from the disinterested standpoint of keeping the whole social machine in good working order. As James Dill, the Wall Street lawyer who helped craft the 1889 law that made the consolidated modern corporation legitimate, forecast back in 1900: "Industrial combinations are producing a new class of financiers, a new order of corporate men . . . prepared to assume the burden that went along with functioning as the general staff for the nation's political economy."[4]

Beck's singling out the midwifing of the Federal Reserve as an insidious plot of the "money cartel" was deranged. Yet it also echoed President Woodrow Wilson, who had grounded his victorious 1912 campaign on a promise to bring the Money Trust to heel. That was indeed the moment when publicly traded corporations of the sort that Dill alluded to, owned by an anonymous mass of transient shareholders and run by a separate cadre of salaried managers, supplanted traditional family capitalism in which ownership and management were vested in the same private circle of founding patriarchs, partners, and their heirs. That was when the peculiar form of class struggle Beck invokes began.

ERECTING THE IRON CAGE

Around the turn of the twentieth century—Beck's primordial moment—the antitrust movement waged war against the new corporate order. It was one member of an extended family of insurgencies, of which populism was the most celebrated, directed at financial and corporate capitalism. It indicted high finance and the trusts for destroying livelihoods and ways of life. It attacked big business as well for undermining democracy. It condemned the amorality and decadence of Wall Street, the way the new corporate order corroded the moral and religious armature protecting the family. It reverberated with a sense of violation.

Today we take for granted as the furniture of modern life what was back then not merely new, but strange, at once promising and ominous. While there had been publicly traded corporations for many years (railroads principally), only at the turn of century did they come to dominate the economic landscape; United States Steel, for example, the world's first billion dollar corporation, was invented in 1901. Moreover, family patriarchs no longer ran them. They required instead a multifunctional corporate bureaucracy, managements possessing great power, but not the rights and prerogatives nor the loyalties attached to ownership. That precious possession of family capitalism was now diffused among a vast sea of anonymous shareholders.

Americans had been well known for their aversion to government and kept theirs weak and on short rations. That began to change too. The sheer size and complexity of an industrial and urbanized society demanded some supervision. Public bureaucracies grew up to look after the transcontinental and interurban transportation systems; or to ensure public health and sanitation; or to inventory and protect the natural environment and manage its exploitation; or to make sure schools were training young people properly to make them fit to join the labor force; or to police urban ghettoes; or to supply great concentrations of people with potable water; or to classify and institutionalize the aberrant; or to codify and inspect tenement housing; or to process and channel the tidal wave of immigrants disembarking on American shores; or to watch after at-risk children; or to maintain the infrastructures of urban living; or to monitor the worst hazards of the workplace; and so on.

Even the biggest businesses found themselves the objects of bureaucratic scrutiny, as for example in the food and drug industry or on the railroads or in the case of public utilities. This too was new. Once big business had put up a mighty resistance to such outside interference and had largely succeeded in nullifying those laws passed by state governments designed to check their power. But, as the birth of the Federal Reserve suggests, this new regulatory state, while still in its infancy, was becoming a collaborative project, no longer treated as an alien intrusion by at least certain elements of the commercial community. In some instances and in some industries, government regulation promised to even out the dangerous oscillations of the marketplace, place a floor under competition, drive under the most unscrupulous cost-cutters, and reassure members of a mass buying public that they could trust what they were being persuaded to buy. After all, increasingly the economy was coming to rest on mass consumption. For these and other reasons specific to specific industries, the old laissez-faire hostility to public regulation had begun to fade away.

Modern managerial capitalism and modern government bureaucracy grew up together. They encouraged what is today a familiar reliance on social science "expertise"; on the multifunctional and hierarchical bureaucracy; and on impersonal, data-based classifications and evaluations. They bred a belief in meritocracy that soon became the reigning ideology of modern democratic society. A new milieu of middle class professionals, technocrats, corporate managers, and public sector administrators populated the interstitial zone between the working classes and the command centers of the new order. They often considered themselves a vanguard of rational reform, social engineers standing at some remove from the prejudices and narrow-minded self-interest, not to mention the corruption, that seemed to characterize the still uncivilized badlands of industrial and urban life.

When the duck-hunting bankers decamped to Jekyll Island, America was still in many respects a rural society made up of farms, villages, and small towns. But the world these "conspirators" hailed from was decidedly urban. Metropolises of more than a million people and lesser but still sizeable cities dotted the continent from coast to coast. There, corporations set up headquarters, and mammoth factories dominated the cityscape. There, government agencies set up shop and sent their emissaries out to do their monitoring and supervising, their licensing and regulating. There, immigrants from all over Europe, speaking dozens of languages, professing all sorts of religions, dressed in strange, Old World costumes, and practicing strange, disconcerting customs, lived mashed together in shabby, unhealthy, and dangerous tenements and neighborhoods. There too, the titillating sensations of modern life, everything from nickelodeons and amusement parks to automobiles and the latest fashions, were at hand. Cities had always aroused a cultural uneasiness and suspicion among country folk. But the great urban conurbations that accompanied the rise of industrial capitalism magnified these anxieties. They were moral, sexual, and social all at once. *Cosmopolitan* was well on its way to becoming a curse word in the national vocabulary.

The elementary forms of this whole way of life first took root during this Progressive Era in American history, encompassing the two decades surrounding the turn of the century. The reforms of the New Deal and later the Great Society would go much further in the direction of state regulation and social engineering. So too would the relationship between big business and government grow more intricate. And the invasive spread of consumer culture would enter intimate domains that would have seemed out of bounds in these formative years. But by the time of the Jekyll Island gathering, the skeleton of the bureaucratic, administrative welfare and regulatory state and its cosmopolitan setting, which today arouses so much animosity, was in plain sight. For many it would be a lifesaver. Others resented its presumptuousness, the way its elitist creators and advocates cavalierly overturned the way things once were.

CAPITALISM AGAINST CAPITALISM

Anonymous, impersonal, and amoral, corporate capital was then and is now radical. In the end, nothing—no matter how ancient or revered—can stand in the way of its irresistible quest to accumulate. It may profit from racial segregation or patriarchy, for example, but it does not depend on those arrangements to exist and may at any particular historical moment find they get in the way. Its commitment to the family and to religious and traditional values is contingent, subject always to the higher mathematics of the bottom line. As John Maynard Keynes once observed, "Modern capitalism is absolutely irreligious, without internal union, without much public spirit . . . a mere congeries of possessors and pursuers."

Family capitalism, however, in which property and marriage are bound together to make up what we know as the bourgeoisie, is conflicted; it's eager to grow but only within the circumscribed confines of the propertied, morally disciplined individual and the dynastic household. At every moment the entrepreneur, or that vast population of wannabe business people, attach their pecuniary behavior, accomplishments, and desires to distinct local communities, regional attachments, family aspirations, ideals of manhood, specific products and forms of workmanship, peculiar historic traditions, religious values, and protective racial or ethnic enclaves—a whole social universe.

Foes of the Money Trust, along with populists and others suffering dispossession at the hands of the new corporate order, rose up to defend a society of independent producers, a familiar society of Christian virtue, hard work, self-reliance, and family continuity. Some, such as future Supreme Court Justice Louis Brandeis, who in 1912 coined the term "other people's money" to impugn the behavior of the Money Trust, were otherwise entirely comfortable with the elementary forms of modernity: urban living, technological innovation, government administration, and the ethos of social engineering. Others, however, felt stronger attachments to the hallmarks of small-town America: its racial homogeneity and piety, its patriarchal family, and its cherished cultural traditionalism. Hatred for what would later come to be known as limousine liberalism first took root among this latter group.

All those beliefs, sentiments, and prejudices that had been cherished by generations raised up in the austere but familiar world of family capitalism were foreign matter inside the hierarchies of the publicly traded corporation that first began to dominate the economy at the turn of the century. This new species of capitalist enterprise was "owned," for the most part, not by a family, dynasty, or a handful of business partners, but by a vast sea of shareholders. Those "owners" had little if anything to do with running these companies, leaving that to a managerial cadre captained by lavishly rewarded chief executives. The family attachments and local traditions, those customary community mores, long-standing religious and racial prejudices, ingrained patriarchal authority and inspiring dynastic ambitions, the hallmarks of an older style of capitalism counted for little if anything to those running these complex bureaucratic machines. For those manning the barricades in rural and small-town America and even for urban dwellers caught up in the romance of family capitalism—an indigenous American romance after all—something more than money or property was at stake. This was a matter of "to be or not to be," an existential struggle.

Much of this is far removed from what Glenn Beck alludes to. Still there is a kinship, a real genealogy that joins the animosities, cultural forebodings, and economic anxieties of the Tea Party to this bygone universe of family capitalism under siege.

THE PEOPLE'S TYCOON

Henry Ford, improbable as it may seem, was the first to wage holy war on behalf of family capitalism against a distinctly Semitic version of Mario Procaccino's bête noire. By World War I, already an American folk hero, Ford had identified the heartland's mortal enemy: limousine liberalism *avant la lettre*.

The automobile magnate was the country's iconic family capitalist. That may seem odd—after all, he employed tens of thousands in dozens of sophisticated factories, some the size of several football fields. But the Ford Motor Company was a privately held family firm whose founder meant to keep it that way. For years he'd resisted turning to the investment houses for credit and to meet his longer-term capital needs, preferring instead to draw on his company's earnings. He reacted angrily when Wall Street interests tried to buy up shares in his newly opened British manufacturing operations.

Like it was for so many anonymous entrepreneurs before him in midsized cities and towns across Middle America, the independent family-owned enterprise was a precious achievement for Ford, a point of honor, as much as it was a source of patrilineal continuity. Amid a society increasingly overtaken by gigantic, impersonal corporations run by faceless men in suits—managers, not owners—Ford stood as an outsized emblem and champion of an imperiled way of life. He was family capitalism's superhero, as close to a romantic figure as the inherent workaday counting-house spirit of the bourgeoisie is likely to produce; as good as it got.

Ford hailed from, loved, and in people's minds personified all the cherished virtues of small-town America. He was born during the Civil War on a farm in Michigan to an Anglo-Irish father and a mother of Belgian ancestry. They were Episcopalians. Henry worked hard and harbored ambitions, beginning his rise first of all as an apprentice machinist, then later as a farmer, before finding his way into the car business. By the time of the Jekyll Island get-together, Ford was a popular presence in public life. In 1918, President Wilson asked him to run for the Senate as a Democrat from Michigan. He did and nearly won. A poll conducted in 1923 rated Ford among the two or three most admired men in America. Semi-seriously people talked of Ford as a presidential possibility; the numbers showed him beating President Harding easily.

In the minds of millions, Ford exemplified an older, earlier America, one with rural roots, committed to the godly verities of abstemious hard work and endowed with that peculiar national genius for practical-minded inventiveness. He neither drank nor smoked; he dressed modestly and showed up for work at dawn. Like all legends, Ford's was partly true, partly concocted. Whatever the exact proportions, he was beloved and missed no opportunity to express his own love for the American folk.

But he was a hater as well. Especially he hated Jews, bankers, and Bolsheviks. This was not a case of serial hatreds. Rather it was a composite animosity in which that trio of Jews, bankers, and Bolsheviks in collaboration loomed up, in Ford's eyes, as a singular threat to the continued existence of the American folk, to that whole integrated universe of private property, the patriarchal family, and God—the bedrocks of bourgeois society.

Starting in 1920 and continuing for nearly two years, Ford published a series of articles in *The Dearborn Independent* (a paper he controlled) under the inflammatory title of "The International Jew." The series was discussed all over the country and was reissued as a book that became a best-seller.

Anti-Semitism had always been part of American life; Ford wasn't breaking new ground there. The articles frequently referred to and sometimes excerpted the "Protocols of the Elders of Zion," that infamous forgery concocted by the Okhrana, the czar's secret police, back in the 1890s to help foment pogroms against the Jews. Ford bought into the "Protocols" notion that an international Jewish conspiracy, one dominated by leading Jewish financiers in Europe and America, was poised to take control of the world, to exercise an "economic pogrom against a rather helpless humanity." In his view, World War I had been perpetrated for this purpose (Ford ran for the Senate as a peace candidate in 1916). The great Jewish investment houses had profited, vampire-like, from the blood of the belligerents. A stateless tribe after all, the Jews were devoid of patriotic sentiment and cynically exploited that feeling in others to accomplish their own nefarious objectives. This cabal of international financiers was the only real victor in the war, which otherwise laid waste to much of Europe and exhausted its resources. Such devastation meant nothing to these Jewish bankers, who coldheartedly calculated its costs in profit and loss and in a power over mankind long plotted for and now nearing consummation. They threatened to overturn all of Western civilization. What else was one to expect from a race of parasites and shylocks that over generations had fine-tuned the art of living off the labor of others?

Obnoxious and loony as this scaremongering was, it was also garden-variety Jew baiting. Ford was hunting something new, something related, but much grander. What first of all particularly exercised him was the power of finance capitalism, whether deployed by Jews or not (like Glenn Beck he loathed the Federal Reserve). That power was in the ascendancy. Elite circles of investment bankers had helped birth the publicly traded giant corporation. Those great combines were now managed and directed by emissaries from the banks. Their presumptuous overlordship was repellent to Ford. "It is the function of business to produce for consumption and not for money and speculation," he declared. He was so committed to this producerist view of the world, the credo of family capitalism, that when he set up his gigantic tractor plant at River Rouge (and at the same time made his whole company an entirely privately held concern), he noted, "In the new tractor plant there will be no stockholders, no directors, no absentee owners, no parasites."

Even this amalgamated suspicion about Jews and banking parasites, however, had been common currency before the carmaker came along. Where Ford really played the pioneer was in uncovering a missing link that could explain just why the Western world was in such dire circumstances.

Fiendishly clever, these elite conspirators from the world of high finance enlisted the aid of their apparently inveterate enemies, those

Bolsheviks (especially those Jewish Bolsheviks), whose tyranny in Russia was a foretaste of a world to come. Back home in America, Jewish financial circles secretly plotted with the Industrial Workers of the World and the Socialist Party to make war on the world of gentile capitalism. Bernard Baruch, head of the War Industries Board, was America's Trotsky, who had exercised an autocratic control of the nation's capital resources, honeycombing the agencies of war mobilization with his coreligionists and coconspirators. These financiers and their servitors, their Judaism notwithstanding, would not scruple even at allying themselves with the avowed enemies of all religion, not to mention capitalism itself. Citizens of Middle America had been experiencing night sweats about communists since the Paris Commune. But no one had ever imagined they might combine forces with the ruling classes they presumably were out to overthrow.

Ford's epiphany was the moment when limousine liberalism was first imagined: when the ruling class was first conceived as subversive. "The International Jew" might be thought of as the folk Marxism of the middling classes. And what lent its ravings real grit was the way it managed to connect disparate anxieties about the changing nature of American life to the insidious doings of this diabolically clever cabal. What the auto tycoon wanted to alert his countrymen about was a profound existential threat. Wall Street in league with a godless Kremlin was the fount of a pervasive hedonism that mocked all that the heartland held dear while driving it out of existence.

The Dearborn Independent articles ranged widely across the terrain of modern life in a painstaking effort to unearth the hidden pathways linking this satanic conspiracy to every Sodom and Gomorrah of postwar America. Here the conspirators were peddling pornography through their control of the movie business. There they were organized Jewish gangsters befouling the national pastime in the "Black Sox" scandal of the 1919 World Series. With tentacles extending into the criminal underworld, they ran vast stock frauds to loot the innocent. Determined to undermine what was left of the nation's self-discipline, they saturated the country in bootleg gin. Because they were the masterminds of the publishing industry, they arranged for an endless flow of sex and sensationalism in newspapers, magazines, and pulp novels. They fed the nation the same titillating diet of cheap thrills and sexual innuendo in one scandalous Broadway production after another, thanks to their backstage domination of the Great White Way. "Jewish jazz," bankrolled by the same circles, was on its way to becoming the national music, its mood and rhythms an open invitation to the lewd and lascivious. Encouraging every form of vanity and self-indulgence, pandering, and promoting an ethos of immediate gratification, the conspiracy was the incubator of a modernist debauch.

Every Ford franchise in the country was obliged to carry and distribute these articles. Readership approached three-quarters of a million people. But success was fleeting, and "The International Jew" turned out be a colossal misstep. The main currents of American society were running in a different direction from the one Ford invoked. The articles were denounced by Woodrow Wilson, William Howard Taft, William Cardinal O'Connell, and other luminaries of official society. The American Jewish Committee joined with the Federal Council of Churches to organize a boycott of Ford cars, demanding an apology and retraction. Ford dealers, normally a subservient lot who for years had helped finance the company by accepting consignments of cars on onerous terms, felt the pinch and added their pressure on the auto baron to give in. Finally, he did, forced to retreat by the very forces of consumer capitalism his mass-produced, cheap cars had helped to unleash. The book was withdrawn from circulation, and Ford issued a rather mealy-mouthed mea culpa.[5]

All was not lost, however. Heinrich Himmler hailed Ford in 1924 as "one of our most valuable, important, and witty fighters." For Adolf Hitler, Ford's financial anti-Semitism and denunciation of the Versailles peace treaty rang a bell. He made references to it in *Mein Kampf,* where he praised Ford's independence "from the controlling masters of the producers." The Fuhrer kept a life-sized portrait of the auto tycoon in his Munich office. Later on, in 1938, he awarded Ford the Grand Cross of the Supreme Order of the German Eagle, the first American to receive that honor. These accolades don't prove Ford was a Nazi. He wasn't one. Nor are they important because they may besmirch his reputation. What they suggest is that a new kind of populism of the right was emerging all across the world of organized industrial and financial capitalism. Frustrated, dispossessed, wedded to traditional ways of life, these movements nurtured a hatred for both communists and the economic elites those "Reds" purportedly wanted to eliminate. Certainly this was the case in the formative years of the Nazi movement.[6]

However, *The Dearborn Independent* was a newspaper, not a movement. Ford's ravings never led to anything remotely like an organized assault on either bankers or Bolsheviks. But the atmosphere it helped conjure up and that no doubt helps account for its literary success was heating up even before "The International Jew" hit the stands.

FEAR AND DESIRE IN THE JAZZ AGE

Choosing the second anniversary of the Bolshevik revolution deliberately, the attorney general of the United States, A. Mitchell Palmer, launched a series of raids in twelve cities on November 7, 1919, aimed at the headquarters of various dissident groups. Radical newspapers were closed, meetings broken up, offices pillaged and wrecked, homes raided without warrants. It was posse-style justice. Three thousand people were held without charges, some of them immigrants who were soon enough deported. Palmer's list of sixty-eight persons allegedly holding "dangerous, destructive, and anarchist sentiments" included social workers Jane Addams and Lillian Wald and the historian Charles Beard.

Vigilante terror ran alongside Palmer's official version. Industrial Workers of the World (Wobbly) organizer Wesley Everett, a lumberjack who had served in France during the war, was cornered in the backwoods of Centralia, Washington, where he was castrated and hanged by an enraged mob of businessmen, American Legionnaires, and local thugs. Private corporate armies in steel country in collusion with local police and magistrates ran organizers out of town.

The Red Scare set off a national hysteria that the Bolshevik revolution and all the insurrections against private property and established order that were sweeping through war-ravaged Europe were headed across the Atlantic. Fearsome and nightmarish for some, these general strikes and mutinies and colonial revolts and especially the soviets set up briefly in Hungary and Germany, seemed a harbinger of a world turned upside down, a pandemonium that would obliterate civilized life. After all, everything held sacred by bourgeois society stood condemned: the patriarchal family, private property, Christianity, the free market, parliamentary democracy, and, above all, individualism.

Panic spread everywhere. Calls went out for mass deportations. Plenty of rough-and-ready "justice" was handed out to immigrants. A Connecticut clothing salesman went to jail for six months for saying Lenin was smart. In Indiana a jury took two minutes to acquit a man for killing an alien who had shouted, "To hell with the United States." General Leonard Wood suggested deporting radicals in "ships of stone with sails of lead." A senator from Tennessee proposed shipping off native-born radicals to a special penal colony in Guam. Evangelist Billy Sunday thought it might be a good idea to "stand radicals up before a firing squad and save space on our ships." Palmer denounced "the hysterical neurasthenic women who abound in communism." He worried about revolutionary heat "licking the altars of churches, leaping into the belfry of the school bell, crawling into the sacred corners of American homes to replace marriage vows with libertine laws."[7]

Finally the fever abated. The Jazz Age followed. Its live-for-the-moment high hilarity, its libidinal abandon when it came to sex, drink, and money, seemed to bury all those gnawing anxieties about the end of Western civilization. Yet as Ford's triumph, however abortive, suggests, these sentiments survived, if at a lower temperature. Ironically, it was the Jazz Age that kept them alive. Everything about the Roaring Twenties aggravated suspicions that an honored way of life was being traduced.

Cities had always occupied a seductive yet demonic zone in the American folk imagination. The Roaring Twenties roared loudest there. It was in the cities that cosmopolitanism thrived. Doors opened up to strangers from all over the world and even to African American refugees from the cotton fields of the South. A new, heterogeneous culture promiscuously absorbed and adapted their customs, their music, their art, their dialects, and their humor, and was indifferent about their religions. The times were brazenly hedonistic. City sophisticates flouted conventions in dress, deportment, sexual behavior, and gender relations. Shedding norms became the norm. The age, at least in those environs where it flourished, was uninhibited. It celebrated the flapper, bootleg gin, the Charleston, and jazz, the "sex music" of that era.

And it had a special place in its heart for Wall Street. The stock market boom for which the decade became famous defined the era as much as the speakeasy and for the same reason; both were places where everybody might let his or her hair down. How odd! For as long as anybody could remember, Wall Street had given off an incandescent glow fired not simply by wealth but by wealth burnished with a patina of prudential sobriety and social preeminence. Inside its monumental piles of granite, steel, and glass, the equations of economic fitness were calculated with mathematical rigor. Like its very nickname—the Street of streets—it exuded a certain quintessential purity. It hovered above and at some remove from the messiness of the workaday world, distilling its numerical truth, compelling obedience to a higher rationality.

Madness, however, had always lurked on the dark side of the Street. Fevers, manias, and frenzies had periodically raced up and down its pavement like hysterics in a lunatic asylum. Irrational ecstasies and depressive panics constituted its psychological life cycle. This netherworld surfaced for all to see during the Roaring Twenties when the stock market streaked across the countryside like a shooting star. The Street became a land of financial "wilding." It indulged all dreams, reckless and carefree, a casino open to everyman. Shucking off its traditional strait-laced dignity, like the city, the speakeasy, the dance hall, and the jazz club, the Street too became a carnival, discarding old shibboleths, irreverent, glamorous, part of the play culture that made the decade memorable.

Viewed from afar, from all the homesteads, villages, hamlets, market towns, and smaller cities that still made up what today we call the heartland, this composite culture, which mixed together races and religions, which defied convention in everything from proper attire to romantic propriety, which seemed to have no use for God and worshipped only money, appeared threatening at the least, or worse, a

curse. Ford's paranoid fantasies and the Red Scare fed on these reali-
ties. And still other outbreaks against this specter of modernist sacrilege and cultural miscegenation occurred throughout the decade. In
each instance, the profile of what Mario Procaccino would later identify as the limousine liberal became more distinct and multifaceted.

MONKEY BUSINESS

Culture war broke out down in the small town of Dayton, Tennessee,
in 1925. There, the Scopes Trial or Monkey Trial staged a face-off between secularism and old-time religion. The trial was supposed to ad-
judicate whether Darwin's theory of human evolution could and
should be taught in public schools. It commanded national and even
international attention. Two hundred reporters covered the proceedings, and thousands of miles of telegraph lines were hung to get the
story out. It was the first trial to be nationally broadcast on the recently invented radio.

Big city lawyer Clarence Darrow, an agnostic who had spent years
defending political radicals, confronted the man who had once been a
populist hero, the "boy orator of the Platte," three-time presidential
candidate, secretary of state under President Wilson, and a believer in
the revealed word of God, William Jennings Bryan. The nineteenth-
century populism Bryan grew up with had always condemned the
new order of finance capitalism as not only unjust, undemocratic, and
inequitable, but also as iniquitous, depraved, dissolute, and godless.
Bryan had never forsaken that faith.

Moreover, it was an outlook forever suspicious of the city as an incubator of a kind of hubris, infatuated with its knowingness and sophistication, not to mention the way it offered up every form of
sensual temptation. Indeed, in the run-up to the presidential election
of 1896, Bryan said this: "Burn your cities and leave our farms, and
your cities will spring up again as if by magic; but destroy our farms
and the grass will grow in the streets of every city in the country." The
Nebraska congressman wasn't inviting the immolation of urban America. Nor was he quite the orthodox fundamentalist that big city papers
depicted. But he was reiterating an ancestral faith that the land was

the natural womb not only of a fecund economy but of moral good health. The city had its uses and was the site of scientific and technological marvels. But without vigilant supervision by a god-fearing people, it could easily descend into a narcissistic fascination with its own powers, living for the moment, forgetting about the hereafter.

Also on trial in Dayton in 1925 was a broader cultural persuasion involving trust in scientific thinking. Much of the animus that surfaced before, during, and after the trial was fired up by an urban, secular conceit that the opinions of experts in all walks of life should instruct an otherwise credulous mass. As a matter of fact, the defense team for schoolteacher John Thomas Scopes intended to introduce a whole bevy of academic experts on natural evolution; that was to be the core of its case. While the judge, clearly partial to the prosecution, only allowed one, the point was made: scientific truth stood ready to triumph over ignorance.

Although the geologists and biologists failed to get their day in court, the confrontation was aired over and over again in the mass media. There small-town America not only lost but was mercilessly ridiculed. *Time* magazine called the proceedings a "fantastic cross between a circus and a holy war." Another national outlet judged that Tennessee was "not up to date in its attitude to such things as evolution." No one, however, was more acerbic in venting his contempt for the whole social universe of outback America than H. L. Mencken of the *Baltimore Sun*. He called Bryan a "buffoon" and pilloried the country and town folk drawn to the trial as hillbillies, peasants, yokels, and morons. Yet Darrow, the media spectacle notwithstanding, was no firebrand atheist. And Mencken spoke as much or more in defense of a genteel literary tradition than he did for some avant-garde modernism.

Scopes was found guilty of violating the state's antievolution law. But the verdict delivered through the main channels of public opinion was a triumph for the other side of the cultural divide. Evangelicals returned to their customary state of political hibernation and would not come out in again in full force for two generations, so searing was their humiliation. Yet the public verdict was not quite so one-sided. By 1927 there were thirteen states, in both the North and South, considering antievolution legislation. All of them except Mississippi and Arkansas ultimately rejected these bills. But clearly animosity against cosmopolitan America continued to simmer years after "The International Jew" was withdrawn from publication.[8]

CHRISTIAN SOLDIERS

Tennessee had led the way, and in more ways than one. It was also a hotbed of Ku Klux Klan activity. The remarkable revival of the Klan in the 1920s was another telltale sign that some people were infuriated by the uprooting of customary ways of life taking place throughout urban America, deviances that were applauded by elites whom one might have at least expected to play their assigned role as guardians of the established order.

Today we think of the Klan as a dangerous but marginal pathological political cult. During the Jazz Age, however, it was a muscular mass movement. It grew not only in the South or in border states like Tennessee, but in the North as well. Estimates of its membership ranged from three to eight million people. Ohio had three hundred thousand members, Pennsylvania about two hundred thousand. Followers came from the city as well as the countryside, from among poor as well as middle class people, and included farmers, clerks, independent professionals, craft workers, and small businessmen. Its biggest "klaverns" could be found in western cities like Portland, Oregon, and Denver. The Seattle chapter had two thousand members. Their rallies were staged as spectacular theatrical events, costumed in white robes and hoods, and torch lit, attracting as many as twenty thousand people.

Politically, the Klan was a force to be reckoned with. It helped elect people to local offices from coast to coast, and that included the mayors of Portland, Maine, and Portland, Oregon. Indeed, it was weighty enough in the office of the Oregon governor to get an anti-Catholic law passed banning private Catholic schools. It was noticeably influential in half of the nation's state legislatures, especially in places like Indiana and Colorado. The Klan was at least partly responsible for blocking the nomination of Al Smith (the Catholic governor of New

York) for president by the Democratic Party in 1924. And the restrictive immigration law passed in that same year was also something the Klan could take some of the credit for.

White supremacy of course remained the Klan's core principle. Nothing had changed in that regard since its founding days after the Civil War, when its vigilante terrorism tried to turn back the clock to pre-emancipation days. So when it resurfaced, it burned crosses and committed other acts of intimidation, but this time not only to terrorize African Americans as it always had. It went after Catholics and Jews, immigrants and labor activists, all those who seemed to put in jeopardy the Protestant fundamentalism and "clean living" that defined the way things once were and should have remained.

Klansmen saw themselves as knights of the realm standing at the battlements of an America under siege. They were Christian soldiers, patriots, proud of their manliness, guarding the virginal purity of white womanhood that had to fend off not only the bestial instincts of inferior races but also the hypersophisticated seductions of the Jazz Age. The Klan hated the new woman, her suggestive way of dressing, her smoking in public, her drinking, and her voting. *The Watcher on the Tower,* the Klan's paper, talked about the "defense of the American home," emphasizing its "stubborn loyalty to the virtue of womanhood and honor among men," men who saw themselves to be on a "manly mission."

Echoes of Ford permeated Klan rhetoric as it inveighed against Jewish business and Jewish radicals, a twinned enemy the Klan described as culturally depraved. Broadsides warned that "Jewish movies urge sex and vice" and that jazz did the same. Like Ford, Klan spokesmen skewered the Jews as parasites: "The Jew produces nothing anywhere on the face of the earth. He does not till the soil. He does not create or manufacture anything for common use. He adds nothing to the sum of human welfare." According to the Klan, Jews worshipped only money and were otherwise "moral lepers who gloat over human tragedy, rejoice in the downfall of the guileless and inexperienced." And like the car mogul, Klan literature conjoined the Jewish financier with the Jewish Marxist, finding them not only repellent but in league.

Jews were hardly the only alien invaders to worry about. Labor organizers in Yakima, Washington, trying to help Japanese farmers, were run out of the region as the local klavern mobilized a huge rally. The Klan singled out all non-Anglo-Saxon immigrants for the harshest censure. They comprised a polymorphous array of "Italian anarchists, Irish Catholic malcontents, Russian Jews, Finns, Letts, Lithuanians of the lowest classes." And because these immiscibles congregated in great urban centers, "our cities are a menace to democracy"; they had become "modern Sodoms and Gomorrahs." Deposited in America, these strangers brought with them "illiteracy, disease, insanity, and mental deficiency." If this continued much longer "the American race is doomed to cultural destruction."[9]

BEFORE THE CRASH

Sexual scandal and corruption at the highest levels undermined the Klan so that by the later years of the decade it was but a remnant. It no longer wielded anything remotely like the political influence it once had, unable, for example, to stop the Roman Catholic Al Smith from becoming the Democratic Party's presidential candidate in 1928. Nonetheless, the Klan's stunning ascendancy when taken together with the wide popularity of Ford's ravings, the mass hysteria of the Red Scare, and the cultural theatrics of the Scopes trial is suggestive. Together these episodes reveal something about the etiology of limousine liberalism in its earliest incarnations as a political idea.

We often associate scapegoating with hard times. But the Roaring Twenties were celebrated then and since for their prosperity. No doubt that reputation was exaggerated. If you were a farmer or a wage earner in a broad range of American industries, prosperity was fleeting at best. Still, even though wealth and income inequality widened, it was a period of measurable economic growth and technological innovation. So the politics of resentment directed against subversions that were perpetrated by an incongruous alliance of radical elitists and radical agents of the lower classes thrived during economic good times. It did so back then and it would again in the future. Yet as we will see, the same passions could be ignited when the economy ground to a halt. Something deeper than material self-interest was at work.

When Attorney General Palmer went Red hunting he did so as a member of the political establishment. Glenn Beck would undoubtedly have applauded his zeal, yet Palmer was otherwise a charter member of that circle of elite Progressives installing the apparatus of the corporate state that Beck despises. Henry Ford hated radicals to be sure, but he also warred against the financial establishment, which Palmer did not. Klansmen were even more ecumenical in their scapegoating, and while Glenn Beck would no doubt sympathize with the movement's animus against the era's hedonism and loss of faith, he would have likely demurred when it came to excommunicating a whole religion. Already apparent therefore in this embryonic phase of limousine liberalism—both as reality and as myth—is its heterodoxy. There is no point in searching for political or intellectual coherence where there was none. What has given the metaphor of the limousine liberal its stamina has been its ability to collect together a disparate array of discontents, anxieties, and sentiments aroused by the advent of modern corporate and finance capitalism, cosmopolitan living, consumer culture, and the growth of a supervisory state that helps keep the whole mechanism running.

Thanks to this menagerie of enemies, the face of the limousine liberal has been extraordinarily plastic. A specter of a sinister league of Bolsheviks and bankers would remain an undercurrent of popular political unease for some time to come. But profiles of the leading protagonists evolved; Jews, bankers, and Bolsheviks slowly receded from view or morphed into pointy-headed corporate and government bureaucrats, effete intellectuals, silk-stocking politicians, social engineers, cultural nihilists, one-worlders, and latte-sipping yuppies—in other words, a breviary of the well-born and well-bred who had gone to seed, become acolytes of a capitalist way of life in which, as Marx so aptly put it, "all that's solid melts into air," and were running and ruining the country.[10]

A society as irreverent about customary beliefs and ways of doing things, so callous about the wake of social and economic destruction it left behind, had naturally inspired resistance for many decades.

Clarence Darrow and William Jennings Bryan at one time would have considered themselves comrades. Neither deserved the caricatures served up by the Monkey Trial. Both were veterans in the war against the economic and social injustices that trailed in the wake of industrial and finance capitalism. Both had been partisans in the struggle to save democracy from the suffocating stranglehold that big business exercised over all the main institutions of political life. Their bitter standoff in 1925 was also therefore a poignant and portentous one. The Roaring Twenties marks a great fork in the road in the history of popular resistance to the elitist proclivities of modern society.

Once, the broad populist persuasion these two had helped articulate had blanketed rural America from the cotton South to the grain-growing Great Plains and the Rocky Mountain West and was echoed by the antitrust movement in urban centers from coast to coast. It indicted high finance and the trusts for destroying the livelihoods and ways of life of independent farmers, handicraftsmen, and small businessmen, the atomic nuclei of family capitalism. It attacked big business as well for subverting the foundations of democracy by capturing all three branches of government, turning them into instruments of rule by a new plutocracy. And it condemned the amorality and decadence of Wall Street, the way the new corporate order encouraged the worship of money for its own sake and corroded the moral and religious armature protecting the family. Still, however much this prolonged resistance to modern corporate capitalism remained loyal to a familiar society of Christian virtue, hard work, self-reliance, family continuity, and a rough equality, it also envisioned a new world. Something transformative, a cooperative commonwealth that would escape the barbaric competitiveness and exploitation of free market capitalism, inspired these tragic movements of the dispossessed.

Darrow and Bryan ending up at loggerheads marks the birth of a right-wing mutation of populist politics. This distinctive form of populism became ever more restorationist and ever less transformative, ever more anticollectivist and ever less anticapitalist. Parasitism would remain a key word in the populist dictionary but increasingly would be deployed to skewer the poor when once it excommunicated the rich. What were subordinate themes in the old-style populism—religious rectitude, racial and ethnic homogeneity, national chauvinism, and the politics of paranoia—gradually came to sound the dominant note. This new species would still bear a family resemblance to its parental ancestors. But it would jettison all that earlier talk about a new world being born. Instead it would fix its sights on saving and restoring an older, cherished social universe menaced by a new enemy: limousine liberalism.

3

Fear Itself

On a December day in 1932, with the country prostrate under the weight of the Great Depression, ex-president Calvin Coolidge—who had presided over the reckless stock market boom of the Jazz Age twenties (and famously declaimed that "the business of America is business")—confided to a friend: "We are in a new era to which I do not belong." He punctuated those words, a few weeks later, by dying. The best of times gave way to the worst of times when Wall Street crashed in 1929 and the rest of the economy collapsed soon after. Second only to the Civil War, the Great Depression was the greatest trauma in the country's history.[1]

It left its mark everywhere: on family life and political institutions; on city businesses, market towns, and family farms; at the workplace, at home, and in church. Dispossession and forced migration unsettled familiar ways of living and where people lived. The nation's political demography and geography would never be the same as old regional, religious, and ethnic loyalties to party machines gave way to new ones. Cherished beliefs inhibiting the role of government couldn't stand up against the desperate need for public action. Immunities once enjoyed by finance and industry from official supervision weakened as the shibboleths of laissez-faire seemed preposterous in the face of the free market's total breakdown. Faith in individualism and self-reliance, sacred elements of the American creed, withered. Instead, yearnings to look out for the commonwealth, to rescue the legions cut adrift by the foundering of the economy, to find new existential meaning in insurgent forms of social solidarity worked their way into the fabric of cultural belief and established an enduring institutional presence. Questions about who was responsible for the disaster, about who ruled America and who ought to rule, about the basic credibility and legitimacy of the ancient regime were opened up for debate after a long season in hibernation.

Capitalism itself seemed to have entered a terminal crisis. What would replace it? Fears of the unknown combined with desires to start over. Salvation beckoned. It might lie in some postcapitalist future. Or on the contrary, it might depend on restoring older, customary ways of living and moral convictions overshadowed, ignored, and disrespected by urban, industrial, and financial capitalism.

In short, the Great Depression entailed far more than an economic meltdown. It liquefied American society.

Confronted with the stark reality that nothing was working the way it was supposed to, those occupying the commanding heights of the economy and the political machinery were first paralyzed by indecision about what to do. Then those elite circles fissured into warring camps. Some wanted to stay the course. That meant keeping the faith in the free market's inherent capacity to right itself, relying on orthodoxies about balanced budgets, keeping the government on short rations, and adhering to the gold standard. Gospel had it that hard times could be and should be managed by looking to private philanthropy to bail out the neediest, letting the "natural" deflationary pressures of the Depression and the unemployment it entailed suppress wages until they reached that level where it would once again make economic sense to hire people. Holding the fort also demanded manning the battlements that protected the owners of private industry against any interference by their employees in their inalienable right to run their businesses as they saw fit. So too, prevailing regional and racial prerogatives would remain in place; in particular the Southern landed and mercantile oligarchy would continue to run the old Confederacy, and the caste system would still define its labor market and social hierarchy.

Working to conserve what had once been taken for granted was, after all, just what elites were supposed to do. But the tide had turned. All of this would be disrupted, sometimes done away with entirely, in other instances threatened—as for example the Southern caste system—if not yet overturned. What is now referred to as the New Deal Order repudiated much of what had been treated for generations as sacrosanct.

It was no surprise to traditional elites to find unsavory agitators from the lower depths instigating unrest among distressed farmers, the unemployed, tenement dwellers facing eviction, industrial workers, and other victims of the national calamity. No surprise to hear them demand a vast expansion of government authority: to license public authorities to breach the rights of private property, to take on responsibilities for social well-being, to open up the black box of the workplace to public scrutiny, to replace industrial autocracy with industrial democracy, to empower the government to violate the *idée fixe* about balancing the budget and instead to countervail the market's pressure to suppress the wage level by running a deficit to jump-start the economy. Moreover, malcontents had for a long time made known their contempt for the traditional patriarchal family as well as conventional sexual and race relations. Predictably these insurgents were calling on the government to intrude into family affairs like schooling and child care, and even to presume to reorder relations between the races.

What was distinctly unnerving and infuriating, however, was to discover that this wholesale reconfiguring of bedrock national institutions and mores was being championed and often steered by elites who, after all, ought to be on the other side of the barricades. Common cause seemed to be fusing the immiscible, the Social Register with the Lower East Side, Harvard professors with coal miners, government bureaucrats with white and black sharecroppers, church patriarchs with reform-minded atheists. Architects of the New Deal included men and women of social preeminence, wealth, and power who seemed prepared to overthrow themselves, or at least to repudiate received wisdom and embrace rather than fend off cries for change. Ancestral forebears of John Lindsay, these were the bearers of the political genotype Mario Procaccino would, a generation later, christen as limousine liberals.

KREMLIN ON THE POTOMAC

Franklin Delano Roosevelt epitomized this strange world turned up-side down. Between Wall Street's Black Tuesday in October 1929 and his assumption of the presidency in March 1933, FDR began to real-ize that the credibility and legitimacy of the ancient regime had been undermined beyond any real hope of recuperation.

Roosevelt was a man of genteel upbringing and a familiar face in the clubby world of Wall Street and corporate patricians—he'd in-vested in blue chips and gambled and lost on oil speculation, although he kept away from risky buying on margin. From a family of Hudson River patroons, he had attended similar prep schools—Groton in FDR's case—colleges, and law schools, frequented the same parties and gentlemen's fraternities, and filled similar executive posts in state and national governments as his patrician conferees. But in 1933 he confided to his old friend and a Morgan Bank partner, Russell Leffing-well, whose very name resounded with noblesse, that the president-elect couldn't consider him for the post of assistant secretary of the treasury because "we simply can't tie up with #23"—a street address familiar even to millions of outsiders as the House of Morgan. A year later when applying the finishing touches to legislation that would es-tablish the Securities and Exchange Commission (SEC) as the public's Wall Street watchdog, the president cautioned his close adviser, Adolph Berle, that "the fundamental trouble with this whole stock exchange crowd is their complete lack of elementary education. I do not mean lack of college diplomas, etc., but just inability to under-stand the country or public or their obligations to keep their fellow men. Perhaps you can help them acquire a kindergarten knowledge of these subjects. More power to you."[2]

Power was indeed the issue. FDR was prepared to wield that power against the upper-crust social milieu from which he sprang. In Britain, this form of upper class political defection had long since ac-quired a name: Tory socialism. In the United States it had never quite assumed the same programmatic or institutional coherence. Nonethe-less, this willingness to bump heads with the rich and powerful sig-naled fateful divisions with the inner circles of the country's powerful elites. Roosevelt was less imperious and muscular in his disdain for the selfishly wealthy than his distant cousin Teddy had been, and was less righteous than Woodrow Wilson when it came to condemning the Money Trust and those Jekyll Island conspirators Glenn Beck got so exercised about. Despite his native geniality, however, and when circumstances forced the issue, he knew his classmates to be woefully untutored about their public obligations, so socially ignorant he would have to take them to school.

Even in the first year of his administration, when the president was still trying to reassure suspicious elements of the business and financial community, he nevertheless warned that responsibility for directing the nation's great economic affairs had resided in special interest groups that, while staffed by men with useful knowledge and experience, were not motivated by the general welfare. "We cannot allow our economic life to be controlled by that small group of men whose chief outlook upon social welfare is tinctured by the fact that they make huge profits from the lending of money and the marketing of securities." Roosevelt confided to Colonel Edward House, Woodrow Wilson's factotum: "The real truth . . . is, as you and I know, that a financial element in the larger centers has owned Government ever since the days of Andrew Jackson. . . . The country is going through a repetition of Jackson's fight with the Bank of the United States—only on a bigger and broader scale."[3]

In the eyes of his peers, he had committed an act of unforgiveable betrayal. Richard Whitney, Roosevelt's old classmate at Groton and head of the New York Stock Exchange (before he was convicted of embezzlement and sent off to Sing Sing) fulminated tirelessly against the two securities acts of 1933 and 1934. So too the Public Utilities Holding Company Act of 1935, designed to break up utilities monopolies (the Samuel Insull empire in particular) was ferociously attacked and partly dismembered by the old guard. Old-money (and new-money) plutocrats rose up in arms as well over FDR's wealth tax act. It threatened dynastic inheritances.

His classmates went berserk: "That man in the White House" was insane, a closet Jew, a drunk, a syphilitic, a "foul" communist, and so on and so on in a Niagara of bilious distemper whose very extremism was a measure of their exile. Henry O. Havemeyer, the head of the American Sugar Refining Company, scorned the emerging "nanny state" and the president's solicitous concern about educating people like him: "Let the buyer beware; that covers the whole business. You cannot wet-nurse people from the time they are born until the day they die. They have to wade in and get stuck and this is the way we are educated and cultivated." Republicans were particularly apoplectic lashing out against Benjamin Cohen and Tom Corcoran (designers of the Securities Act establishing the SEC), "the scarlet fever boys from the little red house in Georgetown." The bill would "Russianize everything worthwhile." The Republican National Committee called FDR the "Kerensky of the American revolutionary movement."

The American Liberty League, an organization of high-echelon industrialists and financiers, adamantly opposed the New Deal on all fronts. It was assembled by John Jacob Raskob of DuPont and figureheaded by the ex-governor of New York, Al Smith. At a dinner early in 1936 held to kick off the league's campaign against FDR's reelection, Smith declared the New Deal smelled of "the foul breath of communistic Russia." Nasty league propaganda circulated false genealogies to prove FDR's Jewish heritage and called his wife a communist. The head of a Wall Street bank told the *New York Times* he considered the president a "pathological case." John W. Davis, a Wall Street lawyer and the 1924 Democratic Party presidential candidate, issued a grim warning that administration legislation "constitutes the gravest threat to the liberties of American citizens that has emanated from the halls of Congress in my lifetime." William Randolph Hearst, who had helped secure Roosevelt's nomination in 1932, denounced the "imperial, autocratic, Asiatic Socialist party of Karl Marx and Franklin Delano Roosevelt."

Even after the New Deal had consolidated its grip, the rancid musings of people like Russell Leffingwell fouled the atmosphere. He had figured it all out: "The Jews do not forget. They are relentless. . . . I believe we are confronted with a profound political-economic philosophy, matured in the wood for twenty years, of the finest brain and most powerful personality in the Democratic Party, which happens to be a Justice of the Supreme Court." Leffingwell was referring to Louis Brandeis, who indeed, as Glenn Beck would be quick to point out seventy-five years later, had been another key player in fashioning the Federal Reserve. Here the ingrained anti-Semitism of the upper class functioned as a warped expression of WASP dispossession, a bitter resentment of the ethnically promiscuous nature of the newly empowered New Deal elite. From Wall Street to Newport to Park Avenue the country's "natural aristocracy" whispered that "that man in the White House" was "morally weak," a "dupe," a "cripple," a "liar," a tool of "niggers and Jews," a megalomaniac dreaming of dictatorship. Slander, denial, bigotry, paranoia, and outrageous bluff: these were the symptoms of an unhorsed elite, disoriented, losing its grip, and thrashing about in search of some traction on slippery political terrain. We may presume that ravings this savage are to be expected from the lower orders, from the ill-bred, ill-educated, and ill-informed, from the populist hoi polloi. But the specter of the limousine liberal incited fury just as great and unreasoning, even more egregious, among the nation's most privileged.[4]

THERE AT THE CREATION

Not all of upper class America was of one mind, however. Recognizing the breakdown for what it was—namely a root and branch indictment of the laissez-faire capitalism beloved by their ancestors—leading elements of the corporate world were prepared to venture down a different road and to go there accompanied by people and organizations outside their normal comfort zone.

Thomas Lamont, Morgan's most senior partner, thought of Roosevelt as a bulwark against social chaos even though he opposed most New Deal economic policy. Other Wall Street eminences like Paul Warburg and Otto Kahn saw the need for outside supervision of commercial life. Warburg was a Roosevelt family friend who had worried for years that "unrestrained speculation" would end in depression. Otto Kahn's avant-garde associations with the modernist art world signaled his rebel temperament. He testified before a congressional committee investigating the causes of the Depression that "a good deal must be changed. And I know the time is ripe to have it changed. Overripe in some ways."

Paul Mazur was another Wall Street analyst who had looked askance at the "sterile" capital funds accumulating in corporate coffers and off-loaded onto suspect foreign bonds or into the highly risky call loan market. He lobbied vigorously for public works and corporate taxation to release dammed up capital resources. Averill Harriman, along with Vincent Astor, started a weekly magazine, *Today* (later reinvented as *Newsweek)*, to support the New Deal. Nelson Rockefeller and Winthrop Aldrich of Chase Bank backed FDR's re-election in 1936, as did James Forrestal of Dillon, Read, and Harriman (though more perhaps because they feared the isolationism of the Republican candidate Alf Landon).

Anxious voices could be heard emanating even from the most conventional warrens of the business establishment. Henry Harriman, president of the US Chamber of Commerce, was ready to countenance some collective monitoring of commercial activity as long as business retained the upper hand. Gerard Swope, president of General Electric, offered up his own plan, a corporatist arrangement in which production and consumption would be coordinated by a national council on which representatives of the country's peak corporations would engage in publicly sanctioned self-regulation, covering matters as essential as pricing, wages, and the allocation of markets. Swope was a poor boy who had made good. As a young man in the 1890s he had taught classes at Hull House and met with socialists like Sidney and Beatrice Webb and the leader of the British Labor Party, Ramsay McDonald. Consequently GE (along with other leading companies) had inaugurated various experiments in welfare capitalism during the 1920s, including unemployment insurance. His Depression-era "Swope Plan" embraced these innovations, calling for a federal workmen's compensation act and a nationwide program of unemployment insurance.

A version of corporatist planning became in fact one salient of what is sometimes called the "first New Deal." The National Industrial Recovery Act passed during Roosevelt's first one hundred days in office established representative bodies not unlike the ones proposed by Swope, to regulate markets under the supervision of industrial councils that were in practice dominated by the largest firms in each sector of the economy. To invite the government to create such institutions, indeed to depend on the government to do that in order to circumvent the "normal" and self-evidently disastrous operations of the free market, signaled a readiness on the part of some captains of basic industry to contemplate a fundamental course correction. The same impulse that led to the creation of the Federal Reserve to supervise the financial system now extended its reach to the economy as a whole.[5]

Bolder initiatives cropped up elsewhere, for instance among certain investment houses and commercial banks more closely allied with mass consumer industries. Goldman Sachs, Lehman Brothers, Bank of America, and newer firms like the one led by E. A. Pierce (which would form the kernel of what became Merrill Lynch), firms that were emerging rivals of the older white-shoe investment houses, could see real value in having the government sanction the honesty of the Street and help ensure that ordinary people had enough wherewithal to absorb the output of an economy that increasingly rested on mass consumption. Indeed, years before the publication of his *The General Theory of Employment, Interest, and Money,* John Maynard Keynes's under-consumptionist analysis of the economic crisis was familiar to reform circles in the United States. Its emphasis on the obligation of the government to prevent the disastrous ups and downs of the business cycle, to adopt tax and spending policies that would sustain consumer purchasing power and so encourage employment and investment, was appealing to elements of corporate America. Major retailers like Macy's and Filenes, for example, advocated this view directly and through institutions like The Rockefeller Foundation and the Twentieth Century Fund. They, along with manufacturers in the textile, shoe, and office equipment business, high technology firms like IBM, and enterprises more directly tied to the mass market were ready to try something new.

It was not a homogenous group, uniform in interests or beliefs, and was often divided by regional and commercial rivalries. But there was nevertheless an organic connection between newer, often technologically innovative enterprises associated with the burgeoning mass market for housing and building supplies and household appliances and furnishings on the one hand, and major retail concerns on the other. Together, they depended on the regular expansion of the universe of mass distribution and consumption. They were linked financially to those newer investment houses, commercial banks, and real estate concerns, including, for example, Giannini's diversified and consumer-oriented banking empire in California, the Greenfield real estate and retail interests headquartered in Philadelphia, and the Bowery Savings Bank of New York. These companies and others like them rose to power in the 1920s, and once the collapse happened they were quick to urge unconventional remedies: the six-hour day, the five-day week, unemployment insurance, banking reform, large public works programs to put people to work and also to draw out savings and investment capital that was otherwise inert as long as no entirely new mass consumption industry like automobiles appeared on the horizon.

Toppling the old order was not, however, something even the most adventurous businessman took to easily or at all. Ratcheting up the degree of state intervention into the economy and public life more generally was counterintuitive for many in these circles. But they had help. People from other walks of life, likewise influenced by pre-Keynesian intuitions about the nature of the breakdown crisis and how it might be fixed, coalesced to form an informal elite vanguard of reform. The novel social type Procaccino would baptize as the limousine liberal was taking on embryonic form.

Jurists like Felix Frankfurter and Louis Brandeis during and after World War I had sided with unionizing campaigns and argued the case for jurisprudence sensitive to changing historical and social needs, freed from the constitutional constraints of "original intent." Members of the scientific management community had been struggling since the turn of the century to come up with ways of winning the allegiance of workers on the shop floor through forms of industrial democracy. Investment counselors like Waddill Catchings and William T. Foster had since the mid-1920s promoted countercyclical government spending long before it became a Keynesian maxim. Policy-oriented economists and political scientists, including Rexford Tugwell and Adolph Berle, had dissected modern managerial capitalism and zeroed in on the need for public supervision and economic planning by the state. Upper-middle-class and upper class social workers like Frances Perkins and Jane Addams and Eleanor Roosevelt had spent careers beginning in the Gilded Age and continuing through the great garment industry sweatshop uprisings of the Progressive Era ministering to exploited

workers, those men, women, and children living in the immigrant barrios of metropolitan America. Municipal-, state-, and federal-level politicians including Fiorello LaGuardia, Robert and Phillip LaFollette,
and Hugo Black lobbied for wage and hour laws and other measures
to boost the purchasing power of working people. Certain leaders of
the trade union world, who had come under the influence of Harvard
Law professors like Felix Frankfurter and the genteel women founders
of the social welfare movement like Jane Addams, were invited to join
this revolution from above. In particular those associated with what in
the 1920s was dubbed the socially conscious "New Unionism," cen-
tered especially among clothing workers, had come to see that the
gross inequalities of income and wealth systematically generated by
laissez-faire capitalism would bring the house down unless reversed by
concerted government intervention.[6]

Under way was a secular reconfiguration of the American political
economy. A newborn liberal elite, incubated in the heat of the Depression, rose to power and would remain there for a half century. Arguably, however, that would never have happened without enormous,
concerted, all-sided pressure from those millions whose lives had been
devastated by capitalism's collapse.

Workers at the core of American heavy industry who had lived for
generations under a reign of industrial autocracy braved an armada
of corporate artillery, espionage, compliant judges, paid thugs and police enforcers, dependent town elders, and fathers of the church, along
with a tidal wave of antiunion propaganda. Yet through strikes and
factory occupations they prevailed, winning a modicum of industrial
democracy no one had thought possible just a few years earlier. The
mid-1930s witnessed an explosive expansion of the labor movement
in the auto plants of Detroit, at the ports of San Francisco and New
Orleans, among the long-haul truckers of the Midwest, in the department stores of New York, on the merchant vessels crossing the oceans,
and in the rubber factories of Akron.

Similar insurgencies erupted among the unemployed, who formed
leagues in cities from Detroit to New York to demand that the government act to put people to work. Dairy and grain farmers in the
Midwest organized to stop evictions, blocked the roads so trucks

couldn't deliver produce to an already depressed market, or over-turned vats of milk rather than sell it and commit social suicide. Mortgage bankers and sheriffs were hung in effigy while auctioned-off farms were purchased for a penny by irate fellow farmers and returned to their owners. Tenant farmers and sharecroppers in the South defied their landlords, merchant-usurers, and the caste system. African Americans there in the South as well as up North agitated against American apartheid and the lynchings used to enforce it.

Tenement dwellers in the cities banded together to protect each other from getting thrown out of their apartments by the local authorities, often waiting for the sheriff to leave and then taking furniture and other belongings tossed onto the sidewalk back where they'd come from. Homeowners, cut off by the electric company, seized shuttered public utilities and turned the juice back on. Trying to survive winters without heat led some out-of-work miners and others to flout prohibitions against trespassing on private property and to dig coal from mines closed by their owners. Local and statewide political parties whose purpose was to unite embattled workers and farmers and who were not shy about indicting capitalism and seeking alternatives sprang to life on the West Coast, in the Midwest, and back East.

More radical rumblings notwithstanding, the alternative settled on turned out to civilize capitalism, not end it. Many of the movements, unions, parties, and other forms of rebellion eventually found themselves at home in the New Deal Order. Room was found for them within the exfoliating social welfare and regulatory bureaucracies of the government as well as inside the councils of the Democratic Party. By the conventional standards of that time (not our own), a remarkably cosmopolitan, ethnically and socially diverse governing elite took shape; it shared a worldview about its responsibility for public well-being and recognized, within limits, the need, when circumstances demanded it, to change the way things were.

However, not everyone who burned with rage and outrage at the depredations of the ancient regime was unequivocal in welcoming Roosevelt's assault on those "economic royalists," "Tories of industry," and "money changers" he promised to chase from the "temples of our civilization." An element of the popular rebellion had no love for a predatory capitalism. But it also worried about what might re-place it if the New Deal triumphed.

THE KINGFISH

Henry Ford's conspiratorial sense of history was an active element of populist cosmology long before the automaker arrived on the scene. However, the 1930s witnessed a portentous shift in the view of those trying to ferret out the secret source of all the trouble: Conspiracy Central migrated from Wall Street and the City of London to Moscow and New Deal Washington.

Huey Long, governor and then senator from Louisiana; Father Charles Coughlin from a parish outside Detroit; Francis E. Townsend, a retired doctor living in California; and William Lemke, a neo-populist congressman from North Dakota led movements of consider-able strength and passion that began by decrying a demonic capitalism and by hero-worshipping Roosevelt, but ended in bitter opposition to the president's New Deal. Legions of their followers came to fear that what was under construction in Washington was a mortal threat to traditional small-town values, local control over matters ranging from race relations to public schooling, and the health and wealth of mid-dling enterprise, that whole universe of family capitalism.

The Kingfish (Huey Long's moniker alluded to the master of the Mystic Knights of the Sea Lodge, a satirical fantasy of the radio show *Amos 'n' Andy*, which Long loved), hailed from Louisiana hill coun-try, a land of marginal farmers who for generations had nurtured a hatred for plantation owners and the business oligarchy of New Or-leans. The Longs were a middling farm family. Huey was home-schooled early on, then attended a Baptist seminary briefly. Although never a preacher, the Kingfish was devout. Eventually he took up the law and made it his specialty to represent small businessmen against big ones.

Winn Parish, Long's home base, had been a populist hotbed and actually elected a socialist to office in 1908. It was a world of evangel-ical hillbillies with no love for the high and mighty. The Cajuns in the southern portion of the state were Catholics but felt the same way, and Long assiduously cultivated support there as well. They all loved his audacious populist assaults on oil companies and landed elites— the "Old Regulars" including especially Standard Oil and the utility companies—that were accustomed to running things in Louisiana. His fearless, spellbinding stump speeches, always delivered in his trademark white linen suit, were enough to catapult him into the statehouse in 1928. There he managed to cajole and bully a compliant legislature into enacting a whole menu of social welfare measures including road, bridge, and school constructions, public housing, and public health facilities designed to address the rural isolation and poverty typical of most of the state. He was a readily recognizable populist hero, lacing his rousing speeches with biblical parables hill folk had grown up on.

But his fire was directed at monopoly control, not capitalism in general, which he defended. He talked about "a Wall Street controlled press," of a "Standard Oil plot to kill Huey Long," about the need to protect small business against the bankers and monopolists. When his ambitions carried him to the US Senate in the depths of the Depression in 1932, he launched a "Share the Wealth" movement. It mobilized millions with incendiary images of fat-cat parasites and gold-obsessed eastern bankers. Thousands of Share the Wealth clubs formed not only in the South but all through the country's midsection. It may have had rubbery economic legs to stand on—its proposal to heavily tax and redistribute great personal fortunes would hardly have had a measurable impact on the stalled economy. But the Kingfish roused a righteous anger when he decried "Rockefeller, Morgan and their crowd" who had "stepped up and took the riches God had created for all, leaving behind but a pittance for the rest of the country to survive on."

Long promised to make "every man a king," a phrase he borrowed from a William Jennings Bryan speech of 1900 that ended with the egalitarian, antiaristocratic flourish, "but no one wears a crown." That kind of egalitarianism rested on a native faith in propertied independence, not on notions of social solidarity circulating through the labor insurgencies of that era. Share the Wealth demands were aimed precisely at restoring that kind of small-holder society. Its outlook, Long insisted, owed nothing to Marx and everything to the bible and the Declaration of Independence: "Communism? Hell no!" he declaimed. "This plan is the only defense this country's got against Communism."

Every family was to be "furnished by the Government a homestead allowance, free of debt." That allowance would provide the "reasonable comforts of life." Hours of work were to be regulated "to such an extent as to prevent over-production." Agricultural output was to be balanced with what "can be consumed according to the laws of God." Pensions would be provided for all those over sixty, and education through college made available to all. A capital levy on all fortunes over $1 million would help pay for this and more.

But of course those pensions, that universal education, the levy on capital and private fortunes to provide the financial wherewithal were all to be the gifts of a government grown much more muscular. Here is where the ambivalence of this subspecies of populism became apparent. These calls to expand the social welfare functions of the state clearly mimicked what many stalwarts of the New Deal and even those circles to the left of the New Deal were also championing. Indeed, some of this had already been achieved under Long's tutelage in Louisiana.

This would be true as well of the movements led by Coughlin, Townsend, and Lemke, which together with Long's we can now identify as ancestral forms of modern-day right-wing populism. They did not yet evince that root and branch hostility to big government characteristic of the Tea Party. Yet something about what was happening in New Deal Washington led them to abandon that ship.

Ruled by his megalomania, Long overreached, thinking his own considerable popularity exceeded Roosevelt's, which it did not. When the new president excoriated the "money changers" and "economic royalists," the Kingfish cheered him on. But then he began attacking FDR for temporizing with the plutocracy. A case could be made that indeed that was just what the president was doing, at least in some respects, especially during the opening years of this administration. For example, Long opposed Roosevelt's initial recovery legislation, the National Industrial Recovery Act, as a sellout to big business. And that is essentially what this corporatist arrangement was in practice; it left the dominant corporations in each industrial sector collectively in charge of setting prices, wages, hours, and other key business decisions.

No matter how just his criticisms, Long was intemperate in his assault on the newly emerging elite. He denounced a whole menagerie of "high-brow Brain Trusters, brutish . . . low brow politicians, [and] top-hatted . . . cigar-smoking Wall Streeters" who, the senator alleged, were plotting with their European equivalents to cheat the American folk. He promised that his Share the Wealth vision—"this plan of God"—had no place in it for government "destroying any of the things raised to eat or wear; nor does it countenance wholesale destruction of hogs, cattle, or milk," which the New Deal's Agricultural Adjustment Administration was then in the process of doing in order to reduce the glut of agricultural products exerting downward pressure on prices and driving farmers and ranchers under. FDR considered Long "one of the two most dangerous men in America" (the other was Douglas MacArthur), and likened the senator to Hitler and Mussolini.

In 1935, not long before he was gunned down in the Louisiana state capitol (by the son-in-law of one of his many political enemies), Long addressed Congress in a peroration about the Share the Wealth movement that recalled a long century of biblically inflected populist oratory. "Will we allow the political sports, the high heelers, the wiseacres, and those who ridicule us in our misery and poverty to keep us from organizing these societies in every hamlet so that they may bring back to life this law and custom of God and this country?" The senator naturally indicted "the financial masters of this country," but also those "wiseacres" filling out the alphabet of New Deal bureaucracies who presumed they knew best how to fix things. "Save the country. Save mankind. Who can be wrong in such a work, and who cares what consequences may come following the mandates of the Lord, of the Pilgrims, of Jefferson, Webster, and Lincoln. . . . Better to make this fight and lose than to be a party to a system that strangles humanity."[7]

Gerald L. K. Smith, Long's right-hand man and after the senator's assassination, his political executor, was even less inhibited than Long, driving the movement in a direction the Kingfish wouldn't go. Smith was a poor boy from a small Wisconsin town of modest farms and businesses. There, unpaid, part-time itinerant preachers sermonized at Disciples of Christ churches. Their congregants resented the pretensions of the more established denominations. Gerald attended a one-room schoolhouse and eventually graduated to attend Valparaiso University in Indiana, "the poor man's Harvard." His father had supported Robert LaFollette Sr., the country's most distinguished Progressive legislator. Gerald was himself influenced by the "social gospel" taught at Valparaiso. In fact, in the 1920s he had helped organize trade union locals for the American Federation of Labor and he had opposed the Ku Klux Klan.

Smith became a fundamentalist preacher in Shreveport, Louisiana. There he chastised the local elite as "the silk-stocking crowd," and opposed the "open shop" antiunion campaign of the local Chamber of Commerce. He took to the radio to inveigh against "coal-mining peonage," and began working for Huey Long in his struggle against the state's "feudal lords." He steeped his hatred for Wall Street in a patriotic Christianity familiar to broad stretches of the pious Southland. At home with the folk language of country populism, he compared the poor man's scant wardrobe to that of the Morgans and Mellons, who he labeled "contemptible hoarders." Clutching the bible, coatless, sweating profusely, Smith exhorted his followers to end the rule of Wall Street, confident that "there are enough good people who believe in the flag and the Bible to seize and control the government of America." That sounded insurrectionary, and he meant it to. At six feet tall, weighing in at 210 pounds, with wavy red hair that flopped over his forehead the way Long's did, Smith could be pure histrionics. He loved showing off his muscular physique and conveyed a kind of roguish glamour. Unlike the "caponized clergy," Gerald was a "he-man." H. L. Mencken described him as "the gustiest and goriest, loudest and lustiest, the deadliest and damndest orator ever heard on this or any other earth." Yet beneath all the theatrics and fire-and-brimstone revolutionary rhetoric, Smith emphasized that America must "democratize wealth without destroying the capitalist system."

After Long's death the darker side of the preacher's Herrenvolk democracy surfaced more prominently. While Smith veered away from outright Jew baiting during the early years of the Depression, he would head back in that direction later. After all, the usurious Jew had always figured somewhere in the populist imagining of a satanic financial octopus.[8]

THE RADIO PRIEST

A local parish priest from the North would update that tradition to take account of what the New Deal had wrought. Like Long, Reverend Charles E. Coughlin would start out loving FDR and end up hating him. He was raised in a lower-middle-class Catholic family in Hamilton, Ontario, where his father, who came from Indiana, worked as a lumberjack and on steamboats. Ordained in 1923, Coughlin was an obscure cleric at the Church of the Little Flower in Royal Oak, a poor, mainly Protestant, industrial suburb just outside Detroit, a hotbed of Klan activity in the 1920s. In fact, Coughlin began sermonizing on the radio in 1926 in response to Klan cross burnings on the grounds of his church. By 1933 he was a national celebrity, the "radio priest" whose weekly broadcasts, listened to by millions (up to thirty million for his Sunday sermons), made him probably the most mesmerizing speaker of that era. He could be alternately and deliberately colloquial, academic, vulgar, and audacious, deploying a musical Irish brogue to convey a drama of high righteousness.

Even before the 1932 elections, Coughlin was denouncing President Hoover as "the banker's friend, the Holy Ghost of the rich, the protective angel of Wall Street." He considered the secretary of the treasury, Andrew Mellon (the most celebrated since Alexander Hamilton, until he became the most reviled ever), a modern Judas. Al Smith, leader of the Democratic Party old guard, was "a lackey of Morgan."

During the first one hundred days of the new regime and beyond, he applauded Roosevelt for leading the "Wall Street battle," a modern "Lincoln leading the fight against financial slavery." He coined the memorable slogan "Roosevelt or Ruin" and the somewhat less long-lived "The New Deal is Christ's Deal." His charismatic radio sermons and gymnastic live performances were spellbinding recitations of an old refrain. His mellifluous voice and trim, athletic body (Coughlin was an ex–football player and coach) charmed multitudes into believing the Depression was first and last the fault of the eastern banking establishment. That establishment cared only about gold. Having built an altar to gold, these "high priests of finance" invented both a liturgy and a worship that they had imposed upon the peoples of the earth. In its pursuit, Wall Street was prepared to beggar the rest of the country. Indeed, "international bankers" had subjected people from every civilized nation to a "torture more refined than was ever excogitated by the trickery of the Romans or the heartlessness of slave owners."[9]

Coughlin's rhetoric, however colorful, was also anchored in that branch of formal Catholic theology that had for a generation wrestled with the economic and social dilemmas presented by the vicissitudes of capitalism. Both the 1891 *Rerum Novarum* of Pope Leo XIII and the more recent *Quadragesimo Anno* (1931) of Pius XI declared it a moral urgency to preserve the traditional institutions of family and local community against the predations of unrestrained industrial and financial capitalism and against the atheism and mammon worship they bred. It was an economic theology that found a place for those state and civil arrangements designed to reinforce organic ways of life, moral strictures, and social hierarchies that had arisen outside of the market relations and before they had become so ubiquitous. So the priest advocated work and income guarantees and even allowed that government must "curtail individualism, that if necessary factories shall be licensed and their output shall be limited." But the state was to steer clear of family matters like schooling, authority over children, and the conventions governing marriage and sexual relations, which were the proper realm of the home and church.

Social conscience Catholicism notwithstanding, the priest's sermons during these early years of the Depression also fell well within the chorus of mainstream populism. To escape the oligarchy's grip, the nation would have to return to the fundamental Christian principle of economic life: "By the sweat of thy brow thou shalt earn thy bread." Labor must always take precedence over capital. Yet he was careful to point out that he was not against capitalism *tout court;* he was "no Socialist, no Communist, no Fascist." Thanks to its atheism and internationalism, communism was anathema. In line with those papal encyclicals, Coughlin pronounced capitalism "the best system of economics provided it does not run counter to the laws of morality." But capitalism had been corrupted by usurious elites. Big corporate capitalism was stealthily "privately sustaining in some instances the worst elements of Communism." It needed wholesale reformation—or else there would be "bloody revolution."

Roosevelt, at first, seemed the most promising agent of that secular reformation. As long as the president seemed to be waging holy war against the "money changers," the priest praised him as a champion, leading the nation in "as great a battle as Runnymede or Gettysburg." But when FDR seemed to retreat from the front lines, Coughlin grew increasingly sour.

In the eyes of Coughlin and others of the populist right wing, the New Deal had become too meddlesome, its regulatory reforms really a disguised version of "financial socialism." The Gold Reserve Act of 1934 and the Banking Act of the next year were, in Coughlin's view, Roosevelt's version of Leninism, contributing to the complete centralization of the money power in the hands of the international banking fraternity. Coughlin wanted the Federal Reserve nationalized to pry it loose from Wall Street. (Like Long and Glenn Beck he hated the Federal Reserve, the überinstitution, apparently, for all those searching for the roots of limousine liberalism.)

Especially in the charged atmosphere of the 1936 presidential campaign Coughlin's invective grew more and more bombastic and theatrical, likening the New Deal to a "broken down Colossus straddling the harbor of Rhodes, its left leg standing on ancient Capitalism and its right mired in the red mud of communism." As FDR's first term drew to a close, the priest began describing the New Deal as a coalition of the White House, communists, and bankers. Like Ford's earlier formulation, it seemed a bizarre amalgam. The Brains Trust had been infiltrated by communists, yet the New Deal had become a "government of the bankers, by the bankers, and for the bankers." At a mass meeting in Cincinnati during the presidential campaign, Coughlin decried FDR as "anti-God and a radical," accused him of plotting to make the United States a "one party form of government," and declared that he was not afraid to "advocate the use of bullets" to accomplish that objective.

While the international banking cabal always remained in his crosshairs, increasingly the radio priest stigmatized their social profile and the types they associated with. "Congressmen from New York," elitists from the Ivy League, bankers off at their "grouse-hunting estates in Scotland who never travelled west of Buffalo," were due a comeuppance. These "big shots" would pay for the years of humiliation they doled out to the country's plain and unpretentious people. Mario Procaccino would do no better than this, invoking the aggrieved feelings of resentment against know-it-all and impious limousine liberals. Loyal followers of the radio priest wrote to the president charging that he had "deceived the working man" with his "pagan methods." The New Deal was after all "surrounded by atheists . . . surrounded by red and pink Communists." Coughlin was trading in a politics of moral panic and emotional revenge.[10]

"Pagan methods" also alluded to the tincture of anti-Semitism that began to creep into the priest's broadcasts and into the pages of *Social Justice,* the magazine of his National Union for Social Justice, the organization Coughlin put together in preparation for the 1936 elections. By 1938 the magazine was publishing the "Protocols of the Elders of Zion" and increasingly reiterated Henry Ford's revelation about the organic connection between bankers, Bolsheviks, and Jews. Like Ford, Coughlin claimed the Jewish banking fraternity had orchestrated the Bolshevik revolution. Moreover, the radio priest's growing sympathy for Nazism was not so shocking. Fascism, after all, had its roots, partly, in a European version of populism, nurtured by a post–World War I disgust with the selfishness, incompetence, and decadence of cosmopolitan elites, as well as a bellicose racial nationalism.

For a while the National Union grew rapidly. During the 1936 campaign, it had 302 more or less functioning units operating in the 435 congressional districts. While that sounds impressive, the electoral results were not.[11]

THE GOOD DOCTOR

Early in 1936 Coughlin had joined in uneasy alliance with Gerald Smith from Long's Share the Wealth movement, and sixty-seven-year-old doctor Francis Townsend, the founder of a nationwide organization advocating a universal pension for all those over sixty: the "Old Age Revolving Pension Plan." Together they formed a new political party, the Union Party, and nominated Congressman William Lemke from North Dakota as their candidate for president.

Townsend was a gaunt, white-haired MD with sunken eyes, dressed in threadbare outfits, who had practiced in the Black Hills of South Dakota, burned-over populist territory for generations. He was born into a poor and religious farming family. Once grown, he followed the bumpy trajectory of many a small businessman on the make. He moved out West and started a hay-farming business in California. That failed. Then he returned to South Dakota, got a medical degree, and ministered to patients on the Great Plains. But he was restless. When done doctoring, he moved back to California and ran a dry ice factory in Long Beach. That too failed. Next he became a real estate agent and dabbled in land speculation without great success, so he became a public health official, but lost his job after three years. Finally, he settled into a modest retirement community in Long Beach.

Dr. Townsend fit the profile of family capitalism with its back up, simultaneously anti–big business and a guardian of small-holder capitalism. His "plan" caught fire. Thousands of Townsend clubs (membership estimated at more than three million) were formed by close-knit patriarchal families proud of their self-reliance and thrift, deferential to their elders, and expressly patriotic. Many ministers joined, and meetings often took on an evangelical air. And, although the movement stood at odds with the administration in Washington, the doctor was at pains to make clear that "the Townsend Plan will save America from Radicalism."

Yet Townsend's plan, like so much of the Depression-era populism that ended up feeling a basic antipathy to the New Deal, actually at the same time displayed a real kinship with it. Arguably the movement prodded the administration to move forward more aggressively with the legislation that became Social Security. Its premise was that the Depression was a function of the inadequate consuming power of the average American, a crisis of underconsumption, which in turn discouraged investment and kept the economy flattened. Townsend argued that paying retirees $200 a month, a sum they would be le-

gally compelled to spend not save, flushing that money into circulation, would jump-start the economy. It was to be funded by a 2 percent
transaction tax on all businesses. Whatever the economic flaws of the
plan—there were many and even Coughlin and Lemke were leery—it
also went beyond where the New Deal was prepared to go and was,
on paper, considerably more generous than what became the law of
the land. A universal tax on business was rejected not only by the
business community, but the inner circles of the administration were
also cold to the idea.

In his own way, Townsend, like Long and Coughlin, was not anticapitalist, but rather was searching for ways to save the system of
private enterprise from the profiteers who were looting it. Like the
South Dakota populists of a generation earlier, he went after the
bankers and the "financial middle men." That sounded New Dealish.
Yet at the same time he decried the new Social Security system as a
"miserable dole." He had no use for "brain trust professors . . . who
don't care a tinker's damn how the old folks live or die." Populism
faced off against populism.[12]

THE GREAT FEAR OF 1936

Looking back, FDR's reelection in 1936 seems a foregone conclusion
(in the end the Union Party garnered less than a million votes—2 percent of the total—and no electoral votes). But it was not perceived that
way then. A great fear infected the ranks of the administration and its
critical allies in the newly risen labor movement that these populist currents antipathetic to the New Deal might pose a serious political threat.
This was already the case by 1935, and when the Union Party formed
the next year, the situation seemed grave. After all, its components—
Share the Wealth clubs, National Union for Social Justice electoral
groupings, Townsend Plan community gatherings—amounted to millions of organized citizens. In Coughlin, Long, and later Smith they
were inspired by captivating leaders. While they disagreed among
themselves (Long liked Townsend's scheme, Coughlin did not; Smith
soon proved too obnoxiously and publicly anti-Semitic and uncom-
fortably close to the Klan to tolerate; Coughlin was far friendlier to

collectivist solutions than Townsend or Long), their presidential candidate, William Lemke, embodied the social and cultural common denominator holding these movements together, at least temporarily.

A pious German Lutheran from a pioneering North Dakota farm family of some means, Lemke had been at various times a lawyer and land speculator. He had spent his congressional career warning about the threat to that indigenous American individualism coming from the forces of bureaucracy. He saw himself as the guardian of the "little man" put upon by big government and big business. The northern Great Plains, including North Dakota, suffered from a prolonged drought, whole towns blacked out by clouds of dust. This was well-worn populist geography. Lemke was elected attorney general and later congressman as a progressive-populist Republican running on the Non-Partisan League ticket. Like his compatriots, he started off as an enthusiast for Roosevelt.

Soon, like the others, his ardor cooled. He inveighed against "the little coteries of bureaucrats in Washington representing the money-changers . . . trying to destroy the farmer." His campaign speeches warned, "We are fast approaching a feudal system, with farmers as the feudal serfs." Vassalage to eastern banks was a venerable populist plaint. But Lemke also spied a modern version of serfdom, decrying the way the government dole corroded the armature of individualism. Yet he shared the ambivalence of his Union Party partners. So he called for a huge government program to rescue farmers—the Frazier-Lemke bill to refinance farm mortgages. He supported, with some reservations, the Townsend Plan, which would have required a sizeable government bureaucracy to administer; Long's Share the Wealth program, which included proposals for public ownership of the railroads; and Coughlin's advocacy of a national bank. Indeed, what most embittered him about the New Deal was the administration's refusal to get behind his Frazier-Lemke bill. Amid this rain forest of prospective bureaucracies, some of which he seemed to both love and hate, Lemke nonetheless made sure to rail against "the Harvard and Yale boys sent to teach our pigs birth control." Such were the living contradictions of "little man" populism caught in the maelstrom of economic disaster.[13]

WHAT NOW LITTLE MAN?

In their purest forms the Long, Townsend, and Coughlin movements echoed a besieged culture of small-town patriarchal and personalized wealth and property, overwhelmed by nationwide industry, national markets, the modern state, and the impersonal bureaucracy of the corporation. But the moral condemnations of concentrated wealth, Wall Street, the "Money Power," and parasitic gain were broadly appealing well beyond the borders of "our town" America. So too, the depictions of the enemy as slothful, profligate, cunning, sensual, and sybaritic, yet distant, impersonal, malevolent, and conspiratorial were music to the ears not only of local merchants, community bankers, petty businessmen, and storekeepers. They resonated as well among Irish and German Catholic craftsmen, uprooted Appalachian Protestants, and East European immigrant Catholic industrial workers.

Especially among the latter the papal encyclicals Coughlin would often cite or quote counted heavily. Many a Polish autoworker, Slavic steelworker, and German carpenter listened intently to both the social Catholicism of Father Coughlin and the social democracy of John L. Lewis, the leader of the new, militant industrial union movement. While the captains of these movements bristled at each other from afar, members of Share the Wealth clubs or the National Union of Social Justice often found themselves together with fellow craftsmen in the more conservative American Federation of Labor or even with their insurgent brethren in the Congress of Industrial Organizations. Blue collar conservatively inflected populism was born long before Richard Nixon invoked the "silent majority."

Anticommunism increasingly preoccupied the ranks of Coughlinites particularly. But the "communism" they really feared, which Lemke and Long also shunned, displayed a striking resemblance to the centralizing, bureaucratic, and statist orientation of the New Deal itself. What these anticommunists hated far worse than the Soviet Union, about which they probably knew little, was precisely those more recent transformations in American political economy and society: the advent of the impersonal, national corporation and the consumer culture it encouraged, and the emergence of an intrusive administrative state regulatory apparatus. It was this equation, at the level of mass politics, between anticommunism and anticapitalism, that combusted to produce early intimations of limousine liberalism.

Observers of right-wing populism over the last generation have found it surpassingly odd that these malcontents from the lower middle and working classes have found themselves in alliance with corporate elites, their putative enemies. How could that be, given that their material interests would seem to be so at odds? History, however, obeys its own logic. It is noteworthy, after all, that while followers of Coughlin were zeroing in on Wall Street shylocks and their New Deal confederates, elements of the business old guard—those very same villains allegedly masterminding things in Washington according to the radio priest and his confederates—took after left-wing Jews allegedly running the New Deal's assault on laissez-faire capitalism. Why would they do that when the New Deal in the eyes of its elite architects was trying to rescue capitalism from what threatened to be its terminal crisis? Try as he might Roosevelt couldn't penetrate the old guard's obtuse refusal to see what he really had in mind: "I am fighting communism, Huey Longism, Coughlinism. . . . I want to save our system, the capitalistic system." They weren't listening.

Although they did not assemble in the same political camp, as they do today inside the Republican Party, traditional conservative elites and hard-pressed rebels much further down the social hierarchy did discover a common enemy in these formative years. Grassroots insurgencies like the Union Party and elite anti–New Deal business-sponsored organizations like the American Liberty League had precious little in common, as one might say today about the Business Roundtable and the Tea Party. But they could together craft a new archetype: an eastern elite that was part Anglo-Saxon, Ivy League financiers, bankers with those "grouse-hunting estates in Scotland," and part Jewish, left-wing government bureaucrats. In total, it was a new aristocracy of money, power, and expertise, one bent on remaking the world.

This ideological confection, part real, part phantasm, took root among struggling small businessmen and family farmers, among precariously positioned white-collar employees and better-off elements of the "lace-curtain" Irish Catholic lower middle classes, and Irish and

German skilled working classes. Their Anglophobia and religiosity found a perfect foil in this bizarre amalgam of banker and Bolshevik. Coughlin's support in particular tracked closely with the lower ends of the income pyramid. Manual workers, the unemployed, even those benefiting from the New Deal's Works Progress Administration were more avid than people in the professions. Still, white-collar Catholics were also drawn to the priest. Farmers were, too, but adherents could more commonly be found among small-town businesspeople in the heartland of the northern Great Plains.[14]

New Deal populism and this renegade version of populism were, in some ways, kindred spirits. FDR may have used it first, but images of "the forgotten man" cropped up in the radio priest's broadcasts, in the pages of *Social Justice,* and in Huey Long's stump speeches. It conveyed that wounded sense of being trampled over by the organized power blocs of modern industrial society—big business and big government. Bruised feelings of exclusion continue to animate the legatees of this "little man" populism. Its echoes are audible today in the fury of Tea Party denunciations of limousine liberals.

Before the Great Depression this emerging form of right-wing populism was also distinctly Protestant and nativist. What the Union Party briefly fostered was a new ecumenicalism among the disaffected that crossed denominational lines, intermixed middling and working class people, and embraced Catholics and immigrants. This "solidarity" would prove fragile in our own time, at least with respect to immigrants. Still, it suggested that the animosity congealed in the image of the limousine liberal could migrate over extensive social terrain. So too, a powerful undertow of patriotism ran through all these movements. In one way or another, Long, Coughlin, and Lemke identified their cause with a defense of what we now call the "homeland." They were mad at the new elitists not only because their cosmopolitanism was morally suspect, but also because it showed insufficient fealty to the nation, that highest expression of patriarchal authority. To this day, although not necessarily in the same way, right-wing populists continue to indict limousine liberals on the same grounds.

A new genotype was taking shape during the Great Depression. It would mutate during the decades to follow. Some traits would prove recessive. The fiery element of anticapitalism that the breakdown of capitalism had ignited would cool yet not die away entirely. The "Jewish question" would likewise fade from view (although it would show up now and then at darker margins of the movement). Limousine liberals of the New Deal persuasion would always be found culpable, but what they were guilty of would shift with the times. When political life was more stable, organized movements of conservative rebels would subside, leaving behind mainly a lingering atmosphere of suspicion and unease. When the temperature rose, so too did mobilizations of "little man" discontent. While what had surfaced in the tumultuous 1930s would never reappear in just that form, its ghost haunted the future.

4

All in the Family

Elites Against Elites

How noxiously wacky it seems to us now: the outlandish canard that Franklin Delano Roosevelt was a closet communist. Yet this conviction was by no means confined to circles of the ill-bred and ill-educated, the credulous and resentful. Hard to imagine perhaps, but that paranoia was shared by the country's best educated, wealthiest, most respected and powerful people, guardians of its weightiest corporations and banks, and leaders of its political establishment, often to the manner born, bred to protect and steer American civilization. Under the stress of the Great Depression and faced with the unnerving transformations of the New Deal, they lost their sangfroid and became temporarily deranged.

One of the greatest of American historians, Richard Hofstadter, published an essay in 1964, when Barry Goldwater was running for president, that went on to become a classic piece of historical literature. He called it "The Paranoid Style in American Politics." Although it ranged widely across the span of American history beginning in the late eighteenth century, it was mainly absorbed then as an explanation for McCarthyism, that peculiar and damaging political paranoia of the early Cold War years that purported to discover communist conspirators at work in every nook and cranny of American life (though for some the essay was perhaps an indictment of Goldwater). Hofstadter argued that this pathology had in earlier times and again during Senator McCarthy's reign, taken root among people suffering economic and social dispossession, out of touch with the main currents of American life, passed over, forgotten, often poorly educated, more likely found in small towns and in fundamentalist congregations, at odds with much about the urbanity and secularism of modern times.[1]

Paranoid "little men" during the Cold War and before may have conformed in some vital respects to Hofstadter's profile. But the essay concealed a striking blind spot. Its explanation could not account for the pathological hatred evinced by the high and mighty of the American Liberty League in the 1930s. Even more immediately misguided than that, it couldn't have been more wrong when it came to grasping the higher order anticommunist conspiracy mongering that captured the imagination of political elites after World War II.

Before McCarthy there was McCarthyism. It originated not in the American outback but at the summit of political power. The Truman administration began purging the government of suspected reds before anyone outside of Wisconsin had ever heard of Joseph McCarthy. Compared to the sore losers and cultural Neanderthals Hofstadter described, the corporate chieftains and investment bankers who ran the Liberty League during the 1930s and the postwar liberal elites ferreting out conspirators in the government's bureaucracies might as well have landed here from another planet. They were the crème de la crème, not the dispossessed but the dispossessors of others, Ivy League–trained, worldly wise, the epitome of rational good sense and good order. Nonetheless, they fostered an atmosphere of fear beyond all reason without which it is harder to imagine the nationwide witch hunt that dragged on for years.

Apologias for this aberrant behavior were offered then and since. But they tend to be self-referential. Thus, the argument goes as follows: there was, after all, a worldwide communist conspiracy whose tentacles reached everywhere—across borders, inside churches, snaking through families, insinuated into the classroom and library, masquerading in the movies. Here disguised as acts of social benevolence, there pretending a passion for racial justice and world peace, the conspiracy Joseph McCarthy would later characterize as "immense" was already depicted that way by precisely those empowered, liberal elites the senator would excoriate for being its witting coconspirators.

What may seem a clinical case of paranoid hallucination when the patient hails from the social down under may look instead like the health of the state if those seeing spooky things in the night come bearing pedigrees of distinction. But then, if we credit the architects of the Cold War political order with a sober estimation of a wily, subversive external threat to the domestic tranquility, why dismiss the imaginings of Long, Coughlin, and others about a Wall Street conspiracy to undermine democracy as the ravings of disgruntled demagogues? After all, the evidence for the latter is, if anything, stronger than the former, although in the end it is rather weightless on both counts. However, to acknowledge that a descent into the swamplands of primitive nightmare can happen even among those at the most empyrean reaches of the established order of things can be profoundly disquieting. Who's running the asylum?

Sometimes believing is seeing. Or in this case, believing can make it impossible to see. The New Deal Democratic Party members presided over the postwar political order at home and abroad, and undertook to purge communists wherever they thought they found them, whether in France or on the assembly line in Detroit or in the US Postal Service. But that same Democratic Party could also claim credit for the victory over fascism and the reconstruction of the European economic and social order afterward. That double triumph made it hard to conceive that these circles of wise men, entrusted with so much power, might also be vulnerable to delusions of their own.

Perhaps they weren't, not really. Arguably, witch-hunting reds was merely a tactical ploy, part of a strategic démarche on the part of the Cold War political establishment, but not an article of faith, never rising to the level of a true conviction and crusade. Use it to defeat the left and re-establish capitalism in the West and to fend off critics on the right at home; discard when finished. No doubt for some it was a bit of both, part ideological fantasy, part down-and-dirty politics. In either case, however, the postwar liberal elites were premature McCar-thyites. And this turned out to be a piece of political dramaturgy they would, at least to some degree, regret having authored.

What by the 1950s had been anointed as "the establishment" had only recently come on the scene to challenge and triumph over an older establishment. The members of the new version, like those of the old, occupied the commanding heights of the economy and the political system. In turn, they found themselves in the crosshairs of powerful rivals who were at odds with the New Deal Order and con-testing for control of the nation's political machinery. As guerrilla in-surgents sometimes do, these malcontents captured the anticommunist heavy artillery of their liberal enemies and turned it on their oppo-nents. McCarthyism zeroed in on the limousine liberal as the arch ac-complice of the worldwide communist conspiracy. While once the object of populist wrath, after the war the limousine liberal became instead the main target of a nasty assault by one elite against another.

WORLDS IN COLLISION

Like a Bessemer converter, war fused the still elastic and impure com-ponents of the New Deal into a more durable political order that would last for decades. It combined the national security state with the welfare state and restored corporate America to its accustomed dominant position in the nation's political economy. While the more daring reform initiatives of the tumultuous 1930s—economic plan-ning, public ownership, guaranteed employment, universal health care, comanagement of industry—had largely been abandoned even before the outbreak of war, what endured was still a distinctly liberal dispen-sation. It bore an ideological and programmatic affinity, albeit a dis-tanced one, with European social democracy. Running it all was a newly composed elite of state managers, social engineering bureau-crats, and labor statesmen, together with the more usual suspects from the country's peak industrial corporations, white-shoe banking houses and law firms, and the war-born military/intelligence apparatus. How-ever committed to the new status quo, this was a milieu for which further reform remained a live option.

After the war, all of this set off multiple alarm bells in other regions of the political universe, mainly among Republicans, but also among Southern Democrats. They worried about what they saw as the leviathan state. It seemed to be metastasizing throughout the body politic. Fiscal and monetary interventions by government administrators had little use for that old-time religion about balanced budgets. Whole sectors of business were subject to the regulatory arms of multiple federal bureaucracies. The state was poking its nose into the labor market and even into the black box of the workplace. As a deliverer and guarantor of social welfare, it threatened prevailing modes of party patronage and opened up an avenue of escape from traditional racial and patriarchal dependencies. And the war had justified extending the reach of the welfare state through the GI Bill. Might that constitute a dangerous precedent? Talk of enlarged low-cost public housing programs and even government health insurance were taking on legislative shape in the halls of Congress. The war had also accelerated a long-simmering racial crisis as civil rights groups threatened mass protests against segregated armed forces. It became severe enough that the Southern wing of the Democratic Party promised to secede if the liberal elite running things in Washington followed through on threats to dismantle the region's distinctive form of apartheid.

Haunting all these anxieties about this unsettling new order of things at home were the dire forebodings let loose by the Cold War. Fear of communism is too simple an explanation for what transpired.

War left European capitalist economies prostrate. The Red Army in Eastern Europe (and soon enough Mao's People's Liberation Army in China) and the Communist Party in the western half of the continent was in the ascendant. The newly ensconced liberal establishment in Washington met that threat by military means of course, with the North Atlantic Treaty Organization (NATO) most prominently. And it also crafted programs and institutions (the Marshall Plan, the International Monetary Fund, the World Bank, and others) designed to reconstruct European capitalism under the supervision of reliable, anticommunist regimes. This made permanent what had been provisionally the case since World War I: namely, a deep involvement in steering global affairs by the American state.

Taking on that role, however, aroused an ingrained resistance to venturing abroad that long predated the red menace. A strange political mythography emerged. In the view of those—both discontented elites and ordinary folk—who opposed the new establishment, it was simultaneously guilty of plotting to Sovietize the American homeland yet too intricately enmeshed in anticommunist machinations abroad. In this view an elite that had already proved its readiness to upset the way things used to be at home was getting the country entangled overseas in alliances and economic commitments that would undermine its traditional freedom of action and cherished immunity from foreign intrigues. It became increasingly hard to tell where the international Cold War ended and the domestic one began. They bled into each other because those occupying the summits of power composed a cadre of state managers present at the creation of new worlds. Who were these people anyway? And did they in fact constitute a new ruling class?

MEN IN STRIPED PANTS

From the outset of the war, the institutions of domestic economic mobilization as well as the military and the State Department were manned by Wall Street and corporate lawyers, bankers, and industrialists. Henry Lewis Stimson, Roosevelt's secretary of war, was the patriarch of this elite corps. Originally a Wall Street lawyer, he first served as war secretary for President Taft at the beginning of the century, and later as secretary of state under Hoover. He was the son of a New York mugwump, a graduate of Phillips Academy, and a member of Skull and Bones at Yale. Stimson was nominally a Teddy Roosevelt Republican, but like so many mandarins of the new postwar order, he was effectively nonpartisan and had been, for example, part of Woodrow Wilson's brains trust at the Versailles peace negotiations. During World War I he volunteered (although he was already forty-nine years old), became an artillery officer, and saw active duty in France. Later Stimson helped found the Council on Foreign Relations, which would become the strategic think tank of the liberal foreign policy establishment.

Equally at home in Washington and on the Street, Stimson acted as elder statesman and éminence grise. He was ably assisted by two younger Wall Street protégés, John McCloy and Robert Lovett. McCloy and Lovett, together with Averill Harriman and James Forrestal, who became undersecretary of the navy after a tour of duty at Dillon, Read, and Harriman, were representatives of a rising generation often born and bred in the upper tiers of the Social Register. They first came of age during World War I.

For these architects of Cold War America, the killing fields of Europe two decades earlier had been a testing ground for acts of self-sacrifice, feats of heroic athleticism, loyalty, and magnanimity that carried with them a kind of secular grace. It was the ordeal that would prove their worthiness to rule. They were to rule through pure acts of voluntary service that mirrored the honorific codes of conduct they so admired in their Tory socialist European (especially British) aristocratic counterparts.

Young men of old money yearned for this moment to prove their valor on the killing fields of Flanders or assaulting the impregnable Siegfried line. For example, Winthrop Aldrich (the son of the then famous senator Nelson Aldrich from Rhode Island) was a devoted yachtsman who joined the Navy Reserve. Called to active duty, he was assigned command of a training regiment that left him frustrated. Finally, his repeated requests for sea duty were honored, and he served on the USS *New Orleans,* convoying merchant ships across the treacherous North Atlantic. With the war over, he returned to his career as a Wall Street banker and lawyer.

This was a telltale footprint of breeding, money, and service. As a young college student at Princeton, James Forrestal early on cultivated his social and business ties to the WASP establishment. Then he interrupted his financial career to serve during World War I as lieutenant junior grade in the conspicuously upper class Aviation Training Division in the Office of the Chief of Naval Operations. Later, after World War II, he became the nation's first secretary of defense.

Robert Lovett's father had looked after the Edward Harriman railroad interests in Texas and helped mobilize the economy for war by serving on the War Industries Board under Bernard Baruch. His son was a playmate of W. Averill Harriman's at the family compound, and the two boys grew up to be business partners. Decidedly patrician in manner and a graduate of Yale, Robert Abercrombie Lovett would go on to become secretary of defense under Truman. But first he became a navy pilot during World War I. Indeed, he joined a flying unit of the Navy Reserve (the first aerial coastal patrol unit or the "First Yale Unit") made up of fellow "Yalies," which was financed by Morgan Bank senior partner Henry Davison. Known as the "millionaires unit," these rakish aviators trained at Davison's Peacock Point, Long Island, estate. Lovett was the squadron's most heroic pilot, who led nighttime dive-bombing raids on German submarines.

Soldiering, along with the right social pedigree, was not the only form of apprenticeship. Some who became essential players after World War II missed the first war but were seasoned by other experiences. Take Averill Harriman. E. H. Harriman, the dynasty's founder, was a kind of sea-dog capitalist, better known as a conquistador than as a statesman. But his son Averill evolved differently. A graduate of Groton and Yale, he'd formed his own shipping line and merchant bank, but then joined the government as a pro–New Deal businessman. Roosevelt sent him off as special envoy to meet with Stalin and Churchill. Known as "the Crocodile" for the placid demeanor that concealed his readiness to act boldly, Harriman was ambassador to the Soviet Union when FDR died.

Dean Goodersham Acheson was the son of an Episcopal bishop, not wealthy but wise and well-connected, a graduate of Groton and Yale. He became a student of Felix Frankfurter's at Harvard Law School; Frankfurter was a key adviser to FDR during the New Deal. Acheson briefly functioned as undersecretary of the Treasury in 1933, but he was let go because he was too critical of FDR. He remained so until 1936 when he joined the Roosevelt bandwagon, as did others from that white-shoe world, including Sidney Weinberg of Goldman Sachs and James Forrestal, then at Dillon, Read, and Harriman. Securely ensconced within the expanding new order, Acheson would go on to become Truman's secretary of state. He was a principal author of the Truman Doctrine (which pledged American assistance, including military aid, to those resisting Soviet aggression or alleged Soviet-backed domestic subversion) and the Marshall Plan. Acheson became the favorite limousine liberal piñata of Joseph McCarthy and fellow McCarthyites from both parties.

Alger Hiss, who would become a principal target in McCarthy's indictment of the postwar governing class as subversive, was a close friend of Acheson with impeccable social credentials. He was a lean, handsome upper class WASP. Offspring of a Social Register family, he prepped at Harvard Law and a tony Washington, DC, law firm for his future roles as a New Deal reformer and designer of the postwar order, including the United Nations.[2]

Whether these men had first shown their mettle in World War I or not, their experience during the interwar years made them intimately familiar with the world of international finance and the delicate political negotiations that invariably shadowed that business. They soberly pondered the prospects, once the war against fascism was won, of the United States assuming the dominant position in the world that was until then occupied by Great Britain. That is, they were prepared to shoulder the responsibilities that their fathers' generation had once been accused of shirking at Versailles. Whatever more Olympian vistas of global stewardship had surfaced back then soon dissolved into sordid episodes of "dollar diplomacy," parochial defenses of business interests in out of the way places like Nicaragua and the Dominican Republic, and rapacious speculations in Latin American securities. Victory in 1945 opened up something far grander among policy-making elites in Washington: a deodorized empire of the free world that no longer gave off the aroma of old-fashioned imperialism.

And so what soon enough would be characterized as the American "establishment" was born. This was a world pithily described by Arthur Schlesinger Jr. as headquartered in the New York financial and legal community whose "household deities were Henry L. Stimson and Elihu Root (McKinley's secretary of war and Teddy Roosevelt's secretary of state and Stimson's tutor in statesmanship), its present leaders Robert A. Lovett and John McCloy, its front organization, the Rockefeller, Ford, and Carnegie foundations, and the Council on Foreign Relations." As this sketch suggests, it was a universe of wise men that spilled well beyond the confines of Wall Street. It intermingled financial statesmen like Harriman and Nelson Rockefeller with captains of industry like Charles Wilson of General Motors or Robert McNamara of Ford, foreign service civilians like Dean Acheson with military strategists like Marshall, Forrestal, and Lovett—and brought them all together in collaboration with policy intellectuals at strategic salons like the Council on Foreign Relations, for years chaired by McCloy.[3]

Many in this charmed circle had grown up together, been schooled together, dined together, done business together, fought together. Cosmopolitan, steeped in transatlantic high culture, they were often deeply private men who shied away from elective office and the hurly-burly of democratic politics. Nelson Rockefeller and Averill Harriman turned out to be noticeable exceptions, but their electoral triumphs did not seriously compromise their commitments to the guideposts of postwar elite liberalism. Although mainly Republican by birth—some like Acheson and Harriman converted to the Democratic Party—they adopted an ecumenical bipartisanship when it came to holding public office. So, for example, D. Douglas Dillon, member of the New York Stock Exchange, international banker, an Episcopalian Republican who served Eisenhower as undersecretary of state, whose father had founded the firm Dillon, Read, and Harriman, later became John Kennedy's secretary of the treasury.

Dillon's career was typical of this world's inbred patrician calling to public service performed out of a sense of stoical duty and honor, infused from boyhood with a belief in their Christian obligation to use their great riches wisely on behalf of God and the nation. They were presumably, at least in their own minds, free of any tincture of self-seeking, either after wealth or personal political power. They bore, too, a sense of entitlement that it was precisely their social training and their careers in the complex world of international political economy that prepared them to deal with the intricacies of global affairs too sophisticated and too dangerous to be left to the less knowledgeable, more mercurial democratic public to decide.[4]

Perhaps no one was more emblematic of this unprepossessing elite than John McCloy. His resume maps the social geography of power in postwar America. He started out in modest middle class surroundings in Philadelphia, where his mother worked as a hairdresser. His father was a high-level clerk in a prestigious insurance company, but when he died at an early age, the family's circumstances straitened. Partly thanks to his father's connections at the insurance firm McCloy managed to attend a second-rank prep school, and from there he was off to Amherst, Harvard Law, and ever upward. At one time or another McCloy was a partner in various top-rank Wall Street law firms— including the Rockefeller family firm Milbank, Tweed, Hope, and Hadley—president of the World Bank, US high commissioner to Germany, chairman of the board of Chase Manhattan Bank, chairman of the Ford Foundation, chairman of the Council on Foreign Relations, legal counsel to the "seven sister" oil companies, director of a dozen or so Fortune 500 corporations, and perennial adviser to American presidents. John Kenneth Galbraith once called him "chairman of the board of the American Establishment."

Yet John McCloy might never have risen so high. It is not so much his distinguished pedigree but the fact that he started out in life without one that is especially illuminating about the character of the liberal establishment. It was without question a clubby milieu. However, it was at the same time and by virtue of its experiences living through world wars and depression one necessarily attuned to disruptions of all kinds, to mastering disorder rather than crushing it or fleeing from it. The rise of someone from the lower ranks of the social order into the most exalted circles of power and privilege was not all by itself unheard of; the American dream after all was premised on precisely that possibility, however remote. Rather it was the collective adaptation of such a milieu to a new order of things—sometimes characterized as Cold War liberalism—which granted power, especially in domestic affairs, to outsiders without any claims to patrician birth or breeding that left its distinctive mark on the postwar New Deal world.

Men like McCloy, indeed McCloy more so than many others who came of age on Wall Street, for some time drew back at what they considered the more dangerous economic and social reforms of the New Deal. They might, as McCloy did, especially resent its investigations of the Street and the major companies their law firms represented: corporations like Bethlehem Steel, RCA, Westinghouse, and the major railroads. But even before the outbreak of war, they had begun to make their peace with the essentials of the New Deal Order. On matters of civil rights, civil liberties, and especially in their approach to avowedly internationalist foreign policy, little if anything separated the views of liberal intellectuals from these cosmopolitan gentry then designing the contours of the "American Century." Henry Luce had come up with that rubric. It envisioned a kind of benign American imperium that would assure global peace while tutoring the nations on the virtues of American capitalism and democracy. The creator of main organs of the mass media, including *Fortune, Life,* and *Time* magazines, Luce was no card-carrying New Dealer. But that he could be simultaneously a Roosevelt critic and a cheerleader for postwar American world hegemony signaled the convergence of an establishment perspective.[5]

Incorporating distinguished figures from the business world within the upper echelons of the Roosevelt administration seemed a stunning refutation of older, more polarized depictions of the class fissures in American politics. Still, a rapprochement was there for all to see. A concord of the enlightened from finance and politics presided over the critical regulatory innovations of the New Deal (including the SEC) and promised to heal any lingering wounds from the past. Averill Harriman, whose legendary father had been a railroad tycoon practiced in the arts and crafts of cold-blooded speculation, voiced the new persuasion in 1946: "People in this country are no longer scared of such words as 'planning' . . . people have accepted the fact that the government has got to plan as well as individuals in this country." Managers, CEOs especially, were depicted in this post–Great Depression world as powerful beings to be sure, but benign ones, their earlier reputation for cruelty and greed leached away. Instead they presented themselves and were often accepted as trustees, public servants, peace-loving men ready to do business with old foes from the labor movement and the government, a new species of management that had in effect expropriated the old-time expropriators. Managers of what one historian has called the "corporate commonwealth" still abhorred the class struggle and fretted over the statist tendencies of the New Deal. But above all, this milieu made its peace with the "limited welfare state" and believed in the possibilities of social cooperation administered by a disinterested elite. All the great social enemies of the recent past—Wall Street, the plutocracy, the bosses, the fascists—receded into the background, blotted out by the radiance of military victory, of postwar prosperity, of the real egalitarian drift in the division of national income and wealth, and by the singular preoccupation with the red menace abroad.[6]

For mainstream liberals especially, the Cold War reconfigured their map of the ideological and social universe. Men like McCloy, Acheson, the Dulles brothers, and Robert Lovett (and a younger, similarly reared generation that included the Bundy brothers, Dean Rusk, Paul Nitze, and Charles Bohlen) seemed to be less plenipotentiaries from Wall Street than they did statesmen who made disinterested decisions on behalf of the whole nation. If their worldly experience in business and finance counted for anything, it was as appropriate training in the complexities of international political and economic affairs. This was an invaluable fund of knowledge for waging a cold war against communist tyranny in which freedom was made to seem synonymous with capitalism.

Moreover, assuming the burden of global overlordship inevitably diminished the attachment of these cosmopolitans to local and regional political hierarchies. While their presence spread horizontally from Western Europe, across the Middle East, and into the Far East, their vertical reach downward into the topsoil of the heartland grew shallower. While they worried about goings on in Paris, Berlin, and Cairo, they were less worried about what was stirring in New York, Boston, and Chicago. This would eventually prove to be a real vulnerability, making it easier to paint this world as extraterrestrial.

Internal divisions compounded this sense that those who ruled were losing touch. On the one hand, among the upper classes generally, some were more prepared than others to accept the postwar dispensation, that is, the New Deal order of things. One observer noted the schizophrenia infecting the outlook of "old money." The "wise men" were ready to allow into their own ranks the meritorious whatever their origins. They became conspicuously bipartisan and shed that old intransigent "colonel Blimpism." But many of their peers preferred to hunker down in bunkers of caste exclusivity, pretending not to notice or offering stiff-necked resistance to the social changes swirling around them.[7]

One metric of this cultural falling out among the elect was the degree to which some were infected by the virus of mass and celebrity culture, were more at ease with it, were even drawn into its orbit. Others however, whose names might also appear on the Social Register, found this polymorphous world offensive to cherished values and traditions. Movie stars, particularly, but also politicians and publicists, businessmen and athletes gathered together in a socially promiscuous night world of glamour and souped-up sexuality that fixated attention on the fast moving and the evanescent. It was a café society of the fashionable, where lineage mattered less than media charisma or off-color notoriety. In the process, more durable insignia of personal and social privilege assumed a lower profile. Dynastic marriages, heraldic and genealogical displays, feudal masquerades, transatlantic alliances of wealth and pedigree no longer commanded the front-page priorities of metropolitan newspapers.

Some members of the Cold War patricianate had long since made themselves at home in the more mercurial and heterogeneous environs of mass culture and the celebrity bazaar. Averill Harriman, for example, after his second marriage to Marie Norton Whitney, became a regular partygoer at the Algonquin in the 1920s, where Alexander Wolcott, Helen Hayes, Harpo Marx, Ernest Hemingway, George S. Kaufman, and Dorothy Parker intermingled. Nelson Rockefeller inherited a fondness for modern art from his extraordinarily open-minded mother, Abby Aldrich Rockefeller, the godmother of the Museum of Modern Art. Her son devoted valuable time to collecting and championing abstract expressionist art, which defied the conventional aesthetic habits of the larger social world he was born into. Later, when already serving as New York's governor, Nelson's sexual and marital transgressions would scandalize his more orthodox Republican colleagues. Other Rockefeller offspring followed Abby's high-brow deviance, especially the eldest son, John, who developed a reputation as a "parlor pink" for his social philanthropies and anti-war sentiments. Robert Lovett likewise cultivated a taste for cultural modernism and became a fan of jazz, movies, and popular mystery novels, entertainments once outside the ken of the Social Register.

For two generations—from 1870 until 1930—Newport, Rhode Island, served as the social capital of the country's East Coast elite. By the time of World War II, the ravages of history and the sea had dealt this gilded getaway a mortal blow. The ocean ate away at the coastline and the Crash of 1929 devoured great fortunes. "Fashionable society," which had once managed to patrol the perimeters of its exclusive enclaves with a reasonable degree of rigor in a society potentially awash in waves of new wealth, after the war found itself dissolving into the more promiscuous world of celebrity culture. Social pedigrees counted for less, and their hallmarks, palatial preserves like those in Newport, receded over the horizon of social prestige.[8]

A process of ecological entropy had set in so that those imposing political and cultural signposts that once helped everyone recognize a Victorian plutocrat when they saw one faded away. Mansions weren't being abandoned, grass tennis courts weren't being paved over, polo fields weren't going to weed, *recherché* country clubs weren't sending out applications to African Americans. But consumer culture was accelerating the erasure of age-old hierarchies of taste, dress, residence, recreation, and everyday manners. And the postwar establishment was, at least partially, opening itself up to or was being opened by the onrushing tides of demotic and democratic mass culture, by its moral relativism and its social fluidity. This peculiar combination of East Coast financial and corporate overlordship, Ivy League know-it-all presumption, and agnostic toleration, even indulgence of the morally and culturally unconventional would raise hackles. Those who felt shut out, denied the political influence their stature and wealth might have normally invited, disrespected as out of touch with or too retrograde to appreciate the liberating iconoclasm inherent in consumer culture, and for whom the kinship between communism and the New Deal had long been an article of faith, struck back.

CLASS STRUGGLE INSIDE THE BELTWAY

Undergirded by a balance of nuclear terror and an extraordinary era of economic prosperity and multilateral diplomacy, the establishment presided for a generation. Vietnam and the American version of racial apartheid blew it apart, not only from the outside but internally as well. By the time of the Nixon administration its fissuring was a matter of public knowledge, headlined in *New York* magazine in 1971 as "The Death of the Eastern Establishment."[9]

Senator Joseph McCarthy, had he been alive to read it, would have derived a visceral thrill from that obituary notice. While others spent the postwar years wondering whether or not a ruling elite still existed, and if so who belonged to it, the senator from Wisconsin and those ignited by his demagoguery were not plagued by those doubts. Years after the passions of the New Deal had cooled, during a time when the country's impressive capacity for social amnesia had buried unhappy memories of privileged plutocrats, the one place it continued to haunt was the dyspeptic imagination of senatorial hotheads like McCarthy. What an irony! Those mahogany-paneled boardrooms, posh eating clubs, and exclusive prep schools that had once inflamed the anticapitalist emotions of millions now stuck in the craw of rival elites in a feverish uproar over the threat of communism: communism abroad and communist subversion at home, but mostly the latter.

Their ire was both genuine and confected. It became the chief weapon in the hands of the Republican political establishment, but one they could not always control. A concerted effort to derail the New Deal in precisely this way had begun even before the war. J. Parnell Thomas, a Republican congressman from New Jersey who would eventually chair the House Un-American Activities Committee purportedly investigating subversive operatives in the federal government, claimed New Dealers had "sabotaged the capitalist system." Southern Democrats like Martin Dies of Texas, who ran the committee in the late 1930s, agreed. With the aid of the FBI, the committee initiated a minor hysteria over this alleged infestation of reds at a time when the best estimates suggest there were probably no more than seventy-five members of the Communist Party scattered throughout a federal bureaucracy of a half-million employees.[10]

Henry Ford and Father Coughlin might be counted the progenitors of this deeply conspiratorial view of how the country was being insidiously undermined by a bizarre alliance of Bolsheviks and bankers. However, as both men were infected with a virulent strain of anti-Semitism, a distinct ethnic parochialism lay beneath their global paranoia. After the war and the Holocaust, Jew baiting was insupportable, beyond the pale. Indeed, McCarthy's aide-de-camp was Roy Cohen, a Jewish lawyer from New York. In any event, the senator was after bigger fish. McCarthy and his immediate congressional predecessors instead went straight for the heart of the WASP establishment and its array of satellite organizations.

Reds could be found everywhere, according to this persuasion: in colleges and universities, among writers and performing artists, in advertising agencies and the mass media, leading trade unions and civil rights movements, staffing grade schools and public libraries, commanding the armed forces, and delivering the mail. Far more worrisome, so the senator averred, was their alleged presence in the highest councils of the government, especially its foreign policy apparatus. There, charged with the mission of defending the country against an implacable and fiendishly clever enemy bent on world domination, they plotted to betray the nation. In an address before the Senate in 1951, McCarthy invoked "a conspiracy so immense and an infamy so black as to dwarf any previous venture in the history of man."[11]

How galling it was, the senator exclaimed, that these traitors came from the most privileged precincts of American society, from places like Groton and Harvard and Wall Street. The country had bestowed on them great wealth, the best educations, the highest social honors, the most eminent public offices. Nonetheless, they had worked to turn wartime triumph into postwar retreat and debacle. Just like their spiritual godfather, FDR, they were in effect traitors to their class. They had lost half of Europe and most of Asia, China most alarmingly. Nor could this be written off as well-intentioned but misconceived policy. It was treachery.

Men like Secretary of State Dean Acheson and German High Commissioner John McCloy woke up one day to find their motives impugned and their social origins mocked. McCarthy mesmerized a sizeable audience that cheered his baiting of these people for their cosmopolitan associations, their Anglophilia, their effete aloofness, their silver-spoon upbringings, their gilded careers as international bankers. McCloy was a pro forma Republican, but more ardent members of his party's right wing considered him a witting tool of the communists. In particular, they railed against his multilateralism, his friendliness toward the United Nations, his early advocacy of international control over atomic energy. Republicans denounced the Marshall Plan as a "bold socialist blueprint," an "international Works Project Administration." When President Truman relieved Douglas MacArthur of his command in Korea (a decision Secretary of Defense George Marshall reluctantly supported), McCarthy used the occasion to tell the Senate that General Marshall was a subversive servant of Soviet interests and that his famous "plan" emerged from an "almost complete blueprint supplied in 1945 by Communist leader Earl Browder."

Nor was this the hyperventilating extremism of political marginalia. Ohio Senator Robert Taft—known as "Mr. Republican," son of a president, leader of the party's Midwestern heartland, again and again talked about as its likely presidential nominee, someone who had offered qualified support for public housing and federal aid to education, who had even, reluctantly, voted for the Marshall Plan—vetoed McCloy's rumored appointment as Eisenhower's secretary of state because he distrusted his intimacy with "international bankers" and "Roosevelt New Dealers." Earlier on, when vying for the presidential nomination in 1952, Taft told his Ohio loyalists that "if we get Eisenhower we will practically have a Republican New Deal Administration with just as much spending and socialism as under Truman." When Taft lost the nomination to Eisenhower, he vented his general resentment against those Wall Street internationalists, claiming, "Every Republican candidate for president since 1936 has been nominated by Chase Bank."

For Taft and other leading figures from the Republican conservative old guard, baiting the Democratic administration as well as the eastern liberal wing of their own party as Bolshevik bankers was probably more a tactical convenience than an ideological conviction. J. Edgar Hoover, on the other hand, was a demon hunter. He stealthily encouraged these sentiments about both McCloy and Acheson. He circulated scurrilous reports about their alleged links to communist spy rings. When Alger Hiss was first accused of belonging to such a ring back in the 1930s, his old friend Dean Acheson came to his defense. Hiss and Acheson were perfect foils: patrician in manner, Harvard Law School–educated, and tainted by their New Deal associations. Revanchist Republican congressmen, offended by Acheson's hauteur, jumped on his defense of Hiss, ridiculed the secretary of state as a pretentious "Yalie," and "overdressed, overeducated wise guy." And when in 1950 McCarthy first unveiled his purported list of underground reds in the government at what became a memorable public performance before a Republican women's group in Wheeling, West Virginia, he referred to Acheson as "this pompous diplomat in striped pants" with his "phony British accent," parading about with his "cane, spats, and tea-sipping little finger," running a State Department infested with spies and their dupes who secretly yearned for the Soviets to win the Cold War. Acheson would later characterize this "attack of the primitives" as a "shameful and nihilistic orgy," a "sadistic pogrom." But in the humid atmosphere of the early 1950s, the "red Dean of the State Department" and his co-architects of the postwar order couldn't escape the political heat.

McCarthy alerted his listeners that the reason the country was losing out to the Soviets was "because of the traitorous actions of those who have been treated so well by the Nation. It has not been the less fortunate or members of minority groups who have been selling the Nation out, but rather those who have had all the benefits that the wealthiest nation on earth has to offer—the finest homes, the finest college education, the finest jobs in Government we can give." This was infuriatingly true about the State Department in particular. "There the young men who were born with silver spoons in their mouths are the ones who have been the worst." They were the soured cream of a spoiled elite. McCarthy portrayed Averill Harriman as "a guy whose admiration for everything Russian is unrivaled outside the confines of the Communist Party."

Paul Nitze was a younger member of the establishment working in the Defense Department when he was fired by Defense Secretary Charles Wilson, who succumbed to McCarthyite pressure. Nitze was amazed that McCarthy went after him not for his foreign policy ideas, not even with accusations that he was a red, but because he was "a Wall Street operator." Meanwhile, McCloy was even charged with sheltering communists in the army during the war. McCarthy warned that men "with a top hat and silk handkerchief" were, at best, ill-equipped to deal with the worldwide communist conspiracy.[12]

Images of tea-sipping, silk handkerchiefs, and silver spoons and charges of unmanly cowardice pointed to a refurbishing of the epithetical arsenal and a subtle shift in the center of political gravity. McCarthyism marked a turning point in the transmigration from economic to cultural right-wing populism. In the global war against communism, after all, hostile talk about capitalism of the sort indulged by Long and Coughlin was virtually verboten. The senator tended to emphasize instead the moral dangers of the New Deal state, infected at its root with communist-inflected collectivism. The archetypical enemy looked the same: Anglo-Saxon, Ivy League financiers, bankers with "grouse-hunting estates in Scotland," and New Deal government commissars, an aristocracy of destruction. It was the grouse hunting, however, more than the economic overlordship, that aroused McCarthyite resentment.

The domestic cold war, whose real enemy for many was the New Deal much more than it was the Soviet Union or homegrown communists, left behind many casualties. It committed a kind of cultural genocide, purging and proscribing whole families of languages—not only traditional populism—whose deep grammar had once interrogated capitalist injustice, exploitation, and immorality.

Indeed, that is partly what made this whole interlude so strange. McCarthy and his beltway allies (not to mention the broad popular audience that hero-worshipped the senator) shared the ideology of anticommunism with his chosen enemies. After all, as the Cold War settled in and before Wisconsin sent Joe McCarthy to the Senate, the Truman administration had launched a loyalty program that aimed at purging the government of anyone faintly suspected of harboring "subversive" beliefs, an elastic category that could stretch to include an overly active commitment to peace, civil rights, or free speech. Liberals, not McCarthyites, were responsible for driving communists out of the Democratic Party and the labor movement. It was a young lion of the liberal establishment, Hubert Humphrey, who introduced legislation in 1954 to outlaw the Communist Party. The Truman administration may have differed with McCarthy and Taft over tactics, but not on matters of political substance, not in this arena anyway.

However, the line between tactical nuance and fateful matters of loyalty and betrayal could grow very hazy. For example, one might assume that the CIA was an institution of unimpeachable anticommunist credentials. Yet, now and then it became a target of McCarthyite attack precisely because its maneuvers abroad included lending support to noncommunist left-wing groups and parties. This didn't sit well with McCarthy. William Bundy, a quintessential establishment functionary—Groton, Yale, corporate lawyer—had been picked to run these operations by CIA head Allen Dulles. But Bundy, Acheson's son-in-law and a former law partner of Alger Hiss, was accused by the senator of belonging to a Communist Party front organization. In this case, the senator's demand for an investigation was thwarted, but he'd made his point.[13]

Why, one might ask, would such a favored few find common cause with those inveterate foes of upper class privilege, with communists who meant to destroy the foundations of their capitalist good fortunes? Partly because, McCarthyites explained, their pampered existence sapped their will and cut them off from the grassroots patriotism of more common folk. At one public appearance, the Wisconsin senator talked about a wounded GI returning from Korea. He suggested that this soldier, Bob Smith, "walk over to the State Department and call upon the Secretary if he is still there. . . . He should say to Acheson, 'You and your lace handkerchief crowd have never had to fight in the cold, so you cannot know its bitterness. . . . You never felt the shock of bullets, so you cannot know the pain. . . . ' That thousands of American boys have faced these killers 'because you and your crimson crowd betrayed us.'" (That a goodly number of these "subversives" had risked their lives in World War I a generation earlier apparently didn't count.)

Presumably a cosmopolitan lifestyle had exposed these privileged circles to an armada of cultural viruses that ate away at their Americanism, at that bedrock pietistic self-reliance that made the country what it was. Their urbanity implied a kind of impiety, a social and psychological dissipation and a loss of frontier vigor. Consequently, homosexuality and other forms of "deviance" were high on the list of stigmata used by McCarthy and his agents to purge the government of undesirables, even at the highest levels. For example, President Eisenhower appointed "Chip" Bohlen as ambassador to Moscow in 1953. Bohlen was a classic limousine liberal *avant la lettre*. He was the rich and cultured product of a prestigious family, private schools, Harvard, the Foreign Service, and minister to France in the late 1940s. However, Secretary of State John Foster Dulles didn't want Bohlen; he was too close to people in the previous administration. So Dulles unleashed Senator McCarthy as his attack dog. The senator circulated a rumor that Bohlen was a homosexual and then convened one of his *ex-cathedra* theatrical hearings. But this even scandalized Republican sachems like Taft, who turned on his Wisconsin colleague.[14]

A GENERAL WITHOUT AN ARMY

Like a raging fever, McCarthyism severely weakened the body politic and then subsided. As Taft's demurral over the Bohlen affair indicated, the Wisconsin senator's accusations became increasingly reckless, culminating in his infamous attack on the US Army in 1954 and 1955. The Republican high command had once found him a useful tool. Taft advised him early on to "keep talking, if one case doesn't work, proceed with another." Eventually, however, the old guard threw him overboard as a political embarrassment. But like a fever, McCarthyism was also symptomatic of some underlying unease with the way the New Deal Order behaved at home and abroad. Its hallucinatory comingling of commissars and capitalists was a striking sign of this condition.[15]

Thumbing his nose at the high and mighty, McCarthy's appeal was personal as well as political in a way not unlike Long's before him or George Wallace's a decade later. Son of an Irish American father and German American mother, McCarthy grew up in the rural, small town world of Appleton, Wisconsin, where his family ran a small farm first settled by his grandfather just before the Civil War. It was a large (seven children) close-knit family. Joe tried and failed at setting himself up as a small businessman, and then got a law degree. He was a tough-looking, beefy, burly man with a perpetual one-day growth of beard. His demeanor was cheeky, sometimes belligerent even. Lawyering led to politics and a local judgeship through campaigns of average unscrupulousness. World War II found him in the US Marine Corps, where he served as an intelligence officer in the South Pacific. Combat experience, which Joe tended to exaggerate, earned him the sobriquet "tail-gunner Joe." A heavy drinker, gambler, and womanizer, he had all the bona fides of a manly man. Back in Wisconsin he resumed his political career by defeating venerable, old-style populist Senator Robert LaFollette Jr.[16]

That profile of a man from the economic and ethnic down under, not cowed by his social superiors, plus an anticommunist politics that took no prisoners appealed to all sorts: Anglophobic Irish and Germans; Slavs with kin and sentimental ties to the "captive nations" under Soviet domination in Eastern Europe; Midwestern isolationists suspicious of the "one worldism" inside their own Republican Party; and all those for whom the state's intrusion into social life, whether under the auspices of the Bolsheviks or the New Deal, represented a new species of slavery. The writer and scholar George Lukacs remembered how amazed he was to read in 1949 that "an American Legion post in Philadelphia accused the directors of the Philadelphia chapter of United World Federalists of un-Americanism. The names of the accused were, without exception, English, Welsh, or Scottish; their accusers' names were Ukrainian, Italian, and Slovak." In his home state the Wisconsin senator tended to poll well in rural areas and small towns, and poorly in big cities like Milwaukee where organized labor was potent, even among blue collar Polish Catholics.

A distinguished group of American intellectuals, most famously Richard Hofstadter, writing not long after McCarthyism had died away, attributed his popularity to the status anxieties of upwardly mobile working class ethnic (Irish and German) Catholics in places like Boston, where hatred for Ivy League WASPs was virtually genetic. This "revolt against elites," they argued, was not really about rational economic and social issues, but a "politics of unreason," driven by resentment. It displayed, so they argued, a kinship with nineteenth-century populism in its social origins and conspiratorial mentality.

Daniel Bell concluded that "what the right wing is fighting, in the shadow of communism, is essentially 'modernity.'" But some rejected this alleged affinity and saw in McCarthyism a revival of the conservatism of traditional Republican elites. In this connection, others treated the whole episode as a power struggle within the Republican Party and between it and its Democratic Party rival.[17]

Unlike the Long, Coughlin, and Townsend uprisings, this postwar assault on limousine liberalism was really not a movement at all. McCarthy polled well when he was riding high, but there was never any serious attempt to translate that popularity into some kind of mass organization. Rural and lower-middle-class sentiment in certain regions of the country, including the Great Plains and eastern cities with sizeable Irish and German populations, did welcome the senator's tough-guy, patriotic diatribes against metropolitan, liberal elites. But the confrontations commanding headlines were taking place mainly in legislative chambers and hearing rooms, not in the streets. All kinds of organizations, including churches, chambers of commerce, school boards, and Kiwanis clubs, channeled the Red Scare to purge civic life of undesirables. But these efforts remained local, decentralized, and fragmented, never achieving or even aspiring to become a national political institution.

Moreover, the Long and Coughlin movements had risen, at least to begin with, to the left of the New Deal Democratic Party, not at the right-wing margins of the Republicans. Neither in the political arena nor outside of it did McCarthyism produce anything more substantial than an atmospheric disturbance. That atmosphere was to be sure a toxic one; it ruined thousands of innocent lives and crippled the country's political imagination. And even after McCarthy himself fell into alcoholic disgrace and obscurity, the wounds it had inflamed festered.[18]

If McCarthyism did not qualify as an updated version of a populist rising, it did, at the time and afterward, flourish among a rising milieu of businessmen outside the charmed circle of the New Deal's corporate commonwealth. Within the middling classes, McCarthy found his reliable supporters among independent businessmen, some small, some quite big-time. This was decidedly truer of McCarthy than it had been of Coughlin. Surveys showed that hostile attitudes about both big business and big labor were good indices of pro-McCarthy feelings.

Robert Young, for example, was a Wall Street speculator—one of several in the 1950s known as "white sharks"—who had managed to take away the venerable New York Central Railroad from its long-time Wall Street managers after a ferocious proxy fight. Young made the case for his proxy wars for corporate control in terms that would become increasingly common in the run-up to the Reagan era. He explained at a congressional hearing that the old Wall Street crowd, Morgan's men, was a deeply antidemocratic cabal. They didn't give a damn about shareholders, manipulated the media, and lorded it over not only major industrial corporations but also government agencies charged with regulating them; in a word, they were, Young argued, just like Soviet bosses.

Young was an ardent McCarthyite. Indeed, from the moment the iron curtain was erected, business patriots issued warnings to Wall Street to root out its communists, claiming there were more there than there were even in Hollywood, including partners of some of the industry's top brokerages. The Midwestern Republican leadership—Taft of Ohio, Everett Dirksen of Illinois, William Jenner of Indiana, John Bricker who was both governor and senator from Ohio—all were staunch advocates of free enterprise and spoke for an entrepreneurial world that feared the intrusions of the New Deal state. Major Wisconsin corporations—Cutler-Hammer, Kimberly-Clark, Allis-Chalmers, Harnischfeger, major Milwaukee breweries—reliably backed McCarthy, as did out-of-state donors like Robert McCormick of the *Chicago Tribune*; Robert E. Wood of Sears; Earl Muzzy, the president of Quaker Oats; Clint Murchison; and H. L. Hunt.

Murchison and Hunt were oil barons and were joined in this political crusade by others who like them had acquired their wealth quite recently, often thanks to the economic mobilization made necessary by the war. As one of these newly rich businessmen put it: "We all made money fast. We were interested in nothing else. Then this Communist business burst upon us. We were going to lose what we had gained." For many of them "this Communist business" meant big government and unpalatable domestic reform. In turn, anticommunism meant free enterprise, the open shop, the racial status quo, and Christianity. So, for example, McCarthy was a big hit among Texas Republicans who were quite culturally distinct and lived apart from the larger business world. But the senator aroused profound uneasiness among the business, managerial, and professional classes living in exclusive precincts back East who feared his appeal to those who chafed at their privileged positions. Henry Ford II, Phillip Reed of General Electric, Paul Hoffman of Studebaker, Roger Strauss of American Smelting and Refinery, and Harry Bullis of General Mills, among others, pressured Eisenhower to finally do something about the maverick senator.

Newer ascending elements of the entrepreneurial world felt otherwise. Liberal commentators tended to dismiss these resentful right-wingers as a dying breed, as "old money," or in the words of Daniel Bell, a universe encompassing the "independent doctor, the farm owner, small-town lawyer, real estate promoter, home builder, automobile dealer, gasoline station owner, small businessmen and the like." They were in his eyes "rearguard activists," carriers of old-time religion, morality, and outdated economics.

However, in the recombinant, supersonic "New World"—that ever-renewable frontier of opportunity first envisioned by our colonial ancestors—old money never gets to be very old. One observer speculated about the McCarthy phenomenon that "it was a movement trying to overthrow an old ruling class and replace it with a new ruling class." This may grossly exaggerate the organizational cohesiveness and durability of McCarthyism (and by the way suggest that in America it only takes a decade for a new ruling class to age and become old). Still, it points to subterranean shifts in the national political economy set in motion by the war.

While the war economy doled out public treasure to many of the country's blue-chip corporations, it also incubated new industries and new companies in newly industrializing regions of the country like Texas, California, and the Southwest. New entrepreneurial fortunes piled up but did not necessarily carry with them political access or social prestige. This could and did cause resentment, as it had many times in the past, among a milieu of nouveau riche who in style and language and emotional tone were much closer to their plebian roots than they were to the transatlantic mores of the establishment. They hailed from German and Irish-Catholic neighborhoods in East Coast cities, from midsize towns in the Protestant heartland or upstart suburbs farther west, from secondary state colleges or unknown denominational schools. In their eyes patrician institutions of the eastern elite like Harvard transmogrified into bizarre hothouses of egg-headed, homosexual, left-leaning financiers.

New men of the free market hated the snobbish exclusivity they associated with the establishment, its air of eastern sophistication and knowingness, its gratuitous and self-serving sympathies for the lower orders. Its social graces abraded the egalitarian nerve endings of men on the make; they seemed presumptuous and irritatingly silly. A rising milieu, fancying themselves the "underprivileged rich," these strivers, men from nowhere, managed, as had many before them, to ignore the origins of their own good fortunes in the government's wartime largesse. On the contrary, they nurtured a zealous distaste for government and its demoralizing welfarism.

Out of this soil flowered a new antiestablishmentarianism of the right growing up not in the exhausted terrain of the dispossessed, but rather in new territories of upwardly mobile abundance. It trained its sights on the New Deal state. Postwar multilateral codicils governing international trade and investment as well as the heavy burden of New Deal domestic economic regulations would only stifle the most dynamic sectors of American business, crushing initiative beneath a mountain of bureaucratic constraints. That rule-bound orderliness might appeal to a risk-averse and imperial-minded financial establishment, but not to audacious new entrepreneurs. Their future had precious little to do with a reconstructed Europe run by Wall Street and blue-chip American corporations, and everything to do with the unfettered expansion of the free market right here in the United States. Their distinctive anticommunism expressed itself as an isolationist aversion to the pink-tinted internationalism—or what they derided as the "one worldism," which entailed the sacrifice of the homeland to some fanciful concord of nations—of the eastern elite. And so even as that establishment warred against communism abroad, this new, incongruous species of elite right-wing populism warred against a communist establishment at home.[19]

5

The Vital Center Trembles

For all of the sturm and drang we associate with the Cold War and McCarthyism, the political life of postwar America was in many respects remarkably stable, placid even. The two mainstream parties orbited around the same life-giving sun of the New Deal: one, the Republicans, a bit further away, cooler and more distant than the other. However, none of the fundamental institutional innovations and reforms of the Roosevelt and Truman years were seriously challenged by the Eisenhower administrations of the 1950s. As that decade drew to a close, a writer in the Sunday *New York Times Magazine* noted that it was virtually impossible to find a major figure in American political life who had an unkind word for liberalism: "anyone who today identifies himself as an unmitigated opponent of liberalism cannot aspire to influence on the national political scene."[1]

Indeed, one measure of that equanimity was the ease with which the notion of a "paranoid style in American politics," invented by Hofstadter and others, became a kind of smug conventional wisdom. Like now, so then whatever fell outside the framework of the corporate liberal consensus was not only treated as a distasteful form of extremism, but was not even regarded as fully grown-up politics. Rather it was deemed a kind of prepolitical acting out, psychoanalyzed, investigated clinically as a form of mental pathology. Any class-inflected view of the world, whether from the right or the left, was deemed antiquated, out of touch with the new order of managerial capitalism and the socially engineered welfare state: in a word, irrational. So, for example, if Gerald L. K. Smith's belief in the "Protocols of the Elders of Zion" was deemed dangerously kooky, so was a work like *The Power Elite* by C. Wright Mills to be treated as a left-wing version of conspiracy mongering. And conversely, it became axiomatic that the postwar liberal dispensation epitomized the rational, functioning as a finely reticulated mechanism for resolving social conflict, the benchmark against which all dissenting views were to be measured and found wanting.

Armies of opposition were nonetheless gathering outside the walls. After the paroxysms of McCarthyism subsided, movements reaching well beyond the beltway, infused with the Wisconsin senator's visceral hatred for the liberal establishment, but with considerably greater stamina, disturbed the country's political geography. Hard hats in the Northeast, rednecks in the South, and prospering entrepreneurs in the western Sunbelt had virtually nothing in common. Except that they all detested the liberal elite running the country. For a decade running through the notoriously uproarious 1960s the reality and myth of the limousine liberal inspired both upper and lower classes at odds with the "vital center."

Rebellious businessmen and techno-professionals assembled inside the Republican Party. Malcontents among blue collar "aristocrats" and put-upon lower-middle-class strivers vented loudly within the Democratic Party. There was little if any intercourse between them. That would happen eventually. What they shared was an animosity for an elite that couldn't seem to leave well enough alone, that seemed hell-bent on disrupting prevailing mores and morals, that was cavalier when it came to protecting the homeland and was insufferably sure of itself and its right to tutor everyone else. Still harboring a sense of class resentment, these movements had nonetheless begun a transmutation of that old-time way of dividing up the social universe.

Years before Mario Procaccino penned his one claim to fame, the remaking of the profile of the American ruling class was well under way. Its more inflammatory features were increasingly defined by its social and cultural attributes. Its economic privileges and superordinate positions atop the nation's peak corporations and government departments were more and more taken for granted. Now and then those qualities, which had once alarmed millions worried about the fate of equality and democracy, were featured by critics zealous about exposing the hypocrisy of the nation's anointed ones. What else was the point of mentioning the limousine except to punctuate their economic and political preeminence? By and large, however, these raw indices of economic command lived on as the background radiation of a social cosmos becoming preoccupied with the cultural delinquencies of the country's "best and brightest." Metaphorically, "parlor pink," connoting an unsavory combination of character and cultural defect, mixing together affectation and effeminacy with ideological deviance, captured the shift in sensibility.[2]

BOURGEOIS REBELS

One axiom of modern liberal teleology long assumed that after the great antitrust movement was defanged in the earlier part of the twentieth century, family capitalism had breathed its last. If it lingered on it did so as an anachronism, outdated by the inexorable march of history. But this turned out to be wrong. The tumultuous evolution of capitalism over the past hundred years has repeatedly offered fresh possibilities for small- and medium-sized family businesses, even while power and wealth were being concentrated elsewhere. This world refused to be consigned to some museum of early capitalist curiosities.

Midsize manufacturers had in fact suffered a sharp decline at the turn of the twentieth century. That had slowed, however, by midcentury, when such firms accounted for 25 percent of total manufacturing employment. In Dixie and through broad stretches of the Southwest, burgeoning suburbs and cities ardently wooed businesses to resettle there. The Sunbelt was an entrepreneurial paradise of no unions, low wages, free land, tax abatements, and subsidies. The federal government fertilized the region's industrial landscape with oil depletion allowances, agricultural subsidies, pipelines, and a network of aerospace and defense installations.

The "New South" coalesced as a metropolitan-suburban social order, ostensibly race blind but in fact one that remained lily white thanks to a matrix of housing, zoning, transportation, and educational initiatives undertaken by governments at all levels. It bred a middle class politics of taxpayer-conscious homeowner neighborhoods and patriarchal families, exquisitely sensitive to its property rights, unconscious about where those rights came from, and full of latent suspicions about liberal elites who might endanger them. All of this served the needs of big business to be sure, but also served as a hothouse for ancillary, smaller and larger independent firms, including oil and gas companies, real estate developers, regional financial interests, and service industry businesses. William Faulkner summed up the emerging new reality: "Our economy is no longer agrarian. It is the Federal Government."[3]

New family fortunes piled up but did not necessarily carry with them political access or social prestige. This stoked resentment among a milieu of businesspeople—not only in the Sunbelt but across out-of-favor sections of the old Midwest—who in style, language, and emotional tone were much closer to their plebian roots than they were to the transatlantic mores of the East Coast establishment. These new men of the free market hated the snobbish exclusivity, the air of sophistication, and the gratuitous, self-serving, tax-laden sympathies for the lower orders (especially African Americans) evinced by liberal mandarins of change.

Barry Goldwater's insurgency inside the Republican Party mainstreamed what up to the 1960s had remained a marginal if influential political persuasion. Was the Arizona senator a rebel? Yes, if you keep in mind his condemnation of the too liberal elites running the Republican Party. In his eyes, and especially in the eyes of his most zealous advocates, they represented a clubby world of Ivy League bankers, media lords, and "one-worlders." Phyllis Schlafly, who a decade later would lead an antifeminist backlash, crusaded for Goldwater. Her campaign booklet, *A Choice Not an Echo,* which became a runaway best-seller, skewered a power bloc of financiers, publishers, and government officials revolving around people like Averill Harriman, the Rockefellers, and Treasury Secretary Douglas Dillon: a Wall Street cabal disloyal to America, a dangerous band of domestic subversives.[4]

Above all, Goldwater was an avatar of today's politics of limited government. He was an inveterate foe of all forms of collectivism, even the most benign, including unions and the welfare state. (And this is not to mention his opposition to civil rights legislation—he was against the Supreme Court's school desegregation ruling—insofar as it interfered with the rights of property owners to buy, sell, hire, and serve whom they pleased.) He might be called the original "tenther"— that is, a serial quoter of the Tenth Amendment to the Constitution, which reserves for the states all powers not expressly granted to the federal government; for Goldwater and others after him, such federal intrusions simultaneously upset the racial order and transgressed the rights of private property. Nor in his view was standing up for property rights a form of vulgar materialism. He explained that "it has become the fashion in recent years to disparage property rights, to associate them with greed and materialism." But "this attack on property rights is actually . . . another instance of the modern failure to take into account the whole man." The welfare state changed "the individual from a dignified, industrious, self-reliant spiritual being into a dependent animal creature without his knowing it." During his run for the presidency in 1964 a Goldwater campaign brochure was emphatic: "The right of a property owner to manage his property as he sees fit is a civil right, a human right, a moral right."[5]

As the Goldwater opposition sank its grass roots into the lush soil of the Sunbelt and the South, its desire to restore an older order of things was palpable. The senator's followers were quintessentially middle class congregants of the church of family capitalism. Yet they were oddly positioned rebels.

Unlike the declining middling sorts attracted to Coughlin and others in the 1930s, they came mainly from a rising and prosperous middle class, nourished by the mushrooming military-industrial complex: technicians and engineers, real estate developers, upscale retailers, military subcontractors, owners of construction companies, middle managers, and midlevel entrepreneurs who resented the heavy hand of big government while in fact being remarkably dependent on it. On this newest frontier of capitalist expansion their way of life relied on an ingenious and bipartisan array of tax breaks, government loan guarantees and subsidies, public works (like roads, bridges, waterworks, and irrigation systems), zoning protocols, federal housing, and urban development agencies and grants. But they were not about to dwell on this element of their ascendancy; that would have spoiled their amour propre about the free market and their self-invention.

An outbreak of measles, a disease once thought eradicated in the United States, caused a minor panic in 2015. It was attributed, at least in part, to the deliberate refusal of some parents to vaccinate their children. Reports singled out people living in more rural areas and devout fundamentalists. But it was also noted that the refusniks included upper-middle-class, well-educated residents of Orange County and other affluent suburban locales who didn't trust the government, balked at its tutelary intrusion into intimate family matters, and were convinced the regnant scientific establishment was deliberately downplaying or repressing the connection between vaccines and such dreaded aftereffects as autism.

Right from the outset, a half century before the measles uproar, Sunbelt conservatives constituted a living refutation of the Hofstadter thesis about just who was prone to political paranoia. The Columbia University historian imperiously dismissed the Goldwater campaign "as a kind of vocational therapy; without which [his supporters] might have to be committed." He and others viewed that world as an anachronism, a remnant of Sinclair Lewis's Babbittry, with a short life expectancy.

How wrong he was. Instead, they were upwardly not downwardly mobile. They thrived in economic good times, not bad. They were well-educated but not shy about censuring dangerous ideas. They received degrees from probably the best public university system in the country, but were suspicious about the government meddling in public education. They were devoutly religious but often working at the cutting edge of modern scientific research and technology. Loyal to the traditional patriarchal family and its moral inhibitions, they were nonetheless enthusiastic participants in all the delights of consumer culture. One observer noted that they lived in "a sort of Norman Rockwell world with fiber-optic computers and jet airplanes." They were not the forgotten, but the up and coming; the future, not the

past. Goldwater insurgents might be described as reactionary mod-
ernists for whom liberalism had become the new communism.[6]

ENEMIES FOREIGN AND DOMESTIC

Communism indeed! Goldwater rose to prominence along with
Dr. Strangelove. Infamously, the senator's shellacking by Lyndon B.
Johnson in the 1964 presidential election is memorably attributed to
his scary nuclear saber-rattling against the Soviet Union, his hair-
raising praise of extremism, and that chilling Democratic Party commercial of a cherubic little girl counting down those last daisies before
nuclear annihilation. The Goldwater campaign was heir to all those
McCarthy-era accusations about treachery festering at the highest
echelons of the bipartisan postwar order, about its dangerous procliv-
ity for giving in to the communists, even for collaborating with them
in Europe, Asia, and elsewhere.

Long before Phyllis Schlafly emerged as the arch foe of the Equal
Rights Amendment, she was drawn to the Goldwater campaign for its
forthright denunciation of liberal betrayal abroad. In fact, she was
thoroughly schooled in strategic military thinking and familiar with
the most arcane matters of ballistic missile throw-weights, multiple
warhead trajectories, and so on. *A Choice Not an Echo* issued a rousing call to back Goldwater in the 1964 presidential election. It spent
most of its pages excoriating the eastern wing of the Republican Party
and its ties to Morgan and Rockefeller interests. These "kingmakers"
(and their collaborators running the Democratic Party), she maintained, had dictated the choice of the Republican presidential nominee
since 1936 so as to preserve their "America last pro-Communist foreign policy." The kingmakers were in her view a bipartisan or rather
nonpartisan cabal. They embraced LBJ's top advisers like McGeorge
Bundy, as well as David Rockefeller, Dean Rusk, and Henry Cabot
Lodge. All the major investment-banking groups were on board, including not only the Rockefellers, but Brown Brothers. Henry Luce of
Time Life, Eugene Meyer of the *Washington Post/Newsweek* publishing ensemble, Gardner Cowles from *Look,* and other media lords
joined these political and financial leaders, all of whom favored "a

continuation of the Roosevelt-Harry Dexter White-Averill Harriman-Dean Acheson, Dean Rusk policy of aiding and abetting Red Russia and her satellites."

It might appear therefore that the Goldwater movement was singularly preoccupied with limousine liberalism as a threat to national survival. But from its beginnings its concerns were more wide-ranging than that nightmare of global Armageddon might suggest. Even Schlafly wasn't so preoccupied with foreign affairs that she didn't spare time to broaden her indictment of the kingmakers. Coming together in 1936, people like Alfred Sloan of General Motors, Thomas Lamont of the Morgan Bank, Winthrop Aldrich, the president of Chase Bank, and others of their ilk had blocked, according to Schlafly, the nomination of Frank Knox for president because "he had attacked Marxism and Socialism in the New Deal." Four years later these wire-pullers got behind the candidacy of Wendell Willkie, otherwise known as "the barefoot boy from Wall Street," head of a large utility company and a lawyer and friend of elite liberal media lords including Luce, John Young and Raymond Rubicam of Young and Rubicam, and J. Walter Thompson.[7]

In Schlafly's eyes Willkie and his backers replicated all the subversive intentions of the New Deal at home and abroad, but insidiously from inside the Grand Old Party, making their exposure and exile all the more strategically important. Indeed, right after the war ended she was employed by the precursor of the American Enterprise Institute to devise critiques of New Deal economic reforms. Addressing the Illinois Republican convention in 1952, she issued this cautionary observation: "The women of this nation are truly aroused by the New Deal invasion of the American home. The New Deal administration has been demoralizing our children by bad example, drafting our men and confiscating family income." If Democrats got elected again, "we can expect socialized agriculture, socialized medicine—and a scarcity of both food and doctors." The problem, she averred, was not mere policy, but "moral corruption."[8]

Schlafly was not from the Sunbelt but from the Midwest, Missouri in fact. From modest social circumstances, her family had struggled to stay afloat in the Depression. But they were nonetheless strivers, and

Phyllis went to a high-quality Catholic school and actually made a debut in St. Louis society. Her father suffered long bouts of unemployment, only got work as an engineer during World War II when hired by the War Production Board, but hated the New Deal. The inventor in him, even if not a successful one, left him believing in his own self-invention and in the Republican Party, which seemed consecrated to that purpose. His daughter was the proud inheritor of that faith. So she became a Taft loyalist, subscribing to the Ohio senator's 1952 pronouncement "if we get Eisenhower we will practically have a Republican New Deal Administration with just as much spending and socialism as under Truman."[9]

Faith in free enterprise, like Schlafly's, was a Midwest heartland birthright. The region was the ancestral home of American heavy industry. Some of these businesses had long ago transmogrified into impersonal public corporations. Many, however, clung to their dynastic roots. John M. Olin, for example, would go on to create an antiliberal family foundation and noted that "my greatest ambition . . . is to see free enterprise re-established in this country. Business and the public must be awakened to the creeping stranglehold that socialism gained here since World War II." Olin rose through the ranks of the family glass business in Illinois, which later morphed into Olin Mathieson, chemical and arms manufacturer. For Olin or Schlafly the danger communism presented was more insidious than its crude appeals to the down and out. Schlafly worried about its appeal to "the financial, educational, and social beneficiaries of capitalism," that is, those whom Mario Procaccino would soon anoint as limousine liberals.

Clarence Manion also hailed from that same part of the country, from South Bend, Indiana, where he'd been a law professor for years. At one time a New Deal Democrat, he'd become increasingly suspicious of the "Wall Street crowd" running both parties. Soon enough he put together a ginger group to promote a Goldwater presidential candidacy (sometimes exceeding the actual ambitions of the Arizona senator himself). Manion's circle rested on a milieu of family-owned or controlled businesses, including some quite large ones like Sears, run by General Robert E. Wood, a longtime New Deal hater. They viewed the "leftwing as strong, well-organized, and well-financed.

Many gigantic fortunes, built by virtue of private enterprise under the Constitution, have fallen under the direction of Internationalists, One-worlders, Socialists, and Communists. Much of that hoard of money is being used to socialize the United States." Chambers of commerce and chapters of the National Association of Manufacturers through-out the Midwest nurtured this outlook. And so it was that convictions about appeasement abroad and economic and moral subversion at home bled into each other.

Charges of communist skullduggery showed up in all sorts of un-likely places as, for example, in grievances that were addressed to the Housing Act of 1961 or that targeted the creation of the new Depart-ment of Housing and Urban Development and its powers to seize property; in the eyes of one Los Angeles landowner this was "a decla-ration of war." In Phoenix a new city manager system was resisted by a right-wing group as a Kremlin inspired plot. According to the histo-rian Rick Perlstein, this radical right-wing conservatism perceived an "organic unity of the American welfare state and Russian imperial expansion." A freshly invigorated gathering of men on the make were determined to put an end to this and to recover the lost soul of the American experiment in self-reliance.[10]

Barry Goldwater was a fair facsimile of that American type. His grandfather was a Polish Jew who fled to America to escape getting drafted into the czar's army. He opened a saloon qua brothel in gold rush San Francisco and then moved to the Arizona Territory, where he entered the retail business and went on to found a dynasty. Gold-water's father developed a reputation as a dandy, converted to be-come an Episcopalian but without much effect on his character, and was eventually ousted from the mayor's office in Prescott. But an uncle was more steadfast, about both his Judaism and his public be-havior. Uncle Morris, reelected nine times as Prescott's mayor and founder of Arizona's Democratic Party early in the twentieth century, was committed to a philosophy of states' rights. His nephew inherited his political interests and outlook if not his party affiliation.

After a year at the University of Arizona, Barry left to take over the family department store business. It was a model of paternal corpo-rate welfare capitalism, antiunion, committed to the open shop, provincial, adhering to prevailing racial norms. Goldwater was known as a risk-taking hell-raiser as an adolescent and channeled that energy into high-energy business promotion and politicking as an adult. He wanted, as did other business circles in the state, to remake Arizona, and the city of Phoenix in particular, where the dynasty was head-quartered, into a magnet for modern capitalist development. There he helped lead a movement to desegregate the city's public schools to make the place less obnoxious to national interests for whom the caste system had become an embarrassment. The Republican Party was back then much more amenable to such sentiments than the Democrats, who were still afraid to offend their Dixiecrat brethren in the South. Goldwater became Arizona's first Republican senator in 1952, the party taking shape as an outgrowth of his commercial and civic boosterism; he was at various times president of the Chamber of Commerce, the YMCA, a bevy of businessmen's clubs, and the Community Chest and trustee of the local hospital. Goldwater was a merchant prince of Sunbelt capitalism.

Arizona's favorite son was rarely seen without his cowboy hat and string tie. It was fitting regalia for a political myth that played well throughout the Sunbelt and elsewhere. It signaled that indigenous pioneering independence that wasn't about to truckle under to the East Coast's Ivy League men in suits. Yet the Goldwater fortune, like so many that surfaced out West after the war, depended utterly on various kinds of government supports: everything from rural mail delivery to the Roosevelt Dam outside Phoenix. Not only that, Barry grew up with a nurse, a chauffeur, and a live-in maid. He might need that sort of help, but he was sure that analogous aid provided by the New Deal state would rot the moral fiber of Americans less lucky than he.

Exactly this kind of paradox ran through the whole world of nouveau family capitalism given life by World War II and the Cold War garrison state that followed. Businessmen native to the Southwest or migrants from outside the region imagined themselves cowboy capitalists who had risen thanks to their own stamina, ingenuity, and resilience even while grazing on a lush landscape of military bases and aircraft plants. Cities like Dallas and Oklahoma City sprang to life out of the agricultural hinterland to become commercial metropolises whose town elders pretended it was all the outcome of their own bootstrapping while they shrewdly manipulated the levers of local and state political machines to put in place the essential infrastructure. Their politics were an extension of this existential delusion.[11]

"YOU WILL KNOW THEM BY THEIR FRUITS"

Eisenhower, in the eyes of people like Goldwater or like-thinking businessmen and political activists in southern California and elsewhere, was part of an establishment that crossed party lines. Men to the manner born had entered into a compact with the unwashed, men like Walter Reuther, whose labor movement militancy jeopardized the freedom of action enterprising manufacturers and merchants valued so highly. Reuther may have been a left-wing Democrat, but there were too many like-thinking people atop the Republican Party, whose sympathies for the welfare state and social reforms were obnoxious to resurgent ranks of family capitalism. Long before he became the bête noire of the Goldwater movement, Nelson Rockefeller fit that profile.

Second son of John D. Rockefeller Jr., Nelson was the first of the clan to enter politics. His father and grandfather were pious. They were Baptist patriarchs entirely devoted to the perpetuation of the dynasty who steered clear of politics except when tribal interests demanded otherwise. Nelson was far worldlier and cultivated broad cultural interests (his fondness for modern art, for example, encouraged by his mother's deep involvement with the Museum of Modern Art), and was far less pious when it came to sexual matters and marital propriety (his dalliances and indecorous second marriage would shadow his quest for the presidency later on). To unfriendly eyes this moral looseness and social unorthodoxy were inseparable from his political views, which seemed infected by excessive solicitude for the down and out.

Apparently disturbed by encountering the pervasive poverty and exploitation that went along with the family's vast Venezuelan oil holdings, Nelson lectured the Standard Oil Board of Directors: "The only justification for ownership is that it serves the broad interests of the people. We must recognize the social responsibilities of corporations and the corporation must use its ownership of assets to reflect the best interest of the people." While World War II raged on, Nelson envisioned an enormous postwar social program for all of Latin America that would include social security and health care programs. Later, when he first ran for governor of New York in 1958, his campaign platform replicated that thinking. His platform based its call for wide-ranging reform on a Rockefeller Foundation report that had been cobbled together by a liberal corporate elite that included Charles Percy of Bell and Howell, Thomas McCabe of Scott Paper, Justin Dart of Rexall, one-time US commander in Europe General Lucius Clay, Henry Luce, and David Sarnoff, along with a bevy of union leaders, university presidents, and foundation presidents. And this was all before the governor became an outspoken proponent of racial equality.

Rockefeller was hardly alone in evincing these views. William Scranton, a rival of Nelson's for the presidential nomination in 1964 and the governor of Pennsylvania, possessed all the bona fides of the limousine liberal. On the maternal side the Scranton family had arrived in the New World on the Mayflower. William's mother was a suffragist. His father was an architect of state-sponsored urban renewal in the depressed city named after the family—a form of state capitalism known as the Scranton Plan. William went to Yale. When he entered the political arena, he made clear his sophisticated approach to what had become a complex economic organism that combined state direction with corporate control. He talked about the need for "labor market coordination" by government agencies to circumvent the dangerous consequences of an overly free market. He was staunch in his defense of civil rights. And he was a favorite of the whole eastern Republican establishment, including such corporations as Chrysler, Procter and Gamble, Scott Paper, the *New York Times,* and the *Herald Tribune.*

Scranton and his fellow party wise men were scared by the strange upheaval among the nouveau well-off out West. New York's senator Jacob Javits warned that a Goldwater victory would "wrench the social order out of its sockets." Card-carrying liberal Republicans like Henry Cabot Lodge, George Romney, and Eisenhower himself tried to counteract the movement's free market hallelujahs. Massachusetts senator Henry Cabot Lodge (he of the family of whom it was said, "The Lowells speak only to Cabots and the Cabots speak only to God") pronounced, "No one in his right mind would today argue that there is no place for the federal government in the reawakening of America. Indeed, we need another Republican sponsored Marshall Plan for our cities and schools." (When the Arizona cowboy capitalist did indeed win the duel with the party's liberal establishment, many of them, including two Cabots; a senior partner at Goldman Sachs, Henry Ford II; Lodge's finance chairman John Loeb; and a host of other patriarchs debarked to the LBJ camp.)

Pundits and scholars would call all this "consensus, managerial, or pragmatic liberalism." The New Deal had set in motion a new way to rule and with it a ruling coalition that conceived of itself as an agent of controlled change. It had jettisoned traditional conservative or reactionary responses to a social order that was inherently disorderly. It existed in some chronic state of liquefaction, the inexorable outcome in a society given over to the flux of the marketplace. Keynesian economics, which had become the prevailing conventional wisdom, was the public policy expression of a mass consumption–based system that welcomed such change, indeed depended on it, but sought to domesticate its sometimes violent perturbations. So, for example, the Committee for Economic Development, an elite think tank born during the war, to which the country's largest national corporations belonged, was a serial promulgator of such recipes for stability through government-sanctioned reform. The committee might be seen as walking in the footsteps of those Jekyll Island conferees who so alarmed Glenn Beck.[12]

AT THE BARRICADES

But the nouveau bourgeoisie found all this repugnant. During Goldwater's first attempt to get the Republican presidential nomination in 1960, he laid out his worldview in *Conscience of a Conservative*, which became a best-seller even though it was published by an obscure press. In it he voiced a cri de coeur against precisely the kind of world Rockefeller and other liberal elitists had become comfortable with: a mass society, populated by featureless mass men, all subject to the leviathan state. And unlike the now discredited conspiracy-minded demagogues on the far right who spent their time ferreting out secret cells of reds here, there, and everywhere, the Arizona senator blamed this state of affairs on highly visible, out-in-the-open elites who had lost their manhood, their belief in the individual's autonomy, and so their will to fight for freedom.

An old catechism, muted since the advent of the New Deal, it now awakened in the hearts and minds of the new bourgeoisie a readiness to challenge an odd foe: rulers who had forsaken the society they were supposed to protect and lost the capacity to rule. The insurgency caught fire among a younger generation of newly minted conservative rebels. During the 1964 California primary, young Republicans denounced Rockefeller as a "left-wing extremist" (the governor would narrowly lose this race and with it any hope of the presidency). As election day neared, Goldwater delivered a more tactile sense of what was at stake when he told a California rally: "When you say to some bureaucrat in Washington, 'you take care of the kids' education'; when they say to you, 'Don't worry about Mom and Pop, don't lay aside any money, enjoy yourself, the Federal Government will take care . . . '; this is the ultimate destruction of the American family. When this happens Communism will have won." The aspirations of family capitalism—no matter how small or dynastic-sized the business—ran counter to the notion that wealth carried with it social obligations. There might be religious obligations, which could be conveyed through philanthropy, but not government-imposed responsibilities to ensure the general welfare. This was a way of life defined by character-building self-discipline and patrimonial power and pride that were profoundly personal. Much like its enemy, limousine liberalism, the tenets of family capitalism were at one and the same time anchored in social reality and self-delusional.

When a well-organized boom for a Goldwater presidential run emerged in 1960, it found a financial welcome among "small, family-owned manufacturing companies," some newly hatched, others, especially in the Midwest, with their origins in the late nineteenth century. These included Acme Steel of Chicago, Wood River Oil and Refining

Company of Wichita, Lone Star Steel of Dallas, Rockwell Manufacturing of Pittsburgh, Roberts Dairy of Omaha, Youngstown Sheet
and Tube, Memphis Furniture Manufacturing, and so on. This was a
world that loved Robert Taft and despised Republican liberals like
Thomas Dewey and Nelson Rockefeller. Its anticommunism was ecumenical in reach, stigmatizing even the most pedestrian forms of trade
unionism. Arizona, in fact, was, in 1948, the first state to pass a right-
to-work law after the passage of the Taft-Hartley Act, which defanged
the labor movement by outlawing sympathy strikes, giving the government enhanced powers to enjoin work stoppages, and purging the
labor movement of its radical leadership. Elected from a state that
had been traditionally Democratic, Goldwater felt compelled to vote
for a higher federal minimum wage and an extension of Social Security. But his heart was elsewhere.[13]

Orange County in California, which became a Goldwater haven,
was a perfect laboratory for nurturing this bourgeois rebellion. After
the war it became a proving ground for entrepreneurial strivings. Yet
all of it rested on an understructure of public investment. "Midwest
transplants from small town Illinois" transformed a once sparsely settled agricultural countryside into a series of commercial boomtowns
and affluent suburbs. Much of the postwar makeover of Southern
California was financed by a new breed of venture capitalists in partnership with the federal government. By 1965 the Defense Department had awarded a quarter of its prime contracts to California firms.
Two-fifths of NASA's contracts were located there. Aerospace accounted for a quarter of California's economic growth.

Once rural, Orange County's population grew from one hundred
thousand in 1940 to one million by 1960. Real estate developments
bred like rabbits as ranches were subdivided into towns. The GI bill
provided financial ballast for the housing boom. Private enterprises of
every conceivable variety—construction companies; retail outlets; legal, medical, engineering, and financial practices; skilled tradesmen
supplying the know-how to keep the water running and electricity
flowing—turned the region into an odd sort of "community." The community was in many respects a private enterprise, developed by land
and real estate companies. Property consciousness was its cultural and

ideological métier. Little room was left for public spaces. Instead a sense of exclusivity prefigured the walled-off enclaves that became so common later in the century. This was a kind of social engineering practiced by private enterprise on behalf of private enterprise, invested in creating a social and racial homogeneity, gated by wealth and racial housing covenants. All in all it was an Eden of family capitalism.

Arguably for just this reason, Orange County became the most fertile terrain for mounting a fiercely passionate war against limousine liberalism. There, what had been a marginal political persuasion of rabid anticommunist conspiracy mongering got mainstreamed. The ravings of candy manufacturer and John Birch Society founder Robert Welch (who judged President Eisenhower had "been sympathetic to ultimate Communist aims, realistically willing to use Communist means to help them achieve their goals, knowingly accepting and abiding by Communist orders, and consciously serving the Communist conspiracy for all of his adult life") had once made him an infamous clinical case study in the laboratories of those studying "the paranoid style" in American politics. Fundamentalist preacher Billy Hargis, who was given to exorcizing the "anti-God Liberal Establishment" (until he was revealed to be a child molester), was offered up as another form of the same pathological species. Talk of the satanic connection between godless communism and domestic collectivism had long been part of the repertoire of this exotic world.

But now in Orange County and elsewhere that "politics of the irrational" was instead establishing a new middle class normal. The John Birch Society flourished there, as it did in similar places in Texas and Florida among better educated, wealthier, self-made entrepreneurial types and with middle class professionals like doctors, stockbrokers, and lawyers. Fears about the cross-fertilization of racial unrest, rock 'n' roll "jungle music," and teenage sexuality heated up the cultural atmosphere.

Many of the region's arrivistes were expats from Taft country in the Midwest. They brought with them a hatred for government interference of all sorts: not just in the economy but in public education, racial matters, and religious affairs. Anything that even faintly smacked of collectivism or regulation or government planning or higher taxes was anathema. In these quarters the felt danger was a new serfdom, vassal-age to the state, a cultural poison confected in Washington and threat-ening to go viral. Here Richard Nixon made his congressional debut in 1946 running against the incumbent Jerry Voorhis, who "toe[d] the communist line." Here elaborate "blacklists" helped purge the private and public sector of suspected subversives, and vigilantes cleansed public and school libraries and classroom curricula of politically or morally unseemly books and ideas.

Whether from outside the state or California-bred, many Orange County denizens were churchgoers. They might have belonged to mainline Protestant denominations. But a large number were funda-mentalists and evangelicals, Baptists of strict moral injunctions and practitioners of local autonomy, and Pentecostal believers in personal salvation. All felt increasingly comfortable merging their political and religious beliefs and behavior. That was unusual in the history of Prot-estant fundamentalism, but anticommunism, about which they were fervent, invited this kind of zealousness. After all, the red menace was perceived as simultaneously a moral threat as well as a political and existential one. Despite the fact that they carried with them all of the accoutrements of modern, secular life, they worried about the moral disarmament that self-indulgence seemed to entail and the way a reli-ance on the state abetted that spiritual demobilization. Perhaps their very rootlessness, leaving old heartlands and moving into a territorial tabula rasa, fed desires to re-create semblances of community life and spiritual solace even while taking pride in their heroic self-reliance and self-invention. That is to say they managed, as people often do, to live in messy incoherence, or, to put it more precisely, to live as eco-nomic libertarians on the one hand and social and moral traditional-ists on the other.[14]

FRONTIERLAND

Family capitalism on the frontier occupies a distinctive place in the American imagination. Well over a century ago Frederick Jackson Turner, a celebrated American historian, suggested that the closing of the Western frontier and with it those limitless prospects for family farming, augured serious consequences for the longevity of social equality and democracy. He argued that the frontier had functioned as an ever renewable terrain on which those qualities refreshed themselves—but the clock was ticking. Then, in the mid twentieth century new frontiers of economic development that, ironically, transformed agrarian regions into high-tech and low-tech industrial ones bred a rebirth of family capitalism combatively at odds with the establishment, and thus the main currents of national life.

But it was also at odds with itself. It feared the state, and resented its intrusions and presumptions not only into economic matters but also into more intimate affairs. Yet it relied on government not only for its material sustenance, but also to restore and reinforce an older moral order when it came to child-bearing, or what kind of literature should be considered tolerable, or when movies and photographs transgressed the lines of decency. Books as diverse as *The Communist Manifesto*; Henry David Thoreau's *Civil Disobedience*; *The Grapes of Wrath* by John Steinbeck; and *Finders Keepers,* the winner of the 1952 Caldecott Medal for children's literature, whose artwork was accused of illustrating a "subversive text aimed at urging North and South Koreans to unite and drive the United Nations out of Korea," were banned or threatened with being banned in California, Indiana, and New Jersey. Still, this moral and political vigilance cohabited uneasily with a vigorous commitment to the free market as a way of life. Yet that was, after all, a zone of amorality where desire dictated what was on offer. In that universe all was permissible.[15]

In bygone days, the suffering and anguish associated with modern times, its poverty, anomie, cultural relativism, and family breakdown, all were blamed on capitalism and the totalitarian reign of market relations. Now instead all those dilemmas and more were laid at the doorstep of the nanny state. Yet the nanny state succored everyone, the privileged as well as the despised. Moreover, the nanny state alone could not account for the vertiginous plague of mass society that left so many at sea, rootless, in search of some more reliable social and personal identity, prey to the manipulations of what Dwight McDonald labeled middlebrow culture. A whole literary cottage industry from David Riesman's *Lonely Crowd* to William Whyte's *Organization Man* wrestled with the dilemma confronting a new middle class no longer tethered to the egocentric pursuit of family proprietorship.

So too, the aspirations of family capitalism were unblushingly about power, about the power that inheres not merely in wealth, but in property, property as self-possession, property as a lineage, property as a dynastic continuity, as a hold on the future. Much better and more proper that power reside there, in the bosom of the family, then in an alien, inherently untrustworthy state apparatus manned by deracinated bureaucrats. Still, the revanchist world that looked to Goldwater and his ilk was invested, literally and figuratively, in the garrison state in multiple ways, believed deeply in the need for all-seeing surveillance, and trusted mainly in armed muscle flexing, even nuclear coercion, to protect the homeland. All that required state power on steroids.

However reminiscent America's new breed of family capitalism was of its nineteenth-century antecedents, it was therefore also quite different. And it played a distinctive role in national political life. On the one hand, it was rooted in an earlier, peculiar culture of anticommunism that had for a half century imagined a conspiracy of bankers and Bolsheviks. And its ostensible preoccupation was the Soviet menace. Yet, this rebellion among a nouveau bourgeoisie began a reconfiguration of the country's mythography that would soon enough redefine public life. Liberalism took on the diabolic resonances once given off by communism. In the eyes first of all of these renegades from Republican orthodoxy and then later informing the outlook of a far broader public, liberalism was the new communism.

When Goldwater was run over by the LBJ landslide in 1964, pundits announced the imminent demise of this discomfiting outbreak of the politics of the irrational. And indeed, many partisans of Arizona's senator inside the Grand Old Party found themselves purged and out of work after the election. While crushed nationally (LBJ won 61 percent of the popular vote and 486 out of 538 electoral votes), Goldwater had notably done well in the Solid South (where, together with Arizona, he won his only electoral votes). This was a harbinger of the region's long-term political transformation. The maverick candidate had also done exceedingly well in Orange County. That too was prophetic although not obviously so. In the years ahead the bourgeois rebellion afoot in the Sunbelt and in parts of the passed-over Midwest would make an uneasy alliance with a parallel rebellion of the "little man" against the limousine liberalism that dominated the Democratic Party. Goldwater was too bourgeois, too business-minded, never populist enough in inclination or belief or rhetoric, never ready to play racial politics boldly enough, and never comfortable enough with the class animosities that the emotions incited by limousine liberalism needed to become politically robust. Others would be more prepared to press those buttons and so bring the crisis of New Deal liberalism to a boil.[16]

6

Country and Western Marxism

Polls taken outside steel mill gates in Gary, Indiana, and South Chicago, Illinois, in the run-up to the 1964 election registered majorities for Goldwater. Yet the maverick senator generally speaking did poorly in those kinds of precincts. His truculent demeanor notwithstanding, the Republican presidential candidate didn't really speak the same language as blue collar steelworkers or white collar clerks or those lower-middle-class homeowners from the outer boroughs of New York who soon would rally around Mario Procaccino. By and large these people identified with the Democratic Party. But more than that they accounted for the chasm that separated the Goldwater campaign from the unwashed.

To become a nuclear device with the power to blow up or do serious damage to the two-party system and the New Deal Order that it sustained, the mythology of limousine liberalism needed to ignite the fires of populism. That was something Sunbelt rebels were wary about doing. They had to find a way to inflame those class animosities that had once made FDR so appealing but without allowing the conflagration to incinerate the prevailing hierarchies of wealth and power. The ranks of the Goldwater movement were feisty enough when it came to denouncing the establishment in striped pants and pince-nez. But these emotions were kept on a short leash. Goldwater followers were angry to be sure, but scarcely could be described as hard-pressed. On the contrary, they were doing well at getting ahead as business people and professionals on the rise and on the make. They felt neither the material pressures nor the indignities of those further down the social pyramid. So they were bound to feel uncomfortable in the presence of a movement that might in some more down-to-earthiness patois say unkind things about big business, concentrated wealth, and the prerogatives of property.[1]

Above all, the race question began to surface as the country's most incendiary issue, but one that did not right away fuse together the gathering armies ranged against limousine liberalism. True, the Goldwater movement was virtually lily white. The senator was known for his opposition to federal civil rights legislation and no doubt attracted support, especially in the South, for that reason. But his opposition was only partial, or rather he supported (and had in the late 1950s supported) a highly qualified version of civil rights reform, as long as it did not infringe on the rights of property or states' rights and left in place the core of the racial status quo. This kind of simon-pure version of equal rights made sense among the rising middle classes of the South and Sunbelt. More openly racist appeals were, on the contrary, embarrassing and bad for business.

Such appeals mixed together with more pungent evocations of class warfare were, however, abroad in the land. As the civil rights movement gathered steam and entered into a testy alliance with the liberal establishment, old-time populist wrath took on racial coloration; or alternately, racial animosities that were a permanent part of the substructure of American life vented to the surface in a volcanic explosion against limousine liberalism. Neither the racism nor the class-inflected populism was camouflage for the other. To some degree establishment eminences could speak the same language as black preachers and seminarians, stigmatized sharecroppers, and a rising generation of college-educated African American youths when it came to advocating universal, formal, legal equality. Their purposes were by no means at all times the same. But the crystallization of this coalition opened up a fissure in political life, especially inside the Democratic Party, into which class and racial resentments and phobias poured and intermingled. Racial confrontation could serve as the pursuit of class warfare by other means. And class ranged against class could become another way of defending the racial order.

BLUE COLLARS, REDNECKS, AND THE LITTLE MAN

Little Man, What Now? is the title of a book by the German novelist Hans Falluda published in the early 1930s. It was intended to capture the confusion and anxiety experienced by Germans of meager means and precarious social position caught in the maelstrom of the Great Depression and tossed to and fro by the mobilized armies of communism, socialism, and Nazism. Many such people looked only for a way of retreating into the recesses of some private safe haven. But that was hard to find. So some enlisted in movements that simultaneously voiced anger at those bigger and littler than they. They inveighed against the big shots, who always seemed to prevail and even prosper on the misery of those beneath them, but then again, made sure to keep their distance from and stigmatize the lower orders (proletarians, the unemployed, immigrant aliens), whether to better defend their own material well-being or as compensation for their own existential insecurity, or both. This might be called the "politics of the little man."

Followers of Father Coughlin, Senator Long, Dr. Townsend, and Congressman Lemke evinced these ambivalent attitudes. So, too, did supporters of Senator McCarthy, although more as a state of mind than in any sustained organized form. Trace lines connect "little man" politics erupting in the 1960s and episodically thereafter to these earlier manifestations. However, the emergence of the race question made these newer insurgencies distinctly different.

With the important exception of the Ku Klux Klan, the country's racial caste system was not at issue in these predecessor movements. Why would it be? It was not in jeopardy, not even at the hands of the New Deal coalition and its expanding state apparatus, which kept clear of the issue so as to avoid antagonizing its Dixiecrat southern wing, which wielded great power in the Congress and in the Democratic Party. Anti-Semitism and hostility to immigrants did indeed crop up. Such sentiments were at times rhetorically important, although rarely did they surface with programmatic import. Moreover, Jew baiting was directed at the upper classes and in some considerable measure so was the animus against immigrants who seemed to be swarming Washington's proliferating bureaucracies to unhorse an Anglo-Saxon establishment.

If "little man" politics in this earlier period felt threatened from below, it was by insurrectionary proletarians, by armies of the unemployed, evicted, and dispossessed. African Americans, who of course were well represented, overrepresented in fact, in these ranks, nevertheless didn't constitute a distinct menace. The civil rights movement and the right-wing assault on limousine liberalism in the 1960s would change all that. It would make George Wallace, the Southland's most flamboyant segregationist, the perfect embodiment of "little man" class and racial anger, targeting an alleged complicity between WASP overlords and the black mudsills of America.

Alabama's governor accelerated the transformation of economic populism of yesteryears into the cultural populism of the late twentieth century. Wallace weighed into privileged know-it-alls using their levers of power over the government, the media, the judicial system, the universities, and the philanthropic foundations to upset the prevailing order of things. "Do we have an elitist government? . . . They've decreed it's good for the people to do certain things. And even though the people don't like to do it, they must do it because this super-elite group is so determined." The governor was addressing, as he put it, "the man in the textile mill," the "barber and beautician," and "the little businessman." He wasn't afraid to taunt the bourgeoisie, to talk outside the box, and to violate WASP taboos against the unsayable. The irony is that once this kind of rhetorical impiety was part of the arsenal of working class defiance of capitalist hierarchy and hypocrisy; now it was retrofitted on behalf of law and order.

No matter! Any movement worth its salt needs this emotional energy. On high school football fields and parking lots, at shopping malls and stock car race tracks, in Elks halls, fairgrounds, and drugstores, speaking to blue collar and first-generation white collar workers and second-generation Okies, Wallace roused feelings of nostalgia for a culture that seemed headed for extinction. He mixed that sentimentality with rage against all those—hippies, atheists, and pseudointellectuals—who might be considered the camp followers of limousine liberals.[2]

Patricians like William F. Buckley, editor of the *National Review,* denounced this kind of politics as "country and western Marxism" creeping in from the hinterland. He had a point: Wallace was all at once an antielitist, a populist, a racist, a chauvinist, and a tribune of the politics of revenge and resentment. His appeal reached into the skilled upper echelons of the white working class and beyond. He defended the hard-hat American heartland mainly by saluting its ethos of hard work and family values. Like other Southern Democratic demagogues, the governor avoided attacking those core elements of New Deal reform that his poor white constituents relied on. But Wallace directed his heaviest artillery at the arrogance of Washington bureaucrats, the indolence of "welfare queens," and the impiety, moral nihilism, and disloyalty of overindulged, long-haired, pot-smoking, antiwar college students. He hated the "Yankee establishment," conflating the "filthy rich on Wall Street" and the "socialist beatnik crowd" running the government.

Still, Buckley, and Goldwater as well, dismissed Wallace as a New Deal populist because the Alabama governor endorsed federal funding of education, job training, an equitable minimum wage, unemployment insurance, public works, and increases in Medicare and Social Security payments. Taken together these were mile markers measuring the distance that still separated the assaults on limousine liberalism from above and those erupting from below. The separate streams of "little man" racial populism and the family capitalism of the Sunbelt would one day converge, but not yet. Shrewd observers, however, had already taken note of the prospects. Right-wing political strategist Richard Viguerie early on sensed the party worth taking over was Wallace's American Independent Party, not the Republicans. Here was a world, unlike the affluent one flourishing in Southern California, Texas, Arizona, and elsewhere, that was feeling squeezed both by the onrush of racial liberation and by an economy that had begun to tip toward decline.[3]

TWILIGHT OF THE GOLDEN AGE

When the sixties began, America was the world's preeminent economic superpower, unchallengeable; this was a position it had assumed even before World War II ended. As the decade drew to a close that was no longer the case. Although America's economy was still stronger than any other nation's, Japanese, German, and other European competitors were visibly muscling up. The US dollar became the object of concerted speculation, and not long after the decade closed the Nixon administration would sever its link to gold and jettison the fixed exchange rate system established after the war, which had rested on the inviolable trust in the dollar and by extension the soundness of the underlying American industrial machine. Government spending on the war in Vietnam and on enlarging the welfare state at home (the war on poverty and Medicare in particular) together not only unmoored the dollar, but generated inflation and a growing tax burden borne increasingly by the country's working classes.

The victory culture that had sustained an indigenous American optimism for generations was losing its grip. Nor was the military quagmire in Vietnam the only reason. A creeping sense of stagnation, cynicism, decline, and defeat coursed through working class neighborhoods by the early 1970s. But even a decade and more before, regions of the country had already begun to suffer the wounds of deindustrialization that would become a national blight. Coal and textile towns particularly were its first casualties. Even in the early 1960s legislation created regional planning boards armed with business financial incentives in the hope of arresting the decline. They failed.[4]

Feeling the first spasms of economic pressure even before the sixties began, white, working class residents of Detroit, for example, were ready to interpret LBJ's war on poverty, one of the constituent parts of the Great Society, as a war on them. Detroit had been the site of violent hate strikes and race riots in 1943 as competition over housing and other vital necessities flared up in response to the mass influx of black workers from down South. Indeed, the great migration of African Americans had changed not only the complexion of the city (blacks had grown from 9 percent to 40 percent of the city's population by 1970), but challenged the local political chemistry. Control over such matters as housing, neighborhood policing, and municipal services was no longer reliably in the hands of the white-run Democratic Party machine. White workers who could afford it moved out to the suburbs, sometimes before and sometimes after the auto plants did the same.

As factories closed and all-white neighborhoods darkened, mythologies about the horrors of slum life became a contagion in the "Motor City." Local movements to protect the racial homogeneity of neighborhoods, including especially their schools, and the property values of their residential homesteads spread here, there, and everywhere, carried along by a politics of fear that was as much moral as it was material. Commercial predators, especially real estate interests, fed on the panic, so that the quest for good housing, once an issue defined by the class antimonies of industrial capitalism, became instead an issue of race. Public housing died and visceral hostility to government as a conduit of aid to the undeserving flourished. A similar dynamic played out in other postwar metropolitan centers.

Ghetto dwellers on the other hand, consigned to an archipelago of poverty and indignity far offshore from the mainland of American postwar prosperity, had had enough. As the civil rights movement migrated to the North in the early 1960s, its militancy rose in response to the hostility with which it was treated by the putative forces of "law and order." It became readier to respond in kind. A rolling series of insurrections qua riots traveled from coast to coast. At the same time, immense antiwar demonstrations whose desire for peace expressed a wrathful disgust for the government's Vietnam debacle also weren't shy about voicing their solidarity with America's internal colonials suffering from a kind of domestic imperialism. These organized mass movements mingled with a kindred, if more vaguely contoured, counterculture. It thumbed its nose at every middle class convention from the nuclear family and sexual propriety to material acquisitiveness, career striving, and Cold War patriotism. All this tumult deeply disturbed the equilibrium of millions still wedded to these values, still expecting the American economy to deliver on its promise, and vulnerable to the virus of scapegoating, racial and otherwise. People viewing this world felt everything they had known or counted on was falling apart. "It's all in danger now. The house you always wanted is in danger, the kids are in danger, the neighborhood is in danger. It's all slipping away," said a Brooklyn man reacting to the chronic turmoil that wracked New York City.[5]

Precariously positioned blue collar workers, beleaguered by taxes, inflation, and the collapse of the racial, sexual, and moral order of things, hunkered down to defend the value of their mortgaged homes, the autonomy of their local schools, and their ethnically and racially familiar neighborhoods. Increasing competition over jobs, housing, and the general wherewithal required to live decently in an economy showing the first serious symptoms of disease were aggravated and given focus by racial animosities. This was a kind of proletarian version of family capitalism—claiming territorial space as its communal property—that enlisted race as another medium of class struggle.

It was politically expedient for liberal elites to dismiss all this as bigotry pure and simple. It was that, but it was also more than that. It is undeniable that primal racial fears and phobias were at work then. Such deeply embedded prejudices and animosities continue to this day to course through the arteries of right-wing populist movements. They create a kind of shadowland of the unsayable surrounding subsets of the Tea Party insurgency. However, the presence of a noxious racism among elements of the populist right has often overwhelmed any inclination by limousine liberals, and even those standing to their left, to appreciate whatever else might be simmering in those precincts of discontent. For elite liberals in particular, racism becomes an encompassing evasion that elides less morally consoling explanations for mass abandonment by people who once comprised the foot soldiers of the New Deal Order.

Limousine liberalism was the metaphor that captured this political ambiguity. Procaccino's campaign bon mot was preceded by and happened amid years of organized protest over discrimination in housing, employment, schools, and unionized jobs, while the first of the ghetto insurgencies erupted in Harlem in 1964. When action to desegregate the housing market seemed imminent, there were fierce defensive outbursts in the outer boroughs. So too with respect to the growing movement to integrate public schools, even before busing students became an incendiary issue. Sit-ins and school boycotts were mounted by "parents and taxpayers" and other "little man" groups. Moreover, by the late sixties New York's economy had noticeably slowed, fueling the fear of which there was already a surplus. All of this reached a climax after Mario Procaccino had faded away. Then a cascade of strikes and boycotts turned Brooklyn schools into a theater of war pitting

African American parents and children along with their allies in City Hall and in the boardrooms of the elite foundations against working class and lower-middle-class white and ethnically self-consciousness parents and students. Similar confrontations, especially over the re-configuration of public education, exploded in other cities.[6]

Wallace's racially inflected anti-statism thus became a workshop for conservatives and segregationists gradually fashioning a common political identity and logic. Soon enough, it would no longer be taken for granted that conservatives were natural-born elitists. On the con-trary! Wallace, a new kind of populist conservative, was an outlier, an outlaw for law and order—defiant, nonacquiescent, and ecumenical. And he aspired to be something more than an unreconstructed red-neck son of the South: "It is basically an ungodly government," he said. "You native sons and daughters of old New England's rock-ribbed patriotism . . . you sturdy natives of the great Midwest, and you descendants of the far West flaming spirit of pioneer freedom, we invite you to come and be with us for you are of Southern mind and Southern spirit and Southern philosophy, you are Southern too and brothers in our fight." He went hunting after a menagerie of enemies—the ultrarich, "welfare loafers," bureaucratic totalitarians, rioters, pro-testers, common criminals—that you didn't have to hail from Dixie to despise.[7]

THE NORTHLAND RISES

When Wallace ran in the Democratic presidential primaries in 1964, he'd polled big numbers not only in the South, but in industrial states like Michigan, Indiana, and Wisconsin. In the Wisconsin primary he won 25 percent of the vote, 30 percent in working class Milwaukee, and in the steelworker precincts of Gary, Indiana, was the winner by a large margin. He collected 43 percent of the Maryland primary bal-lots in the largest turnout for a primary in the state's history. His supporters included working class folk but also people from lower-middle-class suburbs and farms who had loved Joe McCarthy. His earthy, hillbilly wit and his scorching denunciation of Judas-like parasitic elites were aimed at everyman. In Michigan, a large United

Automobile Workers local union endorsed Wallace during the 1968 primaries. A survey found one in three union members in the state preferred the governor, as did 44 percent of all white workers in Flint. In Gary, Indiana, surveys found that the more a voter considered him- or herself working class, the more likely they were to back the Alabama governor, and this included a sizeable proportion of union members. A crowd of twenty thousand attended a Wallace rally in 1968 at a sold-out Madison Square Garden in New York City. When the national count was in, the governor had garnered ten million votes on the American Independent Party line, mainly in the South, but plenty in the Midwest and West.

Under all-sided assault the legitimacy of the postwar liberal order grew ever frailer, and Wallace dug his teeth in. When he ran for governor again in 1970, he railed against the "rich folks" in their country clubs and "big old houses" drinking "those martinis with their little fingers up in the air" who were calling for integrated schools. "And guess where their children go to school. They go to a lily white private school. They've bought above it all." His contempt embraced female welfare recipients who he accused of "breeding children as a cash crop," as well as their ivory tower benefactors "who don't know how to park a bicycle straight."

Before he was shot and nearly killed during the 1972 primary season (he had won 42 percent of the Florida vote, finished second in Pennsylvania and Indiana, and won in Michigan and Maryland), Wallace's campaign registered the early signs of the nation's economic bad news. He championed the tax-burdened middle class and its anxieties about inflation, deploring "welfare loafers" living off "liberal giveaway programs." LBJ's war on poverty and talk about affirmative action in housing, employment, and education offered the governor ample opportunity to lampoon liberal know-it-alls. The authors of those programs were "hypocrites who send your kids half-way across town while they have their chauffeurs drop their kids off at private school." He mocked those intellectuals and bureaucrats who thought, "We got to tell you when to go to get up in the morning. We gotta tell you when to go to bed at night." They were indifferent when it came to addressing the real plight of working people.[8]

"Working people" could be an elastic category, especially in an American context, where class lines were always kept blurry. "Blue collar aristocrats," proud of their work, mingled with modestly salaried white collar people forming a bouillabaisse of discontent stirred by Wallace and others, including tough guy northern charismatics like Frank Rizzo in Philadelphia and Louise Day Hicks in Boston. From the ranks of white collar "little men" came sales and accounting clerks, banking and insurance functionaries—who were often as routinized and subordinate as manual workers but cherished illusions about the stature of their work, their security, and their mobility that set them at a remove, and who considered it a great social accomplishment to have escaped manual labor. Together they fitted into a social space also populated by small retailers, building contractors, and service operators. Sometimes compliant and even admiring of the upper orders, at other moments they simmered with resentment over the privileges and immunities of those protected circles, worried about their own less secure status. Mixing together all sorts the "little man" milieu nonetheless supported a cultural ethos, a lifestyle, and a worldview conveyed in distinctive tastes in dress, deportment, furnishing, orthodox family structure and marriage patterns, leisure habits, and sometimes in political attitudes designed to safeguard "property, family, religion, and order."[9]

So it happened that country and western Marxism, Buckley's snide innuendo notwithstanding, showed up not only in the American outback but also elsewhere in the ranks of an emerging conservative populism. Procaccino's *paesan* from Brooklyn's Italian American Civil Rights League believed that "oil, steel, insurance, and the banks run this country." It was another Italian American, however, who proved more successful taking on the "interests" than New York's comptroller.

Frank Rizzo grew up in a two-story row house in the Italian ghetto of south Philadelphia. His father was a cop, and Frank followed in his footsteps. He climbed through the ranks of the Philadelphia police department, becoming its commissioner in 1967. Then a few years later he became the city's mayor and reigned for eight years. He was a boisterous, tough hombre, notoriously brutish and full of bravado. He was a mountainous man (six-foot-two, 250 pounds, and size 11-E shoes) nattily dressed in handmade suits, his hair sleekly toniced so he looked not unlike some towering, powerful, matinee idol of old. All of which, together with his shoot first, ask questions later demeanor, lent him a certain rough charisma. He was called "the Big Bambino" and "the Cisco Kid."

As police commissioner, he had earned his macho man reputation mainly by intimidating antiwar activists and especially African Americans. Speaking about how he would deal with peaceniks, he assured his followers that, "When I'm finished with them, I'll make Attila the Hun look like a faggot." In the meantime, he was concocting stories about black radical plots to blow up the city, slip cyanide into the police department's drinking water, and other wild phantasms. He fed not only the fears, but also the resentments of the hard-pressed white collar and blue collar folk residing in the city's vast northeastern neighborhoods and the Italian American warrens of south Philadelphia. Rizzo himself, like Procaccino, nursed the wounds left by the stigma attached to his Italian background that he had to confront as he struggled to rise through the city's Irish-dominated police establishment.

And he was a Democrat, so could speak directly to those who shared his feelings and experience. To get to be mayor he first had to vanquish the limousine liberal elite that ran both parties. He took on Rittenhouse Square and Main Line blue bloods like Richardson Dilworth, who ran the school board, and then beat Republican Thatcher Longstreth, who was president of the Chamber of Commerce and also to the manner born. He denounced "the voices of these cuckoo limousine liberals," and wondered "how these cuckoo birds get elected to office." In contrast he pointed to himself: "I'm the voice of the rowhouse guy, the forgotten guy." He got elected to his first term in 1971 thanks to a coalition of Irish, Polish, and Italian voters (including Italian-dominated locals of the Amalgamated Clothing Workers union) who, among the other qualities they liked about the police commissioner, admired his refusal to campaign in black neighborhoods. His braggadocio was an inexhaustible resource, so when he ran for reelection he brushed off his earlier threats and told the city once again, "Just wait, after November you'll have a front row seat because I'm going to make Attila the Hun look like a faggot." This resonated among white ethnics still loyal to the New Deal Democratic Party but restive about its seeming capitulation to racial pandering and do-your-own-thing moral relativism.[10]

Unlike Rizzo, Mayor Sam Yorty in Los Angeles was a real city-bred populist of the left who had broken through to the other side. His family was from Lincoln, Nebraska, but early on had gone West. Sam became a state assemblyman during the Great Depression and stood up for unions and state ownership of public utilities, cheered on the Spanish Republicans against Franco, and was even endorsed by the California Communist Party. He supported the postwar "Ham and Eggs" movement in California, which was heir to Huey Long's populism, led by the Kingfish's first lieutenant, Gerald L. K. Smith. "Ham and Eggs" was simultaneously anticommunist and anticorporate and evangelical Christian and also couldn't abide the state's New Deal–oriented Democratic Party. It drew its strength from Southwestern working class migrants who had been transplanted to California. Like "little man" politics generally, it evinced a love-hate relationship with New Deal liberalism. Jonathan Perkins, a movement leader and preacher, put it like this: "I don't want Communism, but I don't want the rich standing with their feet on the necks of the poor anymore either."

"Ham and Eggs" served as Yorty's segue from left-wing to right-wing populism. He crossed over into the ranks of "little man" politics in the sixties. Known as "shoot-from-the-hip Sam," "mad Sam Yorty," and "the Maverick Mayor," he ran Los Angeles for twelve years. Like Rizzo he was a Democrat who backed Nixon, picking up on the presidential candidate's wooing of the "silent majority." Or was it the other way around: Nixon spying a new road to the White House that had earlier been opened up by people like Rizzo, Yorty, and Wallace? Yorty's populist seduction combined denunciations of the "little ruling clique" of "downtown interests" with opposition to court-ordered desegregation and to feminism and high-decibel radical baiting (he blamed the Watts riots of 1965 on red agitators). He relished taking on and defeating fellow Democrats like James Roosevelt (FDR's son) from the party's establishment wing.[11]

Right-wing populist mayors or mayoral candidates popped up elsewhere: in Minneapolis, for example, or in Buffalo, where Alfreda

Slominski tried to unseat Frank Sedita in 1969 by attacking his plan to achieve racial balance in the city's public schools. Busing students to achieve that purpose had by then become an incendiary issue, perhaps the principal incendiary issue, capable of igniting class and racial passions. Nowhere was that truer than in Boston.

SCHOOLING LIMOUSINE LIBERALISM

Louise Day Hicks tried twice to become mayor of Boston but lost both times. She did get elected to the city council and once to Congress. But by far her most important elected office was as a member and then chairwoman of the city's school board. Her modest electoral achievements notwithstanding, next to George Wallace she led a movement that most effectively aroused the ire of the "little man" against an iniquitous alliance of elite overlords and black troublemakers.

She hailed from a long-established family in south Boston. Her father, although he started out poor, became a real estate dealer and banker. He was a county judge and an elder statesman of what was an insular Irish city within a city. Like her father, with whom she had a close relationship, Louise was a pious Catholic espousing strict and elevated moral standards. One writer noted her "elocution school manner," speaking an "excessively formal, hypercorrect English characteristic of British school teachers turned politicians." And she was ambitious; she went to law school when few women did in the 1950s. When she first ran for a seat on the "School Committee" (Boston's version of a board of education), she was aptly identified as a "lace-curtain Irish" lady, open to reform, ready to work with Yankee do-gooders. By 1963 she was the chairwoman of the committee. Not so very long after that, this epitome of decorum and political politesse was being likened to Hitler or, as James Farmer, head of the Congress of Racial Equality (CORE), saw it, "the Bull Connor of Boston," or as others had it "the Iron Maiden," "the sly bigot," or "Joseph McCarthy dressed up as Pollyanna."

What led to this stunning metamorphosis? An avalanche of demonstrations, boycotts, civil disobedience, sit-ins, street confrontations, gang violence, police actions, and general mayhem pitting neighborhood against neighborhood, all of it over the issue of court-ordered busing to achieve racial balance in the public schools, dominated Boston public life for a decade. It culminated in almost nonstop battling lasting through the whole school year of 1974. There were beatings and stabbings, and during the worst of it the mainstream media labeled Boston the "Little Rock of the North." Nor were schools the only or original field of battle. Antidiscrimination lawsuits had been filed against public employee unions, the police and firemen especially, where the Irish were heavily represented, and against construction unions, where Italians and others made their living and where jobs were treated as a kind of family-ethnic property right bequeathed from generation to generation. These helped fuel the conflagration that then consumed the school system. The city's working class and lower-middle-class Irish and Italian enclaves, anchored there for generations, were up in arms. Hicks was their general.[12]

From the outset, when the charges first surfaced that Boston's school system was a model of de facto segregation, when the first plans were announced to compel its integration, when the first court judgments were issued to enforce those plans, she defied the rationale for busing that had become axiomatic in liberal circles. Shrewdly, Hicks converted an issue the liberal community took for granted was about race into one about social class: "If the Negro lacks mobility in finding housing, the School Committee must not be held responsible. This is a problem for the entire community. . . . Boston schools are a scapegoat for those who have failed to solve the housing, economic, and social problem of the black citizen." She was onto something.

Another observer called Hicks an urban populist who had tapped into feelings of betrayal and abandonment. The local Democratic Party, the church, and the mainline media had sold out their working class constituents, congregants, and readers to Boston's corporate elite, urban developers, and urban renewal policy-makers. Those circles looked down on shabby, unstylish working class settlements and were ready to cash in by uprooting them. In the Irish working class precincts of Boston especially, Hicks could draw on an honored tradition of hostility directed against the city's "codfish aristocracy," which long predated the New Deal. These nouveaux riche had always aroused suspicions of elite outsiders, even if they were Catholic like the Kennedys or the Catholic hierarchs they mixed with and sometimes did a profitable business with. Joseph McCarthy had been well-liked in Irish working class precincts.

Moreover, the Boston Redevelopment Authority had a history of leveling these down-at-the-heel neighborhoods to make way for luxury replacements. All the insignia of a new urban chic—recessed lighting; hanging ferns; skylights; roof decks; Saabs, Volvos, and BMWs in the driveways; KHL sound systems; butcher block furniture; Cuisinart food processors; fashionable boutiques—were showing up here and there in once unfashionable locales. And in a pinch the children of these upscale urban homesteaders could go to private schools (in 1976 over 60 percent of public school pupils came from families at or below the federal poverty line). Indeed, many of the community groups that eventually played some role in the civil wars over schools first took shape in opposition to urban renewal and highway building projects. A complex of banks, real estate brokers, developers, and speculators along with government officials with access to low-interest financing threatened to muscle out the modest row houses, church parishes, schoolhouses, public squares, hangouts, and pubs that had made up the geography and social tissues of a way of life.[13]

Again and again, Hicks singled out the establishment, "the rich people of the suburbs," "the outside power structure," as the real culprits. She was standing in the schoolhouse door, so to speak, to champion "the working man and woman, the rent payer, the homeowner, the law-abiding, tax-paying, decent-living, hard-working, forgotten American." Echoes of FDR, Huey Long, George Wallace, and Richard Nixon reverberated through the streets of Boston's disgruntled. Nor did she confine her invective to strictly educational matters. She excoriated long-haired, countercultural anti–Vietnam War activists, pseudoliberals, and their accomplices in the media. When a federal court commanded the city to bus its students, it was widely characterized, not just by its right-wing critics, as "a Harvard plan for the working class man." The "plan" was seen as a provocation, commanding students be bused between two of the poorest, worst performing, and most antagonistic school districts: black Roxbury and white south Boston.[14]

Hicks and a circle of women of similar Irish propriety created an organization with a decidedly unrefined name to fight back. Restore Our Alienated Rights, or what quickly became more commonly referred to as ROAR, conveyed rather well in its name that bruised sense of being passed over, ignored, and demeaned. Soon enough ROAR had extended its reach into the less decorous zones of working class Boston, where a more and more belligerent language surfaced. One can hear premonitions of today's Tea Party zealotry. So, for example, on the occasion of the bicentennial celebrations, ROAR gathered hundreds of demonstrators at the waterfront: "Led by two drummers, beating a funeral dirge, eight black-clad pallbearers carried a pine coffin marked 'R.I.P Liberty, Born 1770–Died 1974'" (the year of the court order). "Behind them came rank upon rank of marchers, keening in the high-pitched wail long used to mourn the Irish dead."[15]

Hicks would remain at the head of the movement. But increasingly less polished, more militant voices, angry and not shy about inviting direct confrontation, surfaced not only among poorer parts of the Irish community but within Italian neighborhoods as well. When Hicks left for Congress as a Democrat in 1971, her place was assumed by John Kerrigan, a man from working class Dorchester. With enthusiasm he whipped up class and cultural resentments, red baiting the *Boston Globe*, decrying homosexuality and abortion, and taking after the arrogant suburban gentry who were dictating that the buses had to run in Boston, but not where they lived: "Suburban patricians rule urban plebeians." The aggrieved pointed out to Judge Garrity (who had issued the court order) that he had "enough money for your kid to go to private school." An East Dorchester mother put it plainly: "I would love to live there too [suburbia] . . . but I can't because I can't afford a nice house. . . . The majority of the people who live in the city do not have the money to live in the suburban areas." These folk were less legalistic and less bound by the civics of tolerance, flaunted a working class bravado, and were more into street action, boycotts, and beyond. Kerrigan wore a bowling jacket imprinted with his nickname, "Biggo." He was openly racist.

Pixie Palladino, who, unlike Hicks, opposed integration whether by bus or otherwise, emerged out of that same world, closer to its clannish sense of solidarity. Her grandparents were contadini from southern Italy who had migrated to America early in the century, where her grandfather found work in a rubber plant. "Pixie" graduated high school and then worked as a stitcher in a clothing factory and married a fellow factory worker. She was street smart, witty, unwilling to defer to middle class pieties. Catholic, but not pious, "Pixie" was not doctrinaire when it came to matters of birth control or abortion. What she couldn't abide were "the beautiful people" who she thought looked down on "people of color like me." But she was no more fond of "people of color" who were not like her. She was still a Wallace loyalist in 1976 when she tried and failed to oust Hicks.

No matter who was in charge, ROAR was a perfect organizational expression of "little man" ambivalence. In tactics and demeanor it couldn't have been more belligerent, and it was proud of the footprints of American revolutionaries it imagined itself to be walking in. However, the revolution it rallied and fought for marched it back to the future, to the way things used to be or at least as legend suggested it once was. And unlike its putative forebears, the enemy was not some deeply encrusted aristocracy walling itself off from the winds of change, but a New World elite blowing with the winds of change, determined to undo the old order of things. But rarely, if ever, did ROAR or any of the movements like it outside of Boston actually challenge the material prerogatives and the structures of power and wealth that "limousine liberalism" rested on.[16]

THE SILK-STOCKING CROWD

George Wallace was still trying, from a wheelchair, to get to the Oval Office in 1976. He polled quite well in the Massachusetts primary, especially in Boston, where he came away with 29 percent of the vote. For more than a decade he and people like Louise Day Hicks, Frank Rizzo, and Mario Procaccino had been igniting firestorms in the political backyards of the liberal establishment. Wallace declaimed: "Middle America is caught in a tax squeeze between those who throw bombs in the streets . . . while refusing to work . . . and the silk stocking crowd with their privately controlled tax-free foundations." A hard hat, a homeowner, a cop, a steelworker, a taxpayer, a barber: the borders of the aggrieved and angry spilled over class lines: "We're sick and tired of the average citizen being taxed to death while those billionaires like the Rockefellers and the Fords and the Mellons go without paying taxes." A decadent, liberal elite had committed an act of betrayal, stealing away the birthright of the hard-working to a home, to an education, to the right to be safe.[17]

J. Anthony Lukas, who won a Pulitzer Prize for *Common Ground,* his book on the Boston school wars, said this: "The federal court orders of 1974 and 1975 . . . assured that the burden of integration would fall disproportionately on the poor of both races. One need not proceed from a Marxist perspective—as I do not—to observe that class is America's dirty little secret, pervasive and persistent, yet rarely confronted in public policy."

Thanks to the civil rights movement the liberal political establishment was compelled to face the race question. Compelled to or not, these circles genuinely believed in the credo of formal equality, whatever backroom compromises with that idealism they had for decades grown accustomed to making. However, as the 1963 March on Washington for Jobs and Freedom already made clear both in its name and its composition, for those down below the "race question" was a matter not only of equality before the law, but also of material claims on the wealth and opportunity so long denied to the dispossessed pooling in the nation's ghettoes, in the exhausted valleys and mountain passes of Appalachia, and elsewhere.

Poverty had been famously rediscovered in postwar America, by, among others, Michael Harrington. His book *The Other America* described a new kind of poverty, one that did not arise out of exploitation at work as it once had in the nineteenth century. Rather this poverty was the fate of those excluded from work. Hence, in the eyes of the civil rights groups and labor unions that put together the March on Washington, jobs and freedom were inseparable: no real freedom without the economic wherewithal to exercise it.[18]

Even if Harrington's book became reading matter in the LBJ administration, liberal elites saw things somewhat differently. On the one hand, they became increasingly ready to take on the formal system of American apartheid even if that meant a political divorce from the Dixiecrat wing of the Democratic Party. So after some protracted attempts to forestall what seemed inevitable, they joined hands with the civil rights movement to pass the Civil Rights and Voting Rights Acts of 1964 and 1965. First of all, this comported well with the principal axiom of an ancestral liberal faith, a deeply rooted axiom of bourgeois life that equality of opportunity was the ne plus ultra of freedom.

But there was also a more practical political purpose at work. Urban Democratic Party machines were experiencing growing difficulty in mobilizing African American voters. These local parties were run by white, ethnic apparatchiks not inclined to share the wealth, nor as prepared as their liberal social superiors to break bread with their black coequals. From the vantage point of the impoverished ghetto, therefore, why vote anyway? For many slum life had little to recommend it over the indignities and rural miseries they had left behind in the South.

Embracing the civil rights movement was a way for national elites to change that disturbing equation. Getting blacks to the voting booth was one way to sustain their own national political hegemony. For civil rights activists, on the other hand, the alliance offered the leverage with which to topple segregation and open up avenues of real political influence and power. Mayor Lindsay, limousine liberalism's namesake, was at odds with the machinery of both major parties. So he went out of his way to circumvent them; for example, he appointed a black activist, Major Owens, as commissioner of the city's antipoverty programs. Children of privilege and good intentions like Carter Burden and Robert Kennedy established ties with Harlem-based movement people. So a coalition of the most and least fortunate was born and, notwithstanding its share of internal tension, thrived.[19]

More vexing was the poverty question. It inextricably weaved together issues of class and race. On the one hand, the reform-minded establishment was committed to the welfare state. So to choose an improbable example, Henry Cabot Lodge, bearing impeccable Brahmin credentials, was US ambassador to the United Nations when Soviet premier Nikita Khrushchev made his famous visit to America in

1959. Lodge was Khrushchev's host and wanted the Russian leader to understand just how far American capitalism had come, how unlike it was to Marx's nineteenth-century rendition: "I pointed out to him that there was a great deal of difference between capitalism in its American form and the European type of capitalism." Lodge wanted the premier to understand that a sophisticated America had left behind those nineteenth-century "dark Satanic mills" along with the abject poverty and exploitation they were infamous for that had so discolored the capitalism of yesteryear.[20]

Formal equality, on the other hand, was not about to transform the ghetto, leaving it as a holding pen for growing numbers of the black unemployed, underemployed, and superexploited. That would require substantial economic reform, including massive job creation, the kind of housing program once flirted with by the New Deal in its heyday, and a substantial rerouting of the way capital was deployed. But undertaking to change the way the underlying economy was structured was not on the liberal agenda anymore. Public investment in infrastructure or in housing or in public works of the sort the New Deal had once indulged in was no longer much of an option in an economy that had grown used to taking its lead from corporate America. Little of what constituted LBJ's Great Society envisioned trespassing on the prerogatives of the business class.

Ghetto uprisings punctuated this underlying harsh reality all through the decade. In 1966, for example, 38 riots erupted across the nation, killing seven and injuring five hundred. During the first nine months of 1967, there were 164 outbreaks, 38 of them requiring the intervention of state police and 8 others where the National Guard occupied the streets. Even before this turmoil had become epidemic a reform-minded elite responded with the war on poverty. The "war" did expand the welfare system. Otherwise, however, it treated the question of poverty as a matter of inadequate education and outdated vocational training and prescribed plentiful doses of social engineering expertise. That Olympian conceit could be applied across the racial divide. Not only busing, but scatter-site low-income housing, and in what turned out to be the most inflammatory innovation, local control of school districts as well as other social rearrangements, backed by court injunctions and accompanied by layers of moral high dungeon, became nodes of discontent for those benighted neighborhoods on the receiving end of this medicine.

For the general staff of the war on poverty, including its architect and Kennedy family member Sargent Shriver, dysfunction was a matter of inefficiencies, irrationalities, and pathologies that could be resolved by properly trained social scientists and psychotherapists. Desegregation of public schools was supposed to be part of the solution, as were various municipal and regional efforts to mobilize the poor to take over responsibility for their communities, including schools. The Ford Foundation and its president, McGeorge Bundy, collaborated with community activists in devising such a plan. It produced multiple teacher strikes and ethno-racial confrontations in Brooklyn's Ocean Hill–Brownsville neighborhood as the teachers union reacted to summary firings of teachers by the local control board.

The Citizens Committee for Decentralization included such citizens as the president of Time Inc. as well as the ex-president of Harvard. From the standpoint of Bundy's world, this was a cost-free piece of social engineering; no city resources were necessary, no one need pay attention to the serious material deficits that helped account for lousy schools among both the white and black working class, especially when the city's economy slowed as the sixties drew to a close. The embattled head of the teachers union in New York, Albert Shanker, painted a portrait of the limousine liberal that might have come from the pen or mouth of Mario Procaccino: "What you have is people on the upper, upper economic level who are willing to make any change that does not affect their own position. And so it is the middle class interests that are narrow and selfish. . . . I'm not sure that is a WASP attitude. I think it is only human. But what if you said give 20% of Time Inc. or U.S. Steel to the blacks? Who would be narrow then?"[21]

Indeed, the war on poverty, its suggestion of a kind of class combativeness notwithstanding, was widely supported not only by a new class of liberal social engineers but also by broad ranks of the managerial and professional classes and by businessmen like Henry Ford II and Sol Linowitz (a lawyer, diplomat, onetime chairman of Xerox, and a close associate of David Rockefeller's). The Economic Opportunity Act

of 1964 owed a great deal to pressure from below, from the rediscovered poor. But it also owed much to elite circles active in formulating
the whole démarche in public policy. Policy wonk reformers in the end
conceived of the remedy as an administrative matter. Apply just the
right mix of social and psychological expertise, and moral and political
questions tended to drop out of the equation; call it the domestic version of "crackpot realism."[22]

Despite its own war with limousine liberals, the Nixon administration would further expand the welfare efforts of the federal government and the "rights revolution" by empowering the Equal
Employment Opportunity Commission to open up jobs for minorities
(and women). Partly this was a function of the irresistible momentum
of what had been set in motion by the Great Society; partly it was a
matter of more cynical political calculation by the Nixon inner circle.
But in any event, all of this created a parallel political apparatus that
contested with established urban machines for local control. It provided an aspiring and activist black middle class with real entrée: not
trivial accomplishments, but also ones that left the economic status
quo more or less in place.

A marriage of liberal elites with the vanguard of the civil rights
movement refaced America. Whether measured in votes cast, infant
mortality, adult life expectancy, access to health care and nutrition, or
in those less tangible means of exercising some power over the conditions of daily life, this was an historic achievement. This alliance
might be likened to the one between the organizing industrial working class and the inner circles of the New Deal during the upheavals
of the 1930s. Yet from the standpoint of these new circles of elite reform it was different.

The war on poverty (although not the Civil Rights or Voting Rights
Acts) was more a bequest from on high than the result of mass pressure and sustained mobilization (ghetto jacqueries notwithstanding).
While it seeded poor areas with forms of apparent self-organization,
they were in fact fabricated in the policy ateliers of Washington and in
boardrooms of liberal-minded foundations. Ministering in this way
was less risky or fraught than dealing with the independent vehicles of
power that the insurgent labor movement had created a generation

earlier. The "war" flattered the moral self-regard of the country's political class, and earned credits abroad in the Cold War, where America's infamous racial dilemma had proved costly.[23]

More tangible compensations were also in play. To the degree warring against poverty entailed some measure of urban renewal, it could
be a profitable undertaking for real estate and financial interests
backed up by government loans, tax exemptions, and subsidies: a
kind of state capitalism that dared not speak its name. A distinct milieu of what one writer characterized as "finpols" emerged: that is, financial politicians whose economic behavior entailed deep, long-term
involvement with the federal government to ensure a stable, predict-
able, uniform tax and regulatory environment (including corporate
subsidies), in part to counteract the confusing multiplicity and incoherence of these policies at local and state levels of authority. One
might argue that the welfare state ministered at least as much to corporations as it did to citizens. The Higher Education Act of 1965,
considered the closing act of the war on poverty, aimed at opening up
opportunity to the less privileged. In the end, however, it became a
vehicle of bank accumulation backstopped by the federal government
(although that outcome was not connived at by its architects). So, the
leviathan state that became the bête noire of country and western
Marxists (as well as among Adam Smith loyalists of a rising, rebellious bourgeoisie) was the joint invention of New Deal liberals and
more pragmatic-minded corporate circles.[24]

Addressing the race question through these means was therefore
simultaneously a way of skirting the class question about just why
postwar Keynesian capitalism was failing so many. But behind the
backs of its creators, it also at the same time incited the "class question" among those who had once looked to the liberal establishment
to defend its always precarious place in the social order and who felt
aggrieved when that elite turned its attention to a stigmatized caste of
outliers. This helps account for the fury that sustained ROAR and is,
as Lukas noted, the "dirty little secret" of recent American history.
The Kerner Commission, established by President Johnson in 1967 to
investigate the causes of the ghetto conflagrations, put the case in a
way that most elegantly captured the naïveté and the hypocrisy that

captured the limousine liberal imagination: "White racism is essentially responsible for the explosive mixture which has been accumulating in our cities since the end of World War II."

White racism pure and simple was to blame for what was happening to black America. This was of course both self-evident and an evasion. It was a way of spreading the blame to avoid the blame that those occupying the commanding heights of the economy and political power might otherwise suffer. It was a heartfelt conviction, yet soon became a form of self-righteousness. For those who might indeed feel a deep racial animosity but who didn't see that they had played a determining role in consigning African Americans to the mudsills of American society, this righteous conceit could be infuriating; especially when they, not their social superiors, were going to be tithed to remedy the predicament. Amidst the chronic head-to-head battles between John Lindsay and the city's labor movement, one union leader characterized the mayor as a patrician: "Lindsay is a WASP. He treats labor with contempt. He cares only for the very rich and the very poor. The middle class bores him." And in turn, the racial phobias that kept bubbling to the surface in these plebian outbursts only worked to convince liberal elites and their constituents that they were even more right than they had at first suspected: white racism indeed was the infestation that had to be purged particularly from those lower class sinkholes where it festered and reproduced. With each passing year their contempt for these urban and rural hillbillies became more apparent.[25]

THE NEW CLASS

Country and western Marxists were prey to racial prejudice. About this there can be no doubt. Race as a biological category is an elusive one at best. But metaphorically speaking, American culture has been a genetic carrier of racism since birth. So the lower orders were infected along with everybody else. However, what country and western Marxists also evinced but what mainstream American culture after World War II had difficulty seeing or acknowledging was the way social class defined and disfigured national life. The silk-stocking crowd that Wallace, Hicks, and others excoriated was indeed part of the vanguard of reform. Moreover, it gathered around it a new group of adherents. They didn't dress in silk stockings or socialize on Park Avenue. They often opposed the war in Southeast Asia that the silk-stocking crowd had authored; indeed, it would be hard to overstate their visceral hatred. The irony here is palpable, however, because they shared something essential with the world of thoroughbred, ruling class reformers: namely, its self-righteousness and its disdain for the underworld of white "little men."

Postwar American capitalism was evolving. One quarter of the labor force now consisted of professional and technical workers, engineers, managers, public sector bureaucrats, and proprietors. John Kenneth Galbraith identified them in 1958 as a "new class." This was an exceedingly diffuse economic and sociological category. Those loosely fitting into it hardly subscribed to the same worldviews and political allegiances. Nor did they occupy conspicuous positions in public life, neither in the political arena nor as household names in popular culture. They were rather the anonymous legions of the salaried middle classes flooding the arteries of the new service, financial, and high-tech sectors of the economy. Moreover, during the years that followed, especially in the Reagan years or what some might call the "second Gilded Age," which others labeled the era of neoliberal capitalism, this species would grow in number, in the variety of functions it performed, and in the endless novelty of its lifestyles.

Nonetheless, even in this earlier, formative era, prototypes of this new class made their presence felt as they occupied positions of considerable power. Well-educated, cosmopolitan in outlook, and enjoying the material prerogatives of upper-middle-class living, they were proud of their technical and organizational efficiency and expertise. It was, after all, their principal form of human capital, which lodged in the neurons and synapses of their highly trained brains. It gave them a sense of self-confidence when it came to devising or helping manage technical innovation and social upheaval. Insofar as they embraced an ethos of perpetual change and viewed any attachment to tradition as by definition pathological, they embodied the abstract logic of capital itself captured in Marx's celebrated aperçu, "All that is solid melts into air." They were the twentieth century's architects of progress. And in that common cause they tended to identify with the reform-minded liberal corporate elite then running the country.

They didn't summer in the Hamptons or make truly strategic decisions for corporate America, nor were they even necessarily shareholders. What this new class of deracinated, upwardly mobile professionals, technocrats, midlevel functionaries, liberal journalists, editors, and academics did share with their putative betters was a meritocratic worldview and a dismissive repugnance for all those inhibitions and vestigial institutions standing in the way of individual self-empowerment and self-gratification and self-realization. They were no more inclined to interrogate the underlying structural causes of unemployment, declining wages, and global capital flight than were those who really did own limousines. Their antiracism was genuine and zealous. Along with their antiwar sentiments, it made them natural recruits to a Democratic Party that was grudgingly abandoning the war and slowly abandoning the defense of its New Deal working class constituency.[26]

Still, in the passion of the new class for racial justice and the "rights revolution" more generally the Harvard psychiatrist Robert Coles detected something else as well, "a certain snobbish and faddish 'interest' in Negroes from people who would not think of concerning themselves with those many white families who share with Negroes slums, poor schools, uncertain employment." White, working class locutions were subject to mockery; ghetto argot, on the contrary, earned the badge of "authenticity." New in function and style, the new class adopted the condescending position, looking down at the lower middle class as mediocre, provincial, conformist, rigid, and prudish. *Newsweek* reporting on the uproar in Boston described Hicks and her supporters this way: "They looked like characters out of Moon Mullins and she was their homegrown Mamie-made-good. Sloshing beer at the long tables in the unadorned room of South Boston's Social and Athletic Club sat a comic-strip gallery of tipplers and brawlers, tinseled, over-dressed dolls. . . . After Mrs. Hicks finished reading off her familiar recitation of civic wrongs the other night . . . the men queued up to give Louise their best, unscrewing cigar butts from their chins to buss her noisily on the cheek or pumping her arm as if it were a jackhammer under a trailer truck." The same magazine published a less judgmental "Special Report on the White Majority," in which an interviewer concluded that the old virtues were under assault and listed "the work ethic, premarital chastity, the notion of postponing gratification, and filial gratitude for parental sacrifice."[27]

George McGovern's capturing of the Democratic Party presidential nomination in 1972 institutionalized a changing of the guard that would leave the working class adherents of those old-time verities out in the cold. Ironically he was probably the most labor-friendly such nominee in a long time. And the organized trade union movement, although refusing an endorsement, nonetheless split down the middle when it came to working for him, as did the working class electorate when it came to voting for him. But the procedural reforms inside the Democratic Party that accompanied his victory ceded priority to delegates of minorities, women, and youth, registering the triumph of the new politics of the new class.

McGovern did campaign against the war and talked about a "peace dividend" that might alleviate growing economic pressures on working people. Such appeals were drowned out, however, by lavish praise for the liberating reverberations of the counterculture and its antic ethos of self-fulfillment. The candidate's tone-deaf dismissal of busing as constituting a real threat to the cherished turf of white working class neighborhoods also aggravated his estrangement from these onetime loyal Democrats. The iconoclasm and leveling instincts of the counterculture and McGovern's own romanticized fascination with the down-and-out proletariat of bygone days might seem the raw material with which to make common cause with the common man. But the actual existing working class was not down and out; its most vocal segments were highly organized and enmeshed in powerful bureaucratic institutions of their own. It did not seem a suitable vessel for the individualism or the benevolence that coursed through the renovated Democratic Party. It seemed to those running and attracted to the campaign too repressed and authoritarian in makeup, too reluctant to change, too much a prisoner of its patriotic zeal, racial paranoia, and besieged masculinity. A national newsmagazine, invoking the candidate's past as a Protestant pastor, remarked on his "politics of righteousness," and on how his moralizing played well among his natural constituents of the new class but left much of blue collar and lower-middle-class America unmoved or offended.[28]

THE PARADOXES OF LIMOUSINE LIBERALISM

When the 1960s began, the postwar liberal dispensation seemed beyond challenge. Then its components blew apart as if undergoing nuclear fission. Limousine liberalism both as reality and as myth emerged in the aftershock. And it was riddled with contradictions no one was eager to pry apart.

The silk-stocking crowd and the new class were joined at the hip in their commitment to racial reform and the "rights revolution." Yet some elements of the new class—its sixties youth contingent, for example, which by the early years of the new decade had begun to find its place in the new postindustrial economy—had been born in opposition to the establishment. This was true not only in the realm of war and the American imperial footprint abroad. It was also the case insofar as the new class absorbed the antibureaucratic, nonconformist ethos of the counterculture, including its even greater readiness to embrace the morally and sexually heterodox. They might now be working as bureaucrats but they still made fun of bureaucracy. These were inclinations not yet fully welcomed in the boardrooms and council chambers of otherwise reform-savvy ruling circles. So one might talk of two camps of limousine liberals: one, a traditional object of "little man" censure, the world of big business; and a second, newer one of less-propertied but nonetheless influential elites who were becoming the favored object of right-wing populist wrath. Meanwhile, relations between these two subspecies of limousine liberalism could be congenial or tense depending on the issues at stake.

An analogous tension lived inside the mythic world of country and western Marxism. On the one hand, it condemned the liberal establishment. Yet precisely because the movements gathering around Wallace and Hicks and others felt under siege, felt called upon to defend older ways of life and belief that were under threat, they looked to the establishment to act like one and champion the status quo. During the hard-hat riots of 1969, when organized groups of construction workers in New York and in other cities assaulted antiwar demonstrations, their signs included the ironic benediction: "God Bless the Establishment." After all, common sense suggested that an establishment would and should stand up for all those values these right-wing populists still believed in: hard work, patriotism, social decorum, discipline. But now, while the limousine crowd still controlled the corporations, the banks, the foundations, the universities, the mass media, the State Department, the CIA, and so on, it had deserted the streets, lost the college dorm, and commanded a dwindling allegiance among the bureaucracies running the police, the school system, and the social welfare machinery.

This molten state of American society would open up the chance to recrystallize American politics. Limousine liberalism touched down on something real and something imaginary that would make it possible to forge a workable alliance between "little man" populism and bourgeois revivalism. A Brooklyn veteran of the borough's civil wars concluded: "It's not only welfare but the multinational corporations who are ripping us off. . . . The middle class are the lost people." Savvy heads inside the revamping Republican Party were preparing to act on that observation.[29]

7

The Bridge over Troubled Waters

Richard Nixon famously nurtured a visceral hatred for the establishment. The "enemies list" he and his closest aides secretly compiled and singled out for censure (the one that would culminate with Watergate and terminate his presidency) consisted largely of limousine liberals and their camp followers. It included notable people and institutions from the worlds of politics and business as well as from high and popular culture: Edward Kennedy and John Lindsay; the Brookings Institution and the Southern Christian Leadership Conference; the *New York Times,* the *Washington Post,* and *The Nation;* Kingsman Brewster, president of Yale, and Derek Bok, president of Harvard; Arthur Schlesinger of the "vital center" and Noam Chomsky of the New Left; McGeorge Bundy and Robert McNamara; Paul Newman and Bill Cosby; as well as a galaxy of business executives from International Paper, the Dreyfus Fund, Kuhn Loeb, Continental Can, Otis Elevator, and so on. This was a universe of the powerful and stylish (with a sprinkling of high-profile dissidents), people who might conduct business with Nixon but did little to hide their disdain. The president's estrangement and wounded sense of exclusion were political emotions hardly unique to him. They traveled widely across boundaries of social class and partisan loyalties. Limousine liberalism became a metaphor so heated it could fuse together serial antipathies that together worked an extraordinary transformation in American political culture.

Rarely had the Republican Party managed to credibly pass itself off as the party of the common man. Back in the late nineteenth century some substantial numbers of workers in the industrial heartland had voted for the GOP in part because its staunch defense of the protective tariff shielded infant American industry from job-destroying competition from abroad. But the party had always found its natural constituency among the middle classes in town and country, and especially among businesspeople. By the time of the Crash of 1929 and the Great Depression, its reputation as the party of business and big business especially had become axiomatic, no matter how much its leadership might try to run from the enduring stigma left behind by that singular economic calamity.

Part myth, part social reality, limousine liberalism became a pathway out of this political dead end, an escape hatch, a way of turning the tables on the party of the New Deal. Richard Nixon's appeal to a "silent majority" ignored by the nation's liberal elite prompted an historic mutation. However counterintuitive the spectacle might seem, during the closing decades of the twentieth century the Republicans made a persuasive case that they had become the party of the people, assuming one bracketed those who fell on the wrong side of the racial divide or those who clung to their unions or other institutional residues of the New Deal.

An accomplishment of this magnitude depended first of all on finding common cultural ground on which working people and their natural antagonists could comfortably commune together. Only then did those perennial issues of wealth and work, pitting blue collar New Deal loyalists against the GOP's "Tories of industry" and their political enablers, become less abrasive. Or rather class fears and resentments remained just as inflammatory but were transmuted into primordial differences over sexuality, the nuclear family, racial hierarchy, masculinity, patriarchy, patriotism, and the divine. Intimate and profound, these were probes driving deep into the emotional and psychological underlayers of everyday life. This interbreeding of class warfare with cultural antagonisms had been smoldering for decades.

It echoed in the ravings of Henry Ford, Father Coughlin, and Senator McCarthy. Now, however, cultural polarization worked to efface older forms of the class struggle, those head-to-head confrontations between the haves and the have nots. The Chicago journalist Mike Royko called this political alchemy Marxism "turned upside down."[1]

Nor were these stealth attacks smuggled into the mainstream by outside political operatives. Rather, they had been part of the warp and woof of capitalism in America from its earliest familial beginnings through its evolution into the deracinated corporate system it had largely become. Capitalism was always much more than a form of trucking and bartering, of making things and exchanging them. It was a way of life that compelled changes in ways of life and belief that had endured for generations. Now these issues opened up an existential chasm that also seemed to correlate with the skewed distribution of wealth and privilege as those showed up in the upper echelons of the Democratic Party especially.

Culture war did not displace class war. Instead, it shifted the terrain. Class, which had largely been banished from acceptable public discourse with the onset of the Cold War, returned with a vengeance but was camouflaged. Every attempt to shut down an abortion clinic, all the lobbying to defeat the Equal Rights Amendment, the lawsuits to restore the right to pray in school, those book-banning outbursts at local school libraries, the boycotting of outlets of salacious popular culture, the recurring, indefatigable efforts to keep gay marriage illegal, the mutating ideological assaults on affirmative action, the "love it or leave it" hard-hat affirmations of patriotic righteousness, and all the other front-line confrontations over "values"—all carried with them a subtext. This civil war of values was not a disembodied one, but instead was conducted by distinct social classes: on the one side secular elitists and their army of functionaries, intellectual camp followers, trade union bureaucrats, and dispossessed ghetto constituents; on the other an everyman army, people of faith, not only the pious, but all those workaday white folks who remained faithful to the way things once were or were imagined to be or were ordained to be.

Two counterrevolutions account for the frisson of American politics in the late twentieth century and on into the next. One marshaled its forces to dismantle the New Deal administrative, regulatory, welfare state. It seeks to erase the 1930s. The second wants to do the same to the 1960s. It has mobilized to reverse the overturning of traditional race and gender relations and conventional morality that is that decade's principal legacy. An ascending business community, sometimes at odds with the corporate establishment, has been the main torchbearer for erasure of the thirties; a more heterogeneous gathering of "little men" from the working and lower middle classes has stood up against the sixties counterculture. But these two movements have bled into each other. People who were up in arms about the sacrilege of gay marriage or abortion had just as little sympathy for government handouts to the underclasses. An entrepreneurial milieu that felt strangled by the heavy hand of the government's regulatory bureaucracies also flooded suburban megacongregations as part of the Moral Majority. The limousine liberal became a lightning rod channeling all these antipathies.

It would take some time for the reaction against the New Deal Order to gather up a full head of steam and to enlist the big guns of the corporate world. That was not the case when it came to challenging the rights revolution and moral iconoclasm of the sixties. A silent majority was imagined into being and enlisted for that purpose.

A WIFE WITH A CLOTH COAT

The only president compelled to resign the office was an improbable populist and an even less likely moral evangelist. True, Richard Nixon had risen to prominence as a McCarthyite Republican. And he had mastered the populist-inflected language about "striped pants diplomats" and "grouse-hunting" Ivy Leaguers who were presumably selling out the country to the Soviets. But as president he ran an administration notable in part for its liberal-minded reforms. These included the Philadelphia Plan (affirmative action to open up the construction trades to minorities) and the Equal Employment Opportunity Act. (He even offered a lukewarm endorsement of the Equal Rights Amendment.) The Occupational Safety and Health Administration and the Environmental Protection Agency were created on his watch. The president lobbied on behalf of a guaranteed annual income to replace the welfare system, for low-income housing aid, and federal grants to the arts, though these failed to get through Congress. When speculative runs against the dollar forced the administration to abandon the Bretton Woods system of fixed exchange rates, which had defined the postwar international financial order, Nixon went so far as to introduce government wage and price controls to dampen inflation: hardly the remedy of choice for a true believer in the free market. He was a highly functional politician still operating within the framework of postwar liberalism.[2]

Moreover, "tricky Dick Nixon" earned that sobriquet. He was never known to stand on moral principle. Rather he was the consummate pragmatic politician, always ready to make a deal out in the open or behind closed doors. He was if not exactly cynical or sacrilegious, then by and large morally indifferent and pliable. He was a churchgoer in name only and more comfortable dealing with the bread and butter rather than the more spiritual aspects of political debate.

So at first glance Richard Nixon seemed a less than ideal champion of moral rearmament against the ravages of counterculture liberalism. But it was precisely his pliability as well as a deep undercurrent of personal resentment that left him open to a promising new political option when he saw one. Indeed, Nixon's ultimate ignominy was, ironically, a consequence of that political shrewdness and instinct for revenge.

Even as he navigated the slippery climb up the ladder of national political preferment, Nixon never got over his bad feelings about the Northeastern establishment, about his own modest educational and social attainments as compared to the prep school, Ivy League, clubby world he kept running into in Washington. He was an outsider on the inside, made to feel his crudity.

Once, he made memorable use of that status, saving his vice-presidential position as Eisenhower's running mate in 1952 by referring to his wife's simple cloth coat to ward off accusations of corruption. Nixon's Checkers speech defended his integrity by emphasizing his humble beginnings in Yorba Linda, California, his father's grocery store, working his way through college and law school, his own mortgaged home, loans from his parents and against his life insurance policy, the family's two-year-old Oldsmobile, and that he was "proud of the fact that Pat Nixon wears a good Republican cloth coat." He then slyly advised that his TV audience compare that inventory of everyman modesty with the inherited wealth of the Democratic nominee for president Adlai Stevenson, and draw the conclusion first allegedly enunciated by Abraham Lincoln: "God must have loved the common people—he made so many of them."[3]

Although made fun of later, the Checkers speech (named after the family's dog, which the embattled nominee pledged to hold onto no matter what calumnies might malign the way the pet was acquired), was a tour de force and smashing popular success. It saved Nixon's spot on the ticket and his subsequent career. Despite the victory, however, he had ahead of him a near decadelong sentence in political purgatory during the 1960s after serial electoral defeats for president and governor of California had seemingly terminated his prospects. Memories of Pat's cloth coat and the way he had used it to exorcize the limousine liberalism of people like Adlai Stevenson suggested a way back up the mountain.

Republican triumph in 1968 and thereafter rested on communing with an imaginative new constituency—the silent majority—and deploying a "southern strategy" that since the end of Reconstruction had been a dead end for the party of Lincoln and that Nixon's house intellectual Kevin Phillips revived in his 1969 *Emerging Republican Majority*. Limousine liberalism was the enemy that gave the silent majority and the southern strategy life. Nixon's apparent sympathy for the indignities and outrages to customary moral behavior, religious convictions, familial and patriotic loyalties of ordinary folk offended by all the transgressions of the counterculture helped rescue him from oblivion and his party from yet another defeat. And as Lyndon Johnson himself had prophesied, the Civil Rights and Voting Rights Acts would cost the Democratic Party the allegiance of Dixie for at least a generation.

Party strategists promptly went trolling for those votes. The long-haired, the braless, the drugged, the flag and draft-card burners were offered up as stage props in a theatrical auto-da-fé in which the whole heretical debauch of limousine liberalism was forced to do penance.

Now those who had made a mockery of bourgeois conventions were mocked mercilessly in return. A motley array of the dysfunctional and decadent—spoiled rotten, stuck in some kind of arrested adolescence, they were vilified as an insult and embarrassment.

Ghetto dwellers too might be treated as exhibits of depravity, encouraged by liberalism's permissiveness to act on inherent criminal instincts or to live off the liberal state. But in this arena attitudes about race had already shifted. So Nixon and his circle avoided the outright racism that marked George Wallace's insurgency. Its primitiveness offended the sensibilities and the business prospects of middle class suburban residents of the South and the Sunbelt. The party's message was clear enough, however: an intrusive federal government under liberal command threatened to violate constitutional protections for property rights and to cross the color line assuring an evenhanded enforcement of legal equality for everyone. A whole democratically inflected vocabulary—states' rights, property rights, local self-determination, free association—evolved to rationalize subterranean racial instincts that had become verboten in polite conversation. This counterargument hijacked the color-blind assumptions of civil rights liberalism to attack liberalism. The idea was that limousine liberals were too partial and too obliged to their African American allies to faithfully guard this American birthright.[4]

A practitioner of the politically possible, the president could nonetheless dream in his own way. He imagined, as did others in his inner circle, a partisan realignment: a new party of independent conservatives (independent, that is, of the still potent limousine liberals within the GOP) consisting of white Southerners and the transregional silent majority. It would be built around the cultural and social opposition to the counterculture and its betrayals of family and nation. Properly mobilized, it would face off against chic elites, racial minorities, the poor, and alienated youths assembled together under the Democratic umbrella.

Working with those cultural raw materials, Nixon could even break bread with the New Deal's core constituency, organized labor. Waving the flag and praising the work ethic got him the enthusiastic support of the construction trades, who rallied behind his Vietnam policy (that, plus a promise to exempt those unions from the mandatory wage and price controls that followed the dollar devaluation of 1971). In New York City the Building and Construction Trades Council organized a rally of one hundred thousand people carrying signs that read "We Support Nixon and Agnew." Nor did the Nixon camp confine its unprecedented wooing of organized labor to its hard hats. Police, firefighters, teamsters, and others were flattered by the administration's attentions. Meanwhile, the repugnance felt by other elements of the labor movement for George McGovern as the poster boy for limousine liberalism led them to abstain during the 1972 presidential election. George Meany, head of the American Federation of Labor, was practically apoplectic about the "new politics" McGovern crowd and the new class it seemed to speak for. He railed against the snobs, elitists, effete decadent radicals, fags, and abortionists who had kidnapped the Democratic Party.[5]

Stock boy in the family grocery, graduate of under-the-radar Whittier College, barred by social and financial circumstance from getting an Ivy League law degree, Nixon husbanded his affronts. Once in possession of the most powerful office on the planet, however, he was surrounded on all sides by the institutions, laws, and seasoned personnel that had created the liberal order. He had no choice but to move with caution. Boycotting the establishment was simply not an option. Nonetheless, his administrations were increasingly peopled by Babbitts from Main Street and country-club deal-makers. They were Sunbelt real estate developers, oil barons, and others. Eventually half of Nixon's cabinet hailed from the Sunbelt as did a third of his agency chiefs and two-thirds of his senior staff. During his run for reelection some of the financial heavy lifting was done by people like Henry Salvatori, a Los Angeles–based geophysicist and oil equipment manufacturer, and Richard Scaife, overseer of the Mellon fortune and well known for his conservative inclinations. For the businessmen among them their road to wealth and power was the dynastic one, not the one that depended on shinnying up the morally indifferent hierarchies of managerial capitalism. Proud of having turned modest family enterprises into giant undertakings, they were determined that they and their heirs would continue to exercise a kind of absolutist control not possible in publicly traded corporations subject to the will and whims of hired executives and anonymous shareholders. That Napoleonic, dynastic ambition carried with it, however, all the inherited prejudices, regional loyalties, and patriarchal instincts that set them apart from the world of the limousine liberal.[6]

Circumspection and circumlocution characterized Nixon's public persona. Now and then, though, he did come right out with a biting indictment of the moral and psychological decadence of the country's reigning political and business elites, accusing them of losing self-confidence, of being unmoored from their anchorages in the country's bedrock beliefs. It wasn't so much a wayward younger generation of bohemians and hippies that was to blame. Instead his finger pointed at "our leadership class, the ministers, the college professors and other teachers . . . the business leadership class, etc. where . . . they have really let down and become soft." His own party was infested.

Senator Charles Percy from Illinois, for example, was typical of this Republicanism gone to seed. Starting out as a poor boy in the Great Depression, during which his father was thrown out of work as a bank clerk, he managed to get a scholarship to the University of Chicago. After that, he had risen through the ranks to become the president of Bell and Howell. Then he used his elegant (some called it pompous) manner to climb rapidly through the political hierarchy to become a serious contender for the Republican presidential nomination in 1964, deferring in the end to fellow limousine liberal Nelson Rockefeller (Percy's daughter was married to John D. IV of West Virginia). A staunch advocate of civil rights, he proposed in the Senate that the government create a private foundation to fund low-cost housing and low-income homeownership. Percy loathed Nixon.

So did Elliot Richardson. A cultivated New England Brahmin of colonial ancestry, he had held numerous high positions in the government, including undersecretary of state, four different cabinet posts, and the ambassadorship to Britain. His father was a prominent MD and professor at the Harvard Medical School. Elliot graduated from Harvard Law. After winning two Purple Hearts and a Bronze Star for bravery (he had crossed a minefield to rescue a maimed fellow officer) during World War II, he clerked for Supreme Court Justice Felix

Frankfurter. How galling it must have been when as attorney general under Nixon he resigned rather than fire Special Watergate Prosecutor Archibald Cox as he had been ordered to do by the president. He blamed the "political and cultural evolution of 20th century America," by which he was alluding to the character of the Nixon .inner circle, men he considered not evil but "get-ahead, go-along organizational men" short on integrity.[7]

Nixon may have ended in disgrace, but evolution, as Richardson mordantly commented, was moving in the ex-president's direction. A cadre of public intellectuals once associated with the liberal center or even the left who would soon coalesce as neoconservatives—men like Irving Kristol and Michael Novak—lent ballast to Nixon's social portrait. They pinioned that new class made up of knowledge workers, parasitic verbalists expert at manipulating symbols, administrators of social welfare, academics, foundation officers, media and culture producers who were, they argued, rootless, without property except for their wits. Together they were allegedly hostile to capitalism, disdained bourgeois values, were agents of a new permissiveness, and went seeking after power to defend and augment their positions in state and nonprofit bureaucracies.

William Rusher limned an emerging conflict between producers (a category that included manufacturers, businesspeople, hard hats and other blue collar workers, and farmers) and nonproducers, which embraced those in the knowledge industry, the media, the educational establishment, the federal bureaucracy, foundations, and social workers. However muddled a concept, zeroing in on this new class helped channel resentments against government and seemed to illuminate why the well-off and well-educated might nonetheless have turned out to subvert the way things once were. Rusher's version of a class struggle pitting producers against parasites echoed a venerable populist tradition extending all the way back to the American Revolution. And it continues to incite Tea Party partisans today who like to see themselves as productive citizens, doing things that matter, making stuff you can touch and feel, while the overlords of American society shuffle paper and invent arcane and baffling ways of transferring wealth from those who created it to those who didn't.

Nixon's brain trust itself advised borrowing fire from George Wallace. When he was running for reelection in 1972 aides suggested, "We should increasingly portray [George] McGovern as the pet radical of Eastern Liberalism, the darling of the *New York Times,* the hero of the Berkley Hill Jet Set: Mr. Radical Chic." Patrick Buchanan, who functioned as senior adviser and speechwriter (and who may have coined the term *silent majority*), laid out the strategy for undermining McGovern: "By November he should be pictured as the Establishment's fair-haired boy and Richard Nixon as the Candidate of the Common Man, the working man."[8]

By and large, however, the president left the rhetorical dirty work of ostracizing his opponents to Vice President Spiro Agnew. He was by inclination and training an apparatchik not an ideologue, certainly not a right-wing one. Indeed, he made it to the governorship of Maryland by being more in favor of integration than the sitting Democratic governor, who showed white supremacist inclinations. But when drafted as Nixon's running mate he took to his new position as limousine liberalism's bête noire with real verve. During the 1968 campaign he accused Hubert Humphrey of being "soft on communism" and attacked the "tiny and closed fraternity of privileged men" who controlled the media. Washington was overrun and being run over by an "effete corps of impudent snobs who characterize themselves as intellectuals." They were "radical liberals" and not to be trusted. And he was only warming up. Flexing an overdeveloped verbal capacity for alliteration he denounced the "nattering nabobs of negativism" and "pusillanimous pussyfooters" who populated the ranks of those dyspeptic critics of the American way, a "decadent few" misleading the nation's youth.

IDENTITY POLITICS ON THE RIGHT

Agnew's rhetorical flamboyance and fearlessness made him enormously popular for a while; polls had him coming in third behind Nixon and the evangelist Billy Graham. Until he was compelled to resign in 1973 (he was being investigated in Maryland on multiple charges of tax fraud, bribery, and conspiracy), he provided more than good theater. As the economy began a secular decline, one writer noted that the vice president's mastery of cultural politics helped people forget "that their jobs are lousy, that more and more people are out of work, that they don't have medical insurance and will go broke if they have to confront an extended illness, that it's the generals who took their tax money and not the poor, that 'curbing inflation' means exorbitant interest rates and bank profiteering that borders on the obscene . . . that hard work, thrift, and self-denial are, under existing economic arrangements, so much hogwash, that their schools are as rotten as the ones attended by black kids." Whether or not Agnew intended to create this distraction, there is little question that it worked to submerge beneath the surface of public life many of those material concerns that had once inflamed class animosities.[9]

Political alchemy of this sort is not easy to perfect. Agnew, Nixon, and others crafted an artful redressing of social grievances by cultural means. It was an apt if not the only response to a creeping awareness of dysfunction and loss. This premonition of decline and fall touched on matters of the material well-being and social prospects of working people, as well as the unnerving sense that fixed moral certainties and national self-confidence were under assault.

During and after Nixon's presidency, economic doldrums deepened with the collapse of the international monetary system and the first serious signs of domestic economic stagnation and deindustrialization. Prices rose each year and accelerated during the 1970s, eventually exceeding a rise of 15 percent. Unemployment topped 8 percent. Interest rates soared to 18.5 percent by the end of the decade. Capital formation withered. Doctors of economics described a new economic cancer they diagnosed as stagflation, a disease that rendered thrift stupid. Hourly wages and average income peaked in the early 1970s and then began a long, slow descent. Time spent at work rose in America while declining in the rest of the advanced industrial world. Layoffs, plant closings, and outsourcing of jobs were becoming features of a new economic landscape that would only grow rockier. Nearly half of the jobs created between the Carter administration through Reagan's first term paid poverty-level wages, and part-time employment grew at twice the rate of full-time work. Unions conceded and cowered in the face of it, shedding members and influence. A journalist described the massacre of the steel industry beginning on Black Monday in September of 1977 when the huge Campbell Works of Youngstown Sheet and Tube shut its gates: "The dead steel mills stand as pathetic mausoleums to the decline of American industrial might that once was the envy of the world."

Symptoms of social decay cropped up everywhere. Even as Ronald Reagan spied "morning again in America," closer to the ground traveling journalists described "medieval cities of rusting iron." In these blasted ruins health suffered, public services shrunk, and domestic violence, alcoholism, drug addiction, and suicide rates rose. So did the incidence of infant mortality; life expectancy and school enrollment fell compared to the postwar era. Racial conflict, urban blight, epidemic street crime, white flight, and military defeat in Southeast Asia aggravated the atmospherics of disintegration. Neighborhoods, schools, jobs, even basic safety and the sanctity of childhood seemed in jeopardy. One might call it, to paraphrase another writer, the end of a domestic victory culture that took for granted that America's preeminence abroad originated and confirmed its blessed birthright at home. President Jimmy Carter allegedly called it a malaise in a 1979 speech in which he never actually used that word, but conveyed that mood and so a legend was born.[10]

Seeping into the consciousness of working class and lower-middle-class white ethnics was a realization that their social contract with New Deal liberalism was expiring. The universalisms of that once dominant political persuasion—integration, assimilation, the work ethic, popular democracy, blind justice, American preeminence abroad, and goulash capitalism at home—were fragmenting, turning inward, dying. The party that had been the carrier of those promises floundered, fractured internally, and seemed at loose ends about how to redeem its legacy. It had no answer for the structural unemployment, declining real income, and the capital flight abroad that had begun to play havoc with working class life; indeed, the new class running the Democratic Party didn't even think that the question was a high priority. What loomed as social chaos induced a yearning to quell the anarchy, all the libidinal abandon, chronic dissent, and disrespect. Naming those who resonated to these vertiginous feelings of disorientation a "silent majority" might lack rigor and precision. But it was evocative as all good political metaphors are.[11]

Reworking an indigenous blue collar and redneck cultural populism gave the silent majority a voice with which to address this social queasiness. Those relegated to the shadows by the main currents of modern life—by its iconoclasm and disturbing social and racial promiscuity, by its secularism and sexual experimenting, and most of all by its apparent disrespect for the customs and folkways of blue collar America—were open to being flattered.

Revanchism found its natural homeland in the South. So the Republican Party's newborn love affair with the silent majority initially rooted there, not only at the ballot box but metaphorically. For example, Nixon administration operatives opened up lines of communication with the world of country music. Its repudiation of pot and free love, its stalwart salutes to the flag and hymns to the rebel "born free" and determined to stay that way made songs like Merle Haggard's "Okie from Muskogee" a kind of unofficial national anthem for the refaced Republican Party. How better to depict this mésalliance with the common man than through the lyrical celebration of the son of an Okie, growing up dirt poor, working on the railroad, doing time for robbing a bar, but no matter what "livin' right" and "bein' free."

Moreover, the humble origins, kinship solidarities, and masculine self-reliance that allegedly typified redneck country (what was left of it, anyway, as the "new South's" urban, suburban, and industrial renovation was paving over much of what remained) could be celebrated north of the Mason-Dixon Line as well. A whole family of folk idioms once peculiar to Dixie—cowboy, bluegrass, gospel, country western, and hillbilly—formed a musical smorgasbord appealing to the tastes of northern blue collar communities. After all, a sizeable number of these Yankees were actually transplanted southerners having arrived in the North only recently from the mountains and hollows of Appalachia. Up North it suited the temperament of an antielitist populism directed at the managers of the state and society but without interrogating the underlying structures of power that the system served. So, for example, a fundamentalist preacher and singer crooned: "No, we don't fit in with the white collar crowd/ We're a little too rowdy and a little too loud/ But there is no place I'd rather be than right here/ With my red neck, white socks, and Blue Ribbon beer."

Instead, this sometimes religiously inflected populism inculcated a truculent self-assertiveness, hewing to down-home, plain-spoken truths about hard work and hard play, extolling the virtues of loyalty, humility, and stoicism, which became an enduring source of pride, a sourish one perhaps, but a piece of resilient cultural armor nonetheless. It returned contempt for contempt. So media increasingly steeped in the worldview of the new class stereotyped the working class as poor and benighted, addicted to unwise early marriages and even more unwise early parenthood that ended tragically in single motherhood. This was purportedly a world in eclipse, still enmeshed in the stultifying, horizon-shortening web of kinship relations, people imprisoned by rigid routines, prudish inhibitions, easily manipulated, ill-educated and ill-informed and chauvinist. Here was a sea of mediocrity, the land of substandard marginalia—Archie Bunker Land!

Without access to most of the airwaves or national print media, the "redneck" riposte mainly flew under the radar. Nonetheless, it made clear its own disdain for the pretense and the social climbing obsessions of liberal-minded, urban sophisticates clustered together on the East Coast. Indeed, that sliver of territory became a metaphor for the land of sissified Ivy League liberals and Jews hanging out at the intestinal end of Manhattan Island on Wall Street, where sex, socialism, drugs, and money cross-fertilized. For insular working class worlds under duress, where ethnic and neighborhood ties still held, where the church, the union hall, and the tavern still anchored everyday life but felt themselves under siege, this put-down of their putative superiors was welcome recompense. It functioned as a kind of stylized gesture of resistance, and in that way was not so very different from the performance of symbolic politics by identity groups on the left.[12]

So attractive was this refurbished identity in a world overrun with new identities—a proliferating array of sexual, racial, and ethnically derived subgroups all invested in their distinctive and exclusive histories and symbolic affirmations—that it managed to migrate across social borders. "Redneck chic" and "faux Bubbas" became forms of interior decoration and psychological theater among middle class suburbanites and urban hipsters. They paraded around as "half necks," or "sunshine crackers" dressing up in leather boots, driving pickups with gun racks, listening to country music, crowding stock car racetracks. There was apparently no limit to this masquerade. By the 1990s George W. Bush, a Yale preppie, was munching on pork rinds and playing horseshoes. Sometimes it was hard to tell where social satire left off and fealty or credulity began.[13]

Already in 1972 the political arithmetic of the future was apparent. Nixon won a majority of the Catholic vote, the first time a Republican had managed that. Well over half of all manual workers voted for him and even 54 percent of union members did. Richard Viguerie's insight about the George Wallace phenomenon proved prophetic as 80 percent of those who had voted for the Alabama governor in 1968 voted for Richard Nixon four years later. The inventive maestro of politics by direct mail, Richard Viguerie, who collaborated with conservative ideologue Paul Weyrich, computerized the combined mailing lists from the Wallace and Goldwater campaigns. This tidal confluence washed over the redoubts of limousine liberalism in both parties.

Weyrich had first shown up in Washington as a twenty-four-year-old, inside-the-beltway, angry young man sporting a "bright pink sport coat and Barry Goldwater glasses." Born a Roman Catholic, he had converted to the ultraconservative Melkite Greek Catholic Church after Vatican II. His father was a German immigrant to Wisconsin who had worked stoking furnaces in a Catholic hospital. Paul attended the state university in Madison for a while, but didn't finish as he hankered after political action and went to work as the press secretary to Colorado senator Gordon Alcott.

For Weyrich politics was war: "a war of ideology, it's a war of ideas, it's a war about our way of life." He would go on to cofound the right-wing Heritage Foundation think tank and coined the phrase *moral majority*. After Nixon's overwhelming victory in 1972 Weyrich offered a radical reading of the results: "We are different from previous generations of conservatives. We are no longer working to preserve the status quo. We are radicals working to overthrow the present power structure of this country." He was in his own way class conscious. Pay attention, he suggested and, "look at our backgrounds. We're not the product of third generation wealth." The face-off between limousine liberalism and redneck cultural populism during the presidential race seemed to confirm that. And it should receive at least some of the credit for the Republican triumph. "Economic royalists," once public enemy number one of populism from the left had mutated into "cultural elitists" and become the piñata of a new populist right.[14]

THE RULING CLASS VANISHES

Surpassingly odd about the new populism was the way it was embraced by the plutocracy, especially those of more recent vintage. This became truer after Nixon exited the scene. Self-made millionaires (soon to be billionaires) were flourishing in the postindustrial businesses of the Sunbelt—defense and aerospace along with retail, service, oil, gas, agribusiness, and real estate developments—which were, as we have seen, heavily dependent on government subsidies and government-created infrastructure. These populist plutocrats were far more adept than their Gilded Age predecessors were at mastering the protocols and rituals of democratic politics. Beginning in the 1970s, business circles generally became acutely more political-minded, penetrating deeply all the pores of party and electoral democracy. Partly this was fight-back against what during the previous decade had grown to be a widespread repugnance, economic as well as cultural, for corporate America and for the business mentality more generally. So too this deeper and more systematic engagement with political and state institutions signaled that even the most avid sea-dog, go-it-alone, pioneering capitalist had to reckon with the intricate interweaving of economic and government affairs in the modern world. Nor were lone wolf dynasty builders the only adepts at this Machiavellianism. Pin-striped managerial types from all over corporate America also learned to play to the crowd. This meant going so far as to craft alliances with elements of what their predecessors—who might have blanched at the prospect—would have termed the dangerous classes.

Proceeding in fits and starts this strategic experiment proved its viability during the Reagan era, just when the businessman as populist hero was first flexing his spiritual muscle. Conservative think tanks like the American Enterprise Institute and foundations created by right-wing business dynasties—the John M. Olin, Adolph Coors, and Scaife Foundations in particular—were already part of the Reagan inner circle by the early 1970s. So too, Southern California businessmen, some functioning as trustees of the Coors-financed Heritage Foundation, longtime fans of Reagan in his two terms as governor of the state, became converts to the "The Great Communicator's" Herrenvolk politics.

Claiming common ground with the folkways of the "good ole boy" working class fell within the comfort zone of a rising milieu of movers and shakers and their political enablers. It was a "politics of recognition"—a rediscovery of the forgotten man—or what might be termed identity politics from above. Then along came Bill Clinton, first as head of the Democratic Leadership Council running the party and then as presidential candidate, who perfected the art of the faux Bubba for the Democrats. By that time the country was living in the age of the Bubba wannabe—Ross Perot as the simple country billionaire. The implausible became commonplace: capitalists depicting themselves as mavericks, driving Range Rovers and pickup trucks, donning bib overalls as a kind of political camouflage. "Live free or die" might have been their adopted motto. Calls to dismantle the federal bureaucracy carried a populist panache. Huffing and puffing about family values proved a cheap date for an ascendant business class that sometimes might care about defending those folkways and at other times might leave them be.[15]

Often far wealthier than the limousine liberals they crucified for their coddled way of life, populists in suits by this point found this kind of political theater second nature. When, for example, rival candidates for the governorship of Connecticut faced off in 2010, they were both in fact men of stupendous wealth, possessed of all the educational, residential, and other material insignia of privilege—prep and Ivy League schooling, private planes, ocean-going yachts, hotel-sized homes. But the Republican made sure to be seen eating egg

salad at dinner while wearing blue jeans. His Democratic rival dressed
up in a barn jacket and rolled-up sleeves, garb suited to telling tall
tales in awe-shucks lingo about his early struggles to start his own
business: in full flight from all the telltale signs of the limousine liberal
his party was infamous for being.

That same year, Jeff Greene, otherwise known as the "Meltdown
Mogul," had the chutzpah (hardly alone in that, however) to campaign in the Democratic primary for a Florida Senate seat in a Miami
neighborhood ravaged by the subprime debacle—precisely the arena
in which Greene had grown fabulously rich. There he rallied the
people against Washington insiders and regaled them with stories
about his life as a busboy at the Breakers hotel in Palm Beach. Protected from the Florida sun by his Prada shades, he alluded to his
wealth as evidence that he, a maestro of collateralized debt obligation
speculation, knew best how to run the economy he had helped pulverize, punctuating that point by flying away in his private jet securely
strapped in by his gold-plated seat buckles.

Business lobbyists, beginning in the Reagan years, quickly mastered the art of masquerade. Journalist Jonathan Chait noted one
striking case, a rally convened to support George W. Bush's tax cuts
for the wealthy. It was planned according to a campaign memo, so
that "visually this will involve a sea of hard hats. The Speaker's office
was very clear to say that they do not need people in suits . . . AND
WE DO NEED BODIES—they must be DRESSED DOWN, appear to
be REAL WORKER types, etc." Lobbyists who attended the rally
were indeed provided hard hats. In another instance, the political director of the National Association of Manufacturers dressed in a
rugby shirt and a faded blue Farm Credit hat. When the *Wall Street
Journal* attacked renegade rich people who actually favored the estate
tax as "the fat cat cavalry," it confirmed that virtually anyone could
play this game.[16]

Rarely if ever in the past has the plutocrat so rooted himself in
plebian culture, erasing all that remained of the habits of deference
once expected to inform relations between rulers and ruled. Nor did he
before now build bridges to the lower orders by pointing out precisely
what separates them—namely, his unapproachable wealth—using it as

a credential of his all-Americanism. Nor have such alliances, when they existed, lasted nearly as long. Nor have so many businesspeople assumed second careers as elected officials without any prior experience; many have even pointed out their lack of personal political experience as their chief virtue and qualification. Nor was there ever a plutocracy quite as motley as this one. Certainly it was far less defined by a shared ethnic genome or social or intellectual pedigree. These traits, or rather the lack of these traits, came with the territory. That is the point; this was a world in constant motion, as rootless as the capital flows streaming here and there and that define it. And this was a strength, as it made it all the easier to vanish behind the mask of the "Bubba" and his repugnance for the leviathan state bequeathed by limousine liberalism.[17]

Populist plutocracy reconfigured the age-old problem of legitimacy, of the underlying sources of consent on the part of the subordinate classes to the rule of tiny, wealthy elites. The new plutocrat worked to make a convincing case that he was of the people, expressed their deepest desires and aspirations, and governed in their name. Beginning with Richard Nixon and continuing on through the George W. Bush years this assiduously crafted faux democracy married business elites to blue collar, white-skinned cowboy populism. Or it tried to. It was, after all, a disjointed alliance at best, patently brimming over with self-contradictions. How to square the circle between business triumphalism and the long slide into economic decline suffered by millions of working and middle class folk? To make such a marriage work and endure would require divine intervention.

8

The Holy Family

C lass conflict may have been proscribed by the Cold War. But its pulse was once again easily detectable late in the century. A deeply conservative Catholic, Paul Weyrich, who was an admirer of Father Coughlin, even observed that "Big Business is as bad as Big Government. . . . They are in bed together." Indicting big business for its surrender to liberalism had become a conceit in some circles. The corporate world, in this view, had caved in to the unions and curried favor with government bureaucrats. Nor was this indictment limited to Republican outliers. Senators Paul Laxalt of Nevada and Orrin Hatch of Utah excoriated business leaders as "gutless wonders," "inheritors who have never known what it is like to put everything on the line, to meet a payroll." Sentiments of this sort had already surfaced during the Goldwater insurgency. And they would resurface and lend energy to the Tea Party rebellion in years to come.[1]

Ronald Reagan, however, that larger than life hero of a new conservative populism, did not achieve his exalted position by railing against corporate America. Instead The Great Communicator opened up lines of communication with the world of Christian populism whose presence in public life grew weightier as the Reagan era unfolded. He addressed a great throng attending the Religious Roundtable in Dallas during the 1980 campaign and famously said:

Religious America is awakening, perhaps just in time for our country's sake. If we believe God has blessed America with liberty, then we have not just a right to vote but a duty to vote. We have not just the freedom to work in campaigns and run for office and comment on public affairs. We have the responsibility to do so. . . . If you do not speak your mind and cast your ballot, then who will speak and work for the ideals we cherish? Who will vote to protect the American family and respect its interests in the formulation of public policy? I know you can't endorse me because this is a non-partisan crowd, but I . . . want you to know that I endorse you and what you are doing.

By that time the animus against limousine liberalism as a corporate offense against family capitalism and the parallel animosity felt by the "little man"—who all along had more often than not been a subscribing Christian and who saw the liberal order as an offense against the family pure and simple—were converging. That union, the work of the Reagan era and beyond, was far from a perfect one, subject to frequent misunderstandings and suspicions of betrayal. Reagan may have offered his endorsement, but his administrations delivered little in the way of tangible reform to his evangelical allies. Metaphysical matters would drive the parties toward divorce; the more mundane material concerns of family capitalism about taxes and overbearing government regulators were, on the other hand, recuperative. But if this heterogeneous movement retained a resemblance to old-style nineteenth-century populism, it was an increasingly distant one.

Most Nixon and then Reagan era conservative rebels were, after all, hardly proposing an assault on Wall Street and the Fortune 500. On the contrary, the language and style of these latter-day insurgents were infused with managerial locutions. They were prone to defer to and to emulate business leaders for their savvy and braggadocio. Moreover, as the circumstances of the economy straitened; as profit rates fell; as costs, especially labor costs, became insupportable; as competition from rising industrial nations grew fiercer, corporate America itself grew less tolerant of the regulations and welfare state outlays that had defined the New Deal Order. Deregulation, budget

cutting, redistributing the tax burden downward, privatizing functions once considered public, and offering up hosannas to the free
market together constituted common ground: a zone of cohabitation
that could accommodate family and corporate capitalism.

Christian populism, however, yearned for more. It burned with a
fire in the belly, ignited by its fury over the offenses of limousine liberalism, that could help win elections—and Reagan knew it. Back in
1949, Billy Graham, Nixon's confidant until Watergate, prophesized
that, "When God gets ready to shake America, he might not take the
Ph.D. and the D.D. and the Th.D. God may choose a country boy!"
Ronald Reagan was hardly "country" but he could act like he was.[2]

CHRISTIAN POPULISM

A religiously inflected populism had always been part of the American
political makeup, even in the nineteenth century. The historian Darren
Dochuk argues that this tradition was alive and well in the mid twentieth century. It migrated with the dispossessed of the western South
(particularly Louisiana, Oklahoma, Texas, and Arkansas) during the
Great Depression and after the war. Even before the Crash of 1929
Pentecostal congregations provided some of the spiritual energy (not
to mention a fiery vocabulary about the Satanic rich) that infused
sometimes violent confrontations between farm tenants and landlords
and coal miners and operators in places like Arkansas and Missouri.
In particular these birds of passage transformed Southern California,
bringing with them an ancestral evangelical religious tradition that
mixed resentment of upper class wealth and privilege (the "silk hat
crowd") with missionary zeal. They were ardent individualists, yet
just as passionate about hewing to a strict social code of Christian
values when it came to matters of marriage, divorce, drinking, and the
presence of God in the classroom. They were militantly egalitarian (in
religious affairs as well as political ones, holding a dim view of church
hierarchy in any form), and maintained a combative commitment to
local democracy and autonomy. Often they started out as partisans of
New Deal social welfare and reform, but also retained an entrepreneurial derring-do that derived from pioneering days. They tended to

hate the big banks and corporations and bureaucrats. Christian populism was at one and the same time anticapitalist and procapitalist depending on the issues at stake.

As the Goldwater insurgency of the nouveau well-to-do suggests, for some families the move to the West Coast went particularly well; they became modestly or even hugely successful businesspeople or entered the ranks of white collar work and the professions. They were motivated by zoning protocols, taxes, the obstructive power of unions, and government meddling. They lived in the white suburban sprawl that came to define the residential and economic geography of Southern California. They tended to shed an older overt racism, opposing civil rights if they trampled on property rights, but otherwise maintaining a color-blind neutrality.

Others less fortunate or less enterprising found blue collar work in the region's booming defense and aerospace industries and elsewhere. They lived in increasingly dense, impromptu urban barrios. And they grew more agitated about racial unrest, housing shortages, and school busing. Living in the always shifting, multiracial world of Los Angeles and other California cities, they were more prone to voice the racially impolitic. Sam Yorty had counted these people among his constituents during his long run as mayor of Los Angeles. Reproduced in the new South, living side by side, were the middle class devotees of family capitalism and working class rednecks. It was an uneasy pairing that had often kept Goldwater and Wallace partisans at arm's length.[3]

Now, however, no matter their social location or economic prospects or racial unease, all were deeply upset about what they viewed as the moral crisis of the family and the secular elites responsible for it. Dochuk describes this as a cultural amalgam of Jefferson and Jesus. It was founded upon suspicions that had started forming even during the New Deal's heyday. So, for example, the National Association of Evangelicals issued alerts during World War II about New Deal reforms endangering the family:

> These are bills which could be used to control families. If they are passed, these federal medicine bills, it appears it will not be long before you will hear of "baby crop quotas." There are bills classified

under the high sounding phrase "Fair Employment Practices Commission"; FEPC bills would open the way for large numbers of bureaucrats, "investigators", to pry into one's personal business. It is a class of legislation of the worst kind, sailing under the false banner of civil rights. . . . If this bill passes you can anticipate the arrival of that day when the government will tell you where you must work, with whom your children must attend school, whom you must hire. The police state is near at hand if these bills pass.

A few years after the war ended, George Benson, the founder of Harding College in Little Rock, Arkansas, and other evangelical enterprises, warned his radio listeners, "Should we start federal aid to our public schools now, America would see virtual federal control within a decade, to be followed within one more decade by nationalization of industrial production, transportation, public utilities, and agriculture." And the threat was even more insidious than that, because according to one partisan of the education wars, if schooling was left to outside "experts" kids "would come to embody all the same effete traits exhibited by liberal administrators."

All of this had become part of the atmosphere of public debate in the Sunbelt decades before Ronald Reagan addressed and endorsed the evangelical army. Indeed, from the outset of his political career in California in the 1960s, Reagan had carefully cultivated his ties to this evangelical world of transplanted migrants from western Dixie. This consisted mainly of ceremonial and rhetorical gestures. He avoided the moral truculence and absolutism that was lending evangelical politics a new vigor. But times were changing as the growth and persistence of the Christian populist right could not be so easily assuaged.[4]

THE LIMOUSINE LIBERAL AS THE ANTICHRIST

When The Great Communicator delivered his stunning endorsement that day in Dallas, it punctuated a Christian populist holy war against the soulless. Here the most intimate matters were at stake: the raising of children, the relations between men and women, tribal turf, the racial status quo, and God. Nor did this only arouse the passion of evangelical Protestants. Paul Weyrich had not only converted to Greek Melkite Catholicism, repelled by the Vatican's accommodations with modern morality, he'd become a deacon in that church. For Weyrich and the millions enlisting in the ranks of right-wing populism— Protestant or Catholic—the separation of religion from political life was a problem, a fatal mistake whether or not they might agree with the separation of church and state as a formal constitutional precept. Limousine liberalism was more than a political alliance between patricians and their down-and-out clientele; it was more than a malignant and metastasizing "big brother" government; it was more than an insufferable form of know-it-all snobbery. It was a sacrilege.

When a cabinet-level Department of Education was created in 1979, fear and anger about government obtrusiveness, already aggravated by earlier Supreme Court decisions banning prayer in schools and legalizing abortion, crested. An alarmed correspondent in *The Right Woman* (a now defunct journal of the antifeminist new right) wrote, "There is an underlying assumption . . . that the correct education of children is the primary responsibility of the state. . . . This view is contrary to Judeo-Christian tradition which always maintained that the education and care of children is the primary responsibility of parents. . . . To interfere or to attempt to interfere with parents [sic] rights is a violation of the First Amendment rights." This seamless interweaving of moral and religious views with what postwar liberalism customarily treated as strictly secular matters became a hallmark of grassroots conservative populism.[5]

Pat Robertson, the Machiavelli of evangelical politics as the creator of the Christian Coalition (who, by the way, graduated Yale Law School and New York Theological Seminary and whose father had served as a senator from Virginia for twenty years), condemned "the humanistical/atheistic/hedonist influence on American government" that came from its control by the Trilateral Commission (founded by David Rockefeller) and the Council on Foreign Relations. Phyllis Schlafly's Eagle Forum, Beverly LaHaye's Concerned Women for America, and her husband Tim's American Coalition for Traditional Values mobilized to take over a government diseased by "secular humanism" and to restore the moral order, "the traditional values of Western civilization."

Highfalutin bloviating of this kind, however, conceals something more poignant. A society in which the ground is always shifting under everybody naturally gives rise to a contrary yearning to slow down, to find a resting place, especially to restore some moral surefootedness. Many, whether religious or not, can sympathize with the resolve of one evangelical woman: "I have moral absolutes. The majority of the population doesn't even think they exist."[6]

Radical shifts in religious sensibility help measure the distance traveled from the original Gilded Age to our own. Back then religious denunciations of the established order often originated outside the mainstream, even in renegade denominations. They anathematized Mammon worship and reminded parishioners of Jesus' "social gospel." Now, instead, analogous religious circles censure what their ancestors applauded and applaud the free market orthodoxy their forebears censured. What has stayed the same, however, is the thoroughgoing integration of economic and moral perspectives.

Like a prairie fire, what Tom Wolfe described as a "third Great Awakening" spread through evangelical churches beginning in the 1970s and continued to rage after that. One report released in 1978 counted a fourth of the nation as evangelical. By 1986 nearly a third of Americans described themselves as "born again." While liberal denominations (Episcopalian, Presbyterian, Methodists) declined, their doctrinal distinction from the reigning secular orthodoxy harder and harder to detect, Southern Baptists, Assemblies of God, and other less distinguished evangelical and fundamentalist enclaves, Pentecostals and charismatics particularly, gathered in converts by the truckload. Billy Graham's newspaper claimed a circulation of twenty-four million. There were about one thousand Christian radio and one hundred Christian television stations, numbers that would continue to grow geometrically during the 1990s. Televangelists like Jimmy Swaggart, Jerry Falwell, Jim Bakker, and Pat Robertson preached to multitudes.

Evangelical book publishing and bookselling became an industry in its own right, and Christian rock concerts, romance novels, films and musical productions, magazines and comic books, even bumper stickers reading "Beam me up Lord" or "If the Rapture Occurs, This Car Will Be Driverless" provided entertainment not only for country folk and urban rednecks but permeated recently settled middle class suburbs as well. Some of these suburban congregants were descendants of rural migrants from the Southern Bible Belt, becoming what one observer has called "the first modernized generation." They constituted a new Sunbelt lower middle class employed in service and clerical occupations or were self-employed, with some college education. Robertson's Christian Coalition, for example, was a step up the social ladder, reaching as far as the higher ranks of lawyers, doctors, and the upwardly mobile. Falwell's Moral Majority, by contrast, was rooted among less well-heeled and less well-educated circles.

When Falwell and Robertson's organizations faltered, James Dobson's Focus on the Family became the dominant conservative and largely middle class Christian organization of the 1990s. Dobson came from plain-folk, evangelical stock in western Louisiana. His father had been a traveling evangelist for the Church of the Nazarene ranging through Texas and Oklahoma. James got a PhD in psychology from the University of Southern California and did his roaming electronically. Dobson's radio show was carried by two thousand stations to which between six and ten million listened weekly. Focus on the Family, while not shy about proselytizing on behalf of the traditional family, steered clear of the sort of direct intervention into the electoral arena that had backfired on Robertson. Thanks to the labors of people like Dobson, half of college graduates in 1990 were awaiting Jesus's return.[7]

Arguably this organizational rebirth among evangelicals was part of a broader disaffection with modern life, with its bureaucratic rationalism, its giantism, its singular preoccupation with economic growth, its love affair with technology, its obeisance to experts. You didn't have to affiliate with the right wing to feel this way. So, for example, the counterculture had been in flight from all that. Even more explicitly political elements of the New Left originated in reaction against the utilitarianism, the robotic bureaucratic mentality, and anomie of the postwar liberal order and articulated their concerns as first of all moral ones. Later, an infant ecological consciousness gripped the imagination of many and for some that included spiritual if not religious emanations. If not Christian they were nevertheless evangelical and often political.

Indeed, the "born again" pious (whether Protestant or Catholic) were late to politics, as they had to overcome their own scruples about participating. Once in, however, their staying power and influence were impressive. Actually the Catholic church, both its hierarchy and rank and file, was early to mount opposition to abortion, the Equal Rights Amendment (Phyllis Schlafly, a devout churchgoer herself, was acutely aware of the Catholic underpinnings, theological as well as institutional, of the movement she led), and the whole galaxy of family matters—divorce, same-sex marriage, drugs, and praying in school, as well as what was being read and taught in school. Evangelical and Catholic churches transformed into Jacobin clubs and spread across the heartland. And whatever reservations they harbored about the immorality of modern society did not stop them from deploying its technologies and organizational savvy.

Those accused of being limousine liberals placed a premium on their own plasticity and seemed to invite serial revision in quest of the next new thing. Christianity's emphasis on the solidity of the nuclear family was the antidote to that cultural vertigo. That old-fashioned family formation fixed in place traditional relations between men and women and between parents and children. And that microlevel stability reinforced ethnic attachments whose bloodlines ran all the way from small-town squares and urban neighborhoods to the beating heart of the nation; patriotism was, after all, only devotion to the hearth and home writ large, or as our current locution has it, "the homeland." Jerry Falwell's hypothesized Moral Majority (formed in 1979 to do battle with what the preacher labeled "an immoral minority" that had run the country since World War II), Pat Robertson's Christian Coalition, and the Promise Keepers movement led by football coach Bill McCartney, which rallied against the permissiveness licensed by the feminist movement, presumably resonated to all these interconnections.[8]

Falwell and others were tapping into a deep estrangement from the permanent revolution of everyday life and the state institutions that permitted or abetted it. Though they thought of themselves as paladins of the free market, they constituted in this sense a resistance army against the moral corrosions of capitalism, the capitalism in which, according to Marx's famous aphorism, "All that is solid melts into air." No social custom, no sanctified form of authority, no cherished belief seemed safe. This could surface in homely ways like the father explaining his vote for a Republican senatorial candidate in the South: "I can't say prayers at high school football games. I can't say it at the football game when my son is going to be the quarterback? For 240 years in the U.S. people could do and say whatever the heck they wanted, and I want to say a prayer and you're telling me I can't?" James Dobson lamented that tried and true methods of disciplining children had given way to liberal "permissive democracy." Falwell called out new, self-aggrandizing government agencies like the Department of Education and the Department of Health and Human Services for separating children from their parents. No wonder movements of the religiously inspired right sometimes took on telltale names like the Ohio Restoration Project or the Texas Restoration Project and the stillborn American Restoration Project.

But the scene could shift radically from the mundane to the cosmological. For those anticipating a millenarian truth or consequences, the government was a demonic beast ravenous for power; global financial and commercial consolidation signaled the end times when a system presided over by the Antichrist in the guise of the World Bank, the International Monetary Fund, the Federal Reserve, and the Common Market would pulverize the individual. A regimented order, facilitated by Madison Avenue's manipulation of consumer desires to subvert the will to resist, was imminent. For some it would come via a conspiracy captained by the Trilateral Commission, the principal instrument of "the western world's most powerful bankers, media leaders, scholars, and government officials bent on radically changing the world in which we live." So it was that the religious awakening became at the same time a reveille for political rearmament.[9]

Warfare broke out all across the treacherous terrain of the family and was waged with increasing ferocity through the closing decades of the twentieth century and on into the new millennium. Limousine liberalism came armed with a profoundly disparaging view of the old-time ménage that went like this: it was patriarchal, sexist, and repressive. Consequently, it turned out people in thrall to authority figures. Slavishly attached to norms and beliefs from the past, whether about how to raise kids or who should work and who shouldn't, or when and with whom to have sex, its members feared change. Faced with that upsetting state of affairs, it resorted to violence, sometimes in the form of psychological suppression, sometimes with brute force. It hankered after war (though these wars were manufactured by limousine liberals and thus functioned as a kind of welfare for the working classes who actually fought them). This benighted familial old order was, in a word, pathological. It could be ministered to psychotherapeutically, but in the end it stood in the way of progress. New in function and style, just like all elites, this fresh one naturally adopted a condescending position. It looked down at the lower middle class as mediocre and conformist.

Feeling under siege, those still attached to the emotional and social security of family and communal life as well as to its sacramental status fought back. Caricatures of the pretentious world of limousine liberals proliferated. A satirical article published in 2004 in the *Washington Post* spoofed the language of right-wing cultural warriors but also managed to do a credible job of capturing their spirited distaste for everything associated with the liberal way of life, making reference to "pierce-nosed, Volvo-driving, France-loving . . . latte-sucking, tofu-chomping, holistic Waco neurotic vegan weenie perverts." The language of the offended and besieged could also become appropriately warrior-like. Jerry Falwell, for example, rallied his troops this way: "We are born into a war zone where the forces of God do battle with forces of evil." Or as Beverly LaHaye declared: "If we are truly committed to Jesus Christ, we have no other alternative but to wage warfare against those who would destroy our children, our families, our religious liberties." Pat Buchanan famously caught the zeitgeist in his address to the 1992 Republican Party Convention: "There is a religious war going on in the country. It is a cultural war as critical to the kind of nation we shall be as the Cold War itself."

An apocalyptic atmosphere enveloped this movement for moral rearmament and seemed apt. The family, and especially the traditional gender hierarchy upon which it had always rested, was the bedrock of the moral order, an order whose longevity made it seem "natural." Defying it invited chaos. And that seemed to be precisely what the liberal state intended to do: educational elites deciding what school subjects kids had to learn or should not be permitted to learn, federal agencies making available the medical technology that allowed women to avoid their maternal calling, and so on.[10]

If family values for working people entailed "sacrifice, fate, belonging, character, and the sanctity of parenthood," for their antagonists it was all about the right to choose, competitive striving, intimacy, and self-fulfillment at the expense of or to escape the ties that bind. They delighted in what they imagined to be their freewheeling independence. An acute sensitivity to individual rights too long denied or a fertile imagining of individual rights rarely or never before thought of supplanted an earlier yearning for social rights that had sustained working class families for two generations. A chronicler of what by the turn of the millennium was being described as the new "creative class" of symbolic analysts was ecstatic: "People have come to accept that they're on their own—that the traditional sources of security and entitlement no longer exist or even matter."

A liquid, improvised self, coming into and going out of existence as the theatrics of social presentation dictated, had no use for the solidities presumed by the holy family. And about this people enamored with a sense of their liberation could be insufferably smug and holier-than-thou, as if they had seen the light while a provincial working class lived on in darkness. Devout believers in meritocracy, they knew they deserved their privileged positions. But as even the *New York Times* observed: "Merit has replaced the old system of inherited privilege. . . . But merit, it turns out, is at least partly class-based. Parents with money, education, and connections cultivate in their children the habits the meritocracy rewards." Precisely so, but that didn't stop the chosen ones from celebrating their elevation as a great victory over the ancient regime of inbred class hierarchy.

Even as limousine liberals preached the gospel of social engineering, they seemed to behave like spoiled narcissists. They appeared preoccupied with style, self-promotion, and in their own way just as obsessed with piling up material stuff as the working class Visigoths they looked down on for doing just that. Yet at the same time, their opponents pointed out, they rationalized the family dysfunctions and criminal proclivities of the "underclass." Why wouldn't they, since these high-living liberals celebrated sensual release and had no more use for the moral supervision that had once placed constraints on excess than did their clients and political allies in the urban barrios of America?

Quite to the contrary, ever since the racial upheavals of the 1960s, the ghetto family had become, in the eyes of right-wing racial populists, a clinical case of familial disintegration and illegitimacy, personal indolence, and debilitating dependency. And the fault lay with that ensnaring network of state welfare bureaucracies created by their putative champions. The black family was, in a word, the antifamily. Its poverty evoked no sympathy, but rather fear and disgust. An alien, outlaw caste of nomadic pariahs, the black family in the right-wing populist imagination functioned as a withering indictment not only of African Americans but of their limousine liberal patrons. Seeping down from the top, percolating up from the bottom, an inundation of indiscipline and self-seeking was eroding away the cultural terra firma of the middling classes. Since traditional family arrangements were, among other things, a mark of respectability distinguishing "little man" propriety, frugality, self-restraint, and sense of duty from the profligacy and parasitism of the lower orders, the limousine liberal's "bleeding heart" was particularly galling.[11]

Publicists of right-wing populism no doubt romanticized the working class family. Many lived paycheck to paycheck, caught up in a devilish race to stay in place, with only limited psychological or emotional investment in their jobs, increasingly alienated. They were hardly havens of harmony. An undercurrent of anxiety and even shame if they had to resort to outside help to get by shadowed their lives, eroding their social status and, for the paterfamilias, his masculinity. In these circumstances, marriage and the family assumed a "saliency by default" that made them that much more precious, even as their tangible grip loosened. Newsweek issued "A Special Report on the White Majority," which carried an implicit disdain for the hidebound, insular ways of blue collar folk. But it also observed that the old verities were under assault, including "the work ethic, premarital chastity, the notion of postponing gratification, and filial gratitude for parental sacrifice." Instead, government mandarins of change administered housing, health, education, and welfare programs that provided only for the poorest, leaving the lower middle classes struggling to stay afloat, which they could only do by shipping off their maternal homemakers to the workplace.

If this was clearly war, it was also evident who was winning. Between 1970 and 1998 the number of nonmarital births in America rose by 224 percent. So too did the number of women and men aged forty to forty-four who had never married increase by 83 percent and 108 percent respectively. Single-parent families rose by 190 percent, and the number of children living with unmarried couples increased by 665 percent. By the early nineties, more than half of the children of women ages fifteen to twenty-nine were conceived out of wedlock and 41 percent were born out of wedlock. In 1970, more than 80 percent of the sixty-three million American households were family households of which half were traditional ones. By 2000 less than 69 percent were family households, and the largest proportion of those, 28 percent, consisted of married couples with no children. So in three decades the number of "traditional" families dropped in half, from half to a quarter of the country's family stock. While panic over the vanishing of the traditional family is still most acute in the South, this may be because that is the region with the lowest percentage of two-parent households. No wonder the sense of political and moral urgency behind the crusade to save the family.[12]

SEXUAL POLITICS

Erecting a fortress to defend all at once the integrity of the family, racial hierarchy, and the virility of the homeland was a task infused with sexual anxieties and suspicions. Limousine liberalism, even before Mario Procaccino christened it, had always aroused these forebodings. These sentiments boiled over in the cultural warfare of the Reagan era and beyond.

Sexual deviance among a dissolute upper class that had lost its moral backbone was both symptom and cause of its penchant for betrayal. Once it had been a telltale way of marking a ruling class's sissified inclination to compromise and surrender to the Soviets; the striped pants diplomat sipping at a cocktail with that upraised pinky finger was a dead giveaway of the effete and the effeminate character of elites ready to do business with the devil. During the culture wars of the late twentieth century and into the early twenty-first, sexual transgressions continued to function for the Christian right as identifiers of domestic subversives among the privileged. Take the crusade against homosexuality, for example. Populist conservatives were apt not only to portray gay behavior as unnatural, socially destructive, and evil, but also to assume homosexuals belonged to a wealthy and empowered caste using the influence of money to impose their morality. (As a matter of fact, however, the homosexual population earned on average 10 to 20 percent less than heterosexuals.)[13]

Masculinity as traditionally understood seemed imperiled by the new ethos of social liberalism. The work ethic was a point of honor among many working class males who in turn and for generations had instilled it in their sons. It was an austere training that marbled a stoic endurance into that solitary figure of the silent, disciplined, emotionally opaque masculine ideal. Humble working men were supposed to soldier on with the help of their women, whose native intelligence and care were essential but also subordinate. The Southernization of American political culture, which fixated on the image of the husky, bearded redneck dressed in bib overalls, was a regional variation that recalled olden days when men were men. There is, according to one historian, a striking connection between this form of heroic, reactionary masculinity and those "primitive rebels" (in Europe and America) of earlier times who were heralded as defenders of the traditional order, including the family, against the external forces of the state and predatory wealth. However, lone rangers of bygone days hoisted arms rather than a Pabst Blue Ribbon.[14]

Whatever form the modern mutation took, a whole way of life was doubly in jeopardy. First of all, deindustrialization relentlessly eviscerated the workplaces where that ethic was deployed. The male as breadwinner was becoming an endangered species, or at least could no longer perform that role without the help of his wife. (In 1960, 10 percent of women with children under the age of six worked outside the home; three-quarters did by 2005.) Under that stress the family itself struggled to stay intact; drinking, drugs, and divorce fissured kinship ties. That alone was emasculating.

Worse, while that wasting away was happening, the class of "verbalists," paper-pushers, symbol manipulators, organizational climbers, along with those refugees from the counterculture belatedly joining the mainstream, was flourishing—not only flourishing but acting out a very different emotional drama. Protagonists here tirelessly talked about self-realization, weren't shy about emoting, indeed indulged in a kind of open repudiation of the old work ethic's repressions. This was gender bending that mocked old-style masculine, Spartan reserve. *Esquire* magazine captured the experience of the new man: "But my generation . . . has respect for people who manage to create meaningful lives for themselves, doing something other than work. My contemporaries see being laid back as a virtue."[15]

Sexuality has for generations been a political lightning rod of choice (as well as a cultural obsession). It has been the dark matter detonating political emotions, fueling confrontations over matters apparently far removed from the primal scene of the bedroom. A subtext underlying much opposition to integration, for example, has always been the threat of "mongrelization" and emasculation. "Faggot" was a favorite epithet used to vilify Mayor John Lindsay during the hard-hat demonstrations in support of the Vietnam War. What began in the late 1960s as a broadening of radical politics by opening up private relations between men and women ended up displacing them. Sexual politics became instead a stalking horse for the Christian right, a way of charging their enemies with offenses against God and his moral imperatives.

Politicians and others made fun of "girlee men." An alpha male figure from the past was resurrected to fend off the feminization of American life by yuppies, the white collar professional caste, and "dot-com" geeks. These folk were not only getting filthy rich, they were self-indulgent, emotionally weak, timorous, and unmanly. Abortion was not only a sacrilege, but inflicted yet another blow against a besieged masculinity. It undermined male responsibility and authority by calling into question motherhood as the singular fate and future of working class women. So, too, the outlets of popular culture incited the kind of sexual debauchery that originated among the black underclass; rock 'n' roll, left undirected, was no more than "jungle music" encouraging teenage promiscuity that undermined the foundations of the family before they could even get laid down. The Christian right of the 1980s was, according to one historian, the first right-wing movement to position the family and sexuality at the center of its mobilizing efforts.[16]

Feminism and the fate of the Equal Rights Amendment in particular exhibit this emphatically. The ERA was essentially defeated in the Sunbelt states. Revivalism was most potent in this region, which was at the same time the incubator of a new family capitalism. That conjunction suggests how hard it is analytically to separate the economic from the spiritual aspirations and anxieties fueling the uprisings on the right.

Phyllis Schlafly had no doubt about that. In certain respects she was, as many of her opponents noted, the epitome of the liberated woman: well-educated with a career of her own, a public figure of considerable influence, a writer and world traveler, a seasoned Republican political organizer, witty, articulate, gutsy, even a bit glamorous, carrying herself with a kind of patrician dignity. Yet this orthodox Catholic preached that "God intended the husband to be the head of the family." With six children of her own, even if she got a good bit of outside help raising them, she could claim some adherence to this doctrine. Raised in St. Louis, her Depression-era family had depended on New Deal jobs programs to get by during the worst of times. But Phyllis grew up in a household that staunchly believed in the free enterprise system; she inherited that faith.

Nowadays conflating freedom and free enterprise has become axiomatic. Back when Schlafly was first entering public life—to begin with as a witch-hunter chasing after reds in the State Department, next as a tribune for a maverick senator from the outback intent on overthrowing the Republican establishment, and then when she began her long campaign to derail the ERA—this was still a marginal credo, tainted by association with disreputable groups like the John Birch Society. But for Phyllis, trained in good Catholic schools, adhering to a code of conduct that was absolute, there could be no off-loading of guilt onto society. The responsibility of the free individual was inescapable. She warned against letting "our schools and colleges be the citadels of atheism and moral relativism."

When the ERA was again introduced in 1972, the whole of the establishment was on board: liberal senators, the national media, the official labor movement (which signed on in 1975), even President Nixon, not to mention a bevy of high-profile women's organizations and magazines. Both major parties endorsed it. But Schlafly's moral compass didn't budge: "Make no mistake about it. This is a religious war." Later, when what had once seemed to be the inevitable triumph of the amendment came to seem more doubtful thanks to Schlafly's tireless efforts, one of her supporters explained, "The ERA is a religious issue and that's why we are winning."[17]

Champion of free enterprise and the free individual, Schlafly was sensitive to the fact that the ERA had touched off class resentments in a world boiling over with them. This was so notwithstanding the fact that Schlafly lived a solidly middle class life and that her organization, Eagle Forum, was composed of largely middle class women. Feminists were, in her view, inherently New Deal liberals or even socialists. The ERA was among other things a stealth attack whose aims included government-run day care and "the federalization of all remaining aspects of life." The true agenda of the women's liberation movement was "anti-family, anti-children, and pro-abortion." Feminists "view the home as a prison and the wife and mother as a slave." In fact this had been her worry long before the ERA showed up. At the Illinois Republican Party Convention in 1952, Schlafly warned the delegates, "The women of this nation are truly aroused by the New Deal invasion of the American home. The New Deal administration has been demoralizing our children by bad example, drafting our men and confiscating the family income." At stake were more than differences over mere policy, but the "moral corruption" of the Democratic Party by know-it-all mandarins.

Eagle Forum pursued the class dimensions of the struggle with great tenacity. An Ohio handout claimed that those favoring the constitutional amendment were elitist: "Those women lawyers, women legislators, and women executives promoting ERA have plenty of education and talent to get whatever they want in the business, political, and academic world. We, the wives of working men, need you, dear Senators and Representatives, to protect us. We think this is the man's responsibility." Indeed, the group created specifically to block the amendment was STOP ERA, an acronym that stood for "Stop Taking Our Privileges." An Alabama anti-ERA group wrote about how the Supreme Court might interpret the ERA to affect the draft (ordering women into combat), abortion, alimony, same-sex marriage, homosexuality, child support, divorce, public bathrooms, Little League teams, single-sex education, and prostitution. Its enemies made sure to associate the National Organization for Women (NOW) with radicalism generally and especially the cultural radicalism allegedly threatening the home and sexual conventions.[18]

Schlafly could be quite cutting and colorful when it came to depicting the privileged social positions many feminists enjoyed (while conveniently ignoring the considerable support for the amendment among working class women). Defending the patriarchal family, she compared proponents of the ERA to "the 'liberated' Roman matron . . . helping bring about the fall of Rome through her unnatural emulation of masculine qualities which resulted in a large scale breakdown of the family and ultimately of the empire." Here in a single sentence she limned the connection between family and imperial decline at a moment when what was prophesized to be the "American Century" had suffered a unique military defeat abroad and was showing multiple signs of early onset senescence at home.

Believing it intent on subverting the family *tout court,* for Schlafly the menace of the ERA was more global than the amendment's specific provisions let on. So, for example, she stood up for "the right of parents to insist that the schools permit voluntary prayer and teach the 'fourth r' (right and wrong) according to the precepts of the Holy Scripture." Partisans of the ERA were simultaneously zealots for state intervention and extreme individualists who had no room in their lives for that intermediate zone of life where family and holy scripture prescribed social discipline and duty. The "right to choose" was exemplary. The liberal elitists who propounded it rested their case on a strictly private right, but relied on the Supreme Court, not more democratic mediums, to enforce it.

All this touched a nerve not only among fellow Catholics, but also among a wider universe of the religiously committed including fundamentalists, Mormons, and orthodox Jews, which lent social breadth and ballast to the cause. Beverly LaHaye, the Phyllis Schlafly of the Protestant evangelical movement, established Concerned Women for America in 1978 to help kill the ERA. While she and her husband Tim ran a multifunctional evangelical enterprise out of San Diego, LaHaye was all about defending traditional sexual politics, including female "submission" to motherhood, the patriarch, and the nation. The statistics were striking: while 98 percent of those opposed to the ERA maintained some religious affiliation, well under half of its supporters did. Eagle Forum was a secular organization, and the battle to stop the ERA enlisted middle class as well as working class women, Sunbelt arrivistes, and Northeastern urban ethnics. However heterogeneous the movement clearly was, it nonetheless rested on a broad moral and cultural suspicion that women's liberation spoke the language of secularism and privilege. Like the civil rights movement, like the New Deal's more encompassing overhaul of the way public affairs were once conducted, it was a revolution engineered from above.[19]

THE MYSTERIES OF CHRISTIAN POPULISM

Waging the class struggle as a spiritual crusade mobilized millions. It worked as an electoral strategy for the Republican Party. Reagan's historic triumph in 1980 rested in part on the cultural and moral appeals first enunciated by the Nixon administration. And those in turn borrowed heavily from the class and racial counterinsurgencies of George Wallace, Louise Day Hicks, and others.

Politics may usually concern itself with the humdrum, with legislative horse trading, backroom wheeling and dealing, and the quotidian corruption that seems always to shadow the political class. However, now and then it strikes more deeply into the marrow of public life. It confronts—sometimes directly and sometimes by indirection—not only questions of power but how that power is and should be used to fashion social relations, the distribution of resources, and even the way society comports with the divine. That is to say, political life may at times operate in the realm of the nonrational, wrestling with matters not resolvable by the rigorous application of econometric science. The Christian populism that helped reorder the arithmetic of power and the center of gravity of the nation's political culture in the last third of the twentieth century grew strong, as many movements of both left and right had before it, by moving with those deep currents. This did not mean it expressed a politics of the irrational (although at times it crossed over). But it did mean that the "little man" cultural and Christian populism so shrewdly cultivated first by Nixon and Ronald Reagan after him was a prisoner of its own internal contradictions.

Threats to the traditional family were real enough. But the movement deflected that preoccupation onto the underclass. Early marriage, teenage parenthood, single motherhood, domestic violence, drug abuse, and every other measure of kinship dysfunction were attributed to an African American lost continent. But all those traits marked white working class and lower-middle-class life generally. Honoring the work ethic supposedly separated the respectable both from the underclass indolent and upper class parasites. Yet the work ethic had been a torment to working people for generations, functioning as a kind of internal police that demeaned rather than exalted all those powerless to resist while keeping the production line moving. Moreover, the tribes subscribing to limousine liberalism, all those verbalists, yuppies, geeks, and policy wonks, may or may not have contributed much to the general welfare. But they were by no means idlers. Instead, as often as not they were workaholics whose ambitions and elitist self-conceptions made them Olympians of all-day, all-night, wired-up nose to the grindstone, exertion plus. Across the great divide, the caricature of ghetto dwellers as slothful layabouts living off the "nanny state" may have provided some psychic consolation to white working people suffering the pressures of a declining economy. But it had precious little to do with the harsh reality of urban life for millions belonging to the underclass. And if moral resisters decried the decadence of popular culture, they shied away in most cases from confronting the great capitalist enterprises that fabricated and sold it.

Christian populists were not the only ones made apoplectic by the leviathan state. For them, however, it was emphatically the devil's invention. It was the modern world's version of idolatry, the capstone of a secular piety that ate away at the sense of individual responsibility, which was, after all, the essential nature of the relationship between man and God. Nonetheless, the power wielded by this state is what made the Sunbelt shine. Furthermore, Christian populists were not reluctant to call upon that same power to enforce divine injunctions in the public realm, as, for example, in the case of bans on same-sex marriage. Prohibitions like that might ward off the queasiness elicited by sexual confusion and build a fortress around the family of old. Sexual unorthodoxy and women's liberation especially were dangers from the deep. Still, the family allegedly being protected relied more and more on the gainful employment and perseverance of those liberated women. Schlafly had a point when she provoked women liberationists about the skewed middle and upper class composition of their movement. But she avoided observing that many working class women, in part precisely because of the additional burdens they bore in a sagging economy, welcomed the right to abort unwanted pregnancies.

The cultural and moral populism enlisted by the Republican Party to combat limousine liberalism was thus a fragile creation. It was also an unpredictable one. The coalition envisioned by Nixon and Reagan conjoined two fundamentalisms. One invoked the ideology of the free market, the other holy scripture. Yet both had to cohabit a political home that reserved its main councils of strategic planning for the country's corporate elite. No party with ambitions to rule could afford to ignore the unequal division of economic power in America. The business elite remained dominant. Corporate America, however, was neither Christian nor on all matters devoted to the free market. Serious fissures within the ascending world of right-wing conservatism were therefore a chronic possibility. Limousine liberalism as a cultural stigma would continue to work its magic. It kept this uneasy assemblage more or less on message. But if this was a network of power, it would also prove to be a fractious and tumultuous one and subject to short circuits.

9

God, Capitalism, and the Tea Party

When Republican candidates seeking the party's presidential nomination were multiplying like rabbits in the spring of 2015, Rick Santorum, ex-senator from Pennsylvania, joined the madding crowd. Previously known as a strict social conservative of the most doctrinaire sort, Santorum decided to rebirth himself. He, along with a number of his Republican competitors, had discovered economic inequality as a vendible issue. He branded his new political position "blue collar conservatism." He proclaimed that "working families don't need another president tied to big government or big money." Holding a lump of coal in his hand to punctuate his origins as the grandson of a coal miner, Santorum lambasted big business support for immigration reform that would further undermine the well-being of American workers. He urged raising the minimum wage. For good measure he scolded fellow Republicans for their obsession about cutting taxes for the rich.

Fittingly, this whole conversion experience was enacted on a factory floor in Cabot, Pennsylvania (Santorum grew up nearby in rural Butler County). This wasn't just any factory floor, however. Penn United Technologies manufactures equipment for the oil and gas industries. Employees have a stake in its ownership. Most tellingly, it was founded as a "Christian company" whose website announces that "we exist to glorify God." So although Santorum made it clear he was no longer the single note "values" candidate he'd been during the 2012 primaries, when he tirelessly talked about his opposition to same-sex marriage and abortion, he was by no means abandoning that crusade. Rather the symbolism suggested that Christian capitalism and Christian populism could inhabit the same house of being. Nor was the onetime senator the only one on the Republican right to conceive this political architecture.[1]

Ted Cruz, a sitting senator from Texas, had already entered the Republican sweepstakes by the time Santorum announced. Although intensely disliked by many of his fellow politicians, Cruz was a Tea Party favorite. Moreover, his credentials as a social conservative were impeccable. He remained, for example, a staunch opponent of gay marriage as a violation of the country's allegedly religious founding principles. But in that uproarious spring feverish pre-primary season, he had, like Santorum, discovered a new way to pose that dilemma.

In a fit of reckless overreach, the state government of Indiana had just passed the Religious Freedom Restoration Act, which would have allowed businesses and other organizations to discriminate against gay and lesbian people on grounds of religious belief. The reaction against the act was furious and instantaneous and arose from all points on the limousine liberal spectrum. Joining the opposition, indeed often leading it, was a galaxy of national corporations who threatened to stop doing business with Indiana. General Electric, Eli Lily, Angie's List, Levi Strauss, Apple Inc., and others from the upper echelon of American big business compelled Indiana lawmakers to think again and pass a quick "fix."

Cruz, the pious populist, zeroed in on this culprit in particular: "The Fortune 500 is running shamelessly to endorse the radical gay marriage agenda over religious liberty, to say: 'We will persecute a Christian pastor, a Catholic priest, a Jewish rabbi. . . . The Fortune 500 has cast their lot in with that." Earlier the senator had told the *Wall Street Journal* that "one of the biggest lies in politics is the lie that the Republicans are the party of big business. Big business does great with big government. Big business is very happy to climb in bed with big government. Republicans are and should be the party of small business and of entrepreneurs."[2]

Playing the lone ranger, Cruz made it seem like his Republican confederates were "terrified" to stand up to the corporate hierarchs. But that was not really the case. Not only would Rick Santorum soon join the fray against the Fortune 500, but others already had. Paul Weyrich enunciated this view a generation earlier. In fact, this split between established and up-and-coming capitalism gets periodically recycled as the economy changes.

For example, the rising business milieu in Phoenix that put Gold-water on the map was so successful in inviting in national corporations that it gave birth to a corporate elite more accustomed to and dependent on the state. It was a less ideologically driven milieu ready to support some environmental regulation, tax-aided schooling, even long-range planning and corporate welfare programs. Nor were members of this new local establishment particularly religious. Its racial views also became unexceptionable. Eventually, however, they were confronted by a rising generation of independent businesspeople and those motivated by religious passions, both resentful of government interference. By the late 1980s they had managed to elect a populist businessman, Republican Evan Mecham, as governor of Arizona.

A devout Mormon, Mecham grew up on the family farm in Utah. He ran a number of auto dealerships, an occasional newspaper, a mining company, and a racetrack. But he had the political itch and ran so many times for public office in Arizona that he became known as that state's Harold Stassen. His message was a kind of updated version of Jeffersonian democracy to which he added his spiritual anxieties—Mecham blamed the rising incidence of divorce on working women. He even resurrected an old-time populist antitrust rhetoric denouncing "the monopolistic press" for his newspaper failures. A staff member claimed Mecham appealed to "raucous anti-establishment beer bar crowds" of blue collar workers and petty businessmen, and people who "accept that the Bible is the literal word of God." His campaign coordinator in southern Arizona confidently noted, "For every sushi bar in the state, I counted 40 bowling alleys. Working classes see Mecham as the enemy of BMW owners who exploit them." Mecham eventually committed political suicide by attempting to revoke Martin Luther King Jr.'s birthday as a holiday, by defending the use of the word *pickaninny* to describe black children, and by felonious behavior that led to boycotts of the state by leading corporations and celebrities. He was both indicted and impeached. But while he was around he knew how to play the limousine liberal card.[3]

Nowadays on issues ranging from immigration reform to same-sex marriage, from free trade to abortion, from bailouts of banks "too big to fail" to prayer in school, corporate Republicans and Tea Party Republicans do not see eye to eye; on the contrary, the hostility is palpable. Even in arenas where they might seemingly agree, matters are not so simple. Take government regulation of business. Keeping government agencies out of business affairs is something big corporations can handle with their flotillas of lawyers. But the small businessman has to live with it.

Something as apparently innocuous as the Export-Import Bank of the United States can make sparks fly. The bank was created more than seventy years ago as a New Deal measure to help jump-start recovery from the Great Depression. Presumably it was designed to help business in general reach markets abroad, but it turns out not all businesses are created equal. Tea Party partisans, Americans for Prosperity (a Koch brothers creation), and the Heritage Foundation lined up friendly Congress members to block the bank's renewal as an offensive example of "corporate welfare" and "crony capitalism." Renewing the charter was supported by the Obama administration and the US Chamber of Commerce and the National Association of Manufacturers. It seems the biggest corporations like Boeing and General Electric get the lion's share of the bank's loans, which help foreign concerns buy American products. One Texas Tea Party congressman drew a line in the sand: "Do we stand for free enterprise interests and its hope for fairness and its opportunity? Or do we stand for business interests? Because those two are not identical."[4]

Lurking behind the faceless façade of the corporate monolith is the visage of the limousine liberal. For example, conservative Alabama senator Jeff Sessions called for reducing immigration to help American workers and accused the financial and political elite of a conspiracy to keep wages down by opening the doors to foreigners. Sessions excoriated Facebook founder and liberal-minded tycoon Mark Zuckerberg for ignoring the needs of working people for good jobs: "We are a nation and a nation owes things to its people. And the average working truck driver is worth just as much as Mr. Zuckerberg, just as much as the Wall Street masters of the universe." The governor of Wisconsin, Scott Walker, another Tea Party hero, made similar remarks. A group of Tea Party Republicans in the House sent a letter to President Obama in January of 2014 chastising the administration because "the White House has entertained a parade of high-powered business executives to discuss immigration policy, while shutting out the concerns of everyday wage earners."[5]

THE IMPIETY OF DOLLARS AND SENSE

Some treat the Tea Party as the AstroTurf creation of big business. And on many matters—cutting the budget or reducing taxes or opposing trade unions, for example—they tend to hold similar or identical views. Nonetheless, the intermixing of Christian populism with Christian capitalism has given birth to a lively and deeply rooted current in American life. It does not exist at the sufferance of the Fortune 500, even if it shares a general fondness for market society. A potent combination, it has managed to shift the center of political gravity to the right. While points of friction make the alliance between Christian populism and Christian capitalism an iffy one, their common antipathy to limousine liberalism has so far worked well.

Moreover, the resurfacing of the Fortune 500 as a prime target of that antipathy marks the most recent evolution in the mythography of the limousine liberal. During the Reagan era (which lasted well beyond his two presidencies) the profile of the limousine liberal showed fewer and fewer of those manorial markings that had once distinguished the subversive establishment of the New Deal and postwar era. At least that's the way it seemed in the eyes of cloth-coated Republicans, redneck good ole boys, and Mario Procaccino ethnic Democrats. Instead, most right-wing populist censors went after the lifestyle affectations of the new urban gentry, the moral contagions flooding the mainstream from the ranks of the counterculture, the narcissism of yuppies, and the supercilious bureaucratic presumptions of the American *nomenklatura*.

Banks and multinational corporations did sometimes make an appearance on this list of undesirables. But they were rarely in the crosshairs of rebels on the right. Reagan himself, after all, may have mastered the art of courting evangelical country folk, but his regime and circles of support were peopled with corporate honchos. American businesses, facing increasingly stiff competition from Europe and Japan, grew less and less tolerant of government regulation and the costs associated with the welfare state. Reagan's declaration that government was the problem not the solution to the problems confronting the country was welcome news in corporate boardrooms. And the President and his wife welcomed the new atmosphere of luxe that descended on Washington with his inauguration. This was the president who proclaimed, "What I want to see above all is that this remains a country where someone can always get rich." "Above all," indeed! The regime wasn't bashful about its blunt materialism and its conviction that the pathway to freedom involved an end run around the public sphere. The old ruling class, which grew up on the Main Line, went to Exeter, Yale, and Harvard Law, joined a Wall Street investment bank, ran a Fortune 500 corporation, and then proceeded to turn upside down the class and race relations that had once seemed fixed forever, was dead, or rather had been domesticated. No longer the breeding ground of a peculiar form of milquetoast social democracy from on high, it had rejoined the ranks of free market orthodoxy.[6]

Tea Party times are different. Although various grievances stir up the movement, it is noteworthy that it all began with impassioned denunciations of the bailout of the big banks. Glenn Beck, along with others, launched one merciless attack after another on the Federal Reserve (hence his avid hunt for its conspiratorial beginnings a century earlier). On the one hand, this seems surpassingly strange. If the Tea Party movement swore fealty to capitalism, what in the world was it doing excoriating the monuments to that system whose collapse might end everything? Moreover, for a long generation, the core of American big business and finance had tended to line up on the side of conservative fiscal and monetary policy, deregulation, and an aversion to trade unions. Here presumably was common ground to be shared by Tea Party partisans and the Fortune 500. Indeed, by the late

1980s that had become a bipartisan persuasion when the Democratic Leadership Council encouraged the party to join in the neoliberal hosannas for the free market. Just here, however, is where what might be called the "Indiana dilemma" gestated.

Neoliberal capitalism as pursued by the modern, publicly owned corporation has no objection to the social and cultural reforms (racial and gender equality, for example) that so inflame the ranks of the right-wing rebellion. Quite to the contrary: big business's lightning-like reaction to Indiana's misstep in enacting the Religious Freedom Restoration Act proved that with a vengeance! The American corporation—subject not to the whims, faith, and prejudices of a founding owner or his dynastic heirs, but to the more impersonal motivations of managerial functionaries—is among the most politically correct institutions in the country. That is simply a matter of sound business practice. The sense and sensibilities of the Volk, on the other hand, hold no intrinsic appeal for the avowedly multicultural corporation, except perhaps as a marketing strategy. Corporate capital's logic is strictly commercial, a matter of the arithmetic of cold cash, not morals. Politics follows on. Its purified indifference may upset the tradition-minded. But it resonates well with the highly charged self-righteousness and social liberalism of the new class of deracinated, upwardly mobile professionals, technocrats, midlevel financial engineers, new media makers, liberal academics, and so on.

Family capitalism is pious. Corporate capitalism is impious, or will lean that way if it pays. That moral elasticity is what can make it, under the right circumstances, a bedmate of limousine liberalism.

Family capitalism might seem a perfect carrier of the mundane. Workaday routine; the patient piling up of earnings diligently reseeded in the family enterprise; scrimping in the here and now; methodical, frugal attention to every detail of production and sales; and prudential calculation to ward off the unpredictable: all this constitutes the behavioral antithesis of anything resembling a higher calling, or so it would seem. Yet family capitalism has always been an incubator of metaphysical yearnings. And those desires and spiritual ambitions constitute the soulful subsurface of these pedestrian, counting-house traits, which seem to rob it of all romance. Building the family business from scratch or shouldering that burden bequeathed by a founding ancestor is, in its own everyday way, a coming to terms with questions about time, death, and family continuity. Like a homestead, the family enterprise is rooted in a specific locale, is stamped with its peculiarities and customs, becomes a landmark of neighborhood or regional identity and pride, and so at the same time defines a distinct geography of the spirit. Its rigors comprise a moral calisthenics that reach out to the divine and exercise its commandments.

Heroism may be inculcated on the frontiers of risk that surround and threaten the family enterprise. A sense of mastery accretes out of serial triumphs over technological and natural mysteries and puzzles, from directing the labors of other people, from victories over rivals in the marketplace, from the self-control and steely willingness necessary to confront the perpetual mutability of life that capitalism dictates. Here is built up day by day through the rigors of physical effort and cerebral invention what modern society has championed as "self-empowerment." For men and women who've struggled to create their own businesses (or dream of doing so) and whose success at doing that is an affirmation of their self-reliance, ingenuity, discipline, and moral stamina, conflating the free market with freedom, sensing the sacred in the quotidian, is instinctive.

So while family capitalism and corporate capitalism might in unison raise their glasses in a toast to the free market, they may not be celebrating a common host. For many observers, however, what is befuddling is that in our ultramodern day and age, something as apparently anachronistic as family capitalism even exists at all, much less with the muscular robustness it has displayed lately. It was supposed to be so nineteenth century. What happened?

THE RISEN

Limousine liberalism, in its mythic form, has lived a long time in the American imagination—from Ford to Beck, Santorum, and Cruz. Why? It has risen and subsided without any inherent connection to the ups and downs of the economy, although it may be inflamed by either. As a political incendiary limousine liberalism ignites an emotional firestorm over the pretensions of a reform-minded elite, no matter whether that elite presides over a prospering or declining economy. So, the Ku Klux Klan was a mass movement of considerable influence in the boom days of the Jazz Age. Yet even weightier right-wing populist insurgencies rose in response to the Great Depression that followed.

Good times returned after the war. The economy offered abundant opportunities for manufacturing startups to grow, often with the considerable help of the government, especially but not only in the Sunbelt. Ironically, the Goldwater movement was in part nourished by that symbiotic relationship between business and big government. Manufacturing was dying away, however (or being murdered by high finance). But even as conventional industry proved less hospitable, the service sector beckoned. Flood tides of immigrants formed pools of ethnically based entrepreneurs, some in the underground of the informal economy, some quite formidable. If big box retailers dominated the standardized mass market, the infinity of new niche subcultures and their inexhaustible desires could be supplied by boutique lifestyle enterprises. By the end of the 1970s in an otherwise dolorous economy, 40 percent of service workers were employed by small firms with fewer than twenty employees, and this was even more so the case in retail.[7]

"Flexible capitalism" has become the signature arrangement characteristic of the economic order in the United States and in most parts of the "advanced" world. That system is the offspring of multinational corporations in collaboration with local, state, and national governments, as well as with transnational organizations and accords. Yet its creation also abetted the rebirth of family capitalism. In that way, the real-life limousine liberalism of the Fortune 500 fostered its own potential opposition. Under the regime of flexible capitalism the corporation got decentered and labor markets were transformed into pools of casual, part-time, temporary, contract workers. Megacorporations contracted out a range of functions once performed internally. Outsourcing, subcontracting, and licensing production, communications, distribution, marketing, and other activities to outside concerns meant that the universe of small and medium-sized businesses expanded considerably. Think Joe the Plumber (the conservative activist and wannabe entrepreneur famous for challenging Barack Obama during the 2008 campaign) and all those who bought into the dream of self-employment.

Moreover, the military's insatiable appetite for new weapons systems continued to jump-start ancillary businesses, especially throughout the Sunbelt. With the booming of the financial sector itself (where much of the pressure for "flexibility" originated) all sorts of boutique consulting, accounting, legal, research, software, and other essential undertakings nourished entrepreneurial ambitions and ideology. So too the worlds of retailing and service and entertainment opened up space for specialty, small-scale niche businesses and franchises. New business formations doubled and self-employment rose nearly 25 percent in the decades surrounding the turn of the millennium alongside the downsizing of American industry, in part because of it. Corporations found it increasingly easy to off-load functions once performed internally, thanks in part to the information and communications revolution, which facilitated the coordination of far-flung operations. Modern and "archaic" labor systems and firms lived in side-by-side symbiosis.

According to a Small Business Administration report at the turn of the millennium, nearly six million new businesses were created during Bill Clinton's eight years in office, and nonfarm proprietorships rose 34 percent between 1992 and 2000. Furthermore, small businesses received 23 percent of all federal contracts, not to mention loan guarantees.

Still, this remains a precarious economic zone. The failure rate among small businesses during the period 2002–2006 (a prosperous time) was frighteningly high, especially among startups, whether in construction, retail, or wholesale trade, or even in the finance sector. Core corporations today continue to deploy enormous power, enough to drive entrepreneurs and independent professionals under, perhaps even more than they once did, thanks to the near extinction of antitrust prosecutions. In Silicon Valley, for example, the biggest concerns have vacuumed up hundreds of smaller ones. Google all by itself swallowed one hundred. Of course, for some defeat was sweetened by hefty buyouts. Sometimes the whole point was to be bought out. Nonetheless, this expanding universe of family businesses had every good reason to be wary of its Fortune 500 big brothers. Peaceful co-existence might be possible, or it might not be.[8]

Genuine areas of serious acrimony crop up all the time. How else can one explain the nasty exchanges within the Republican Party over the last several years about such matters as NAFTA and the Trans-Pacific Partnership or over immigration reform? What about the brinkmanship of Tea Party politicians in debates over resolving the debt ceiling, which pitted zealots on the right against the US Chamber of Commerce and otherwise powerful business and financial lobbies? Glenn Beck's denunciations of the life-saving billions received by the titans of finance can't be welcome on Wall Street, where the Federal Reserve is a favorite watering hole.

Hostility of that depth naturally cuts both ways. The executives running the country's leading corporations are a pragmatic bunch and tend to avoid adopting hard ideological positions. They are agnostics when it comes to the role of government, welcoming and depending on it to meet the needs of business on many issues, annoyed and in opposition when it becomes too intrusive. On cultural matters they are most at home with the basic tenets of limousine liberalism. Often enough, core national corporations and business institutions don't trust the Tea Party, finding its slogans dangerous, too ideological, and apt to invite too many bad feelings about big business. Meanwhile, a survey of small business owners found a healthy majority favorably disposed toward the Tea Party. A party blogger advised, "Treating small business owners better than we treat real estate and Wall Street investors is an idea whose time has come." Such fighting words convey that indigenous will to "light out for the territories," to refresh an endless frontier of heroic self-creation born of chastening effort. And this is especially the case in the face of limousine liberalism's bureaucratic leviathan state, which is so debilitating and rule-bound. It eats away at the vigorous life and its sacral rationales, makes people craven seekers of material security.[9]

THE LAST UTOPIA

Every time somebody opens a small business they don't apply for membership in the Tea Party. Many remain politically in the mainstream or don't enter the political waters at all. However, the mythos of producer populism—that social cosmology that divides the world into those whose efforts give rise to the tangible and the useful on the one hand and predators and parasites on the other—envelops multitudes. Part Christian, part a secular version of frontier mythology, a compelling idealism supplies the nuclear fuel for entrepreneurial insurgents on the right.

Utopian thinking has been banished from most precincts by horrific twentieth-century history. It is considered disreputable and woolly-headed. Yet utopias have risen again among true believers in the free market (even if they claim otherwise); they see in this "stark utopia" a wondrous, self-correcting mechanism giving forth self-fulfillment, democracy, law and order, peace and justice, and a channel to the sacred. This entrepreneurial romance remains very much alive and at the same time anchored in an imagined past, one of moral steadfastness, racial and ethnic purity, where small towns husbanded the best in human nature. Newt Gingrich called this view of life the "great adventure" in a course he taught at Reinhardt College, "Rescuing American Civilization." This view marries the heroics of cowboy conquest and the resolve of the Christian pioneer settler, "a moral undertaking and an inherent part of the makeup of human beings." A Tea Party website put it like this: "Small business is important for freedom. . . . Every American should be a small business owner. . . . No job unless you own your business is safe."

Note the sense of impending danger. Faith and desire inspire but also feel imperiled. This is in part due to the demographic makeover the country is going through as the economy has come to depend on a vast influx of immigrant workers. It arises also in response to the moral and racial makeover blamed on limousine liberalism. However, the armies of the faithful are not weak. They can call on Jesus, an ever renewable native belief in America as an everyman garden of opportunity, and a freshly minted crop of pious billionaires to carry them through. But in every case they must wrestle with paradoxes of their own making.[10]

As much as the new utopians might wish it otherwise, tension between God and capitalism has been chronic. Plenty of Protestant divines in the nineteenth century sanctioned the quest for wealth. They applauded the way it instilled a certain discipline and self-control. Others, however, decried such pursuits as mammon worship and called on their congregants to adhere instead to Christ's "social gospel," with its solicitations on behalf of the poor. Papal encyclicals in the late nineteenth century and again amid the Great Depression of the twentieth century echoed these criticisms and in particular emphasized the way capitalism put the family in jeopardy. Nowadays religiously inclined critics of limousine liberalism simultaneously champion something they call "The Gospel of Prosperity" yet raise alarms about the iniquities of consumer capitalism.

If wealth once made the pious uneasy, arousing anxieties about the way it might corrupt the soul, adherents of today's prosperity gospel are no longer troubled in the same way. Indeed, freedom from sin through discovering or rediscovering Christ comports well with success in the market in this latest revision of the gospels. Reverend Terry Cole Whittaker, a preacher from the early days of televangelism in the 1980s, kept her audience upbeat about finding Jesus with the help of a prosperity campaign kit. It worked to bring you closer to the Lord, plus made you wealthy while you were getting closer. A Georgia-based minister with the wondrous name of Creflo Dollar runs a Pentecostal church where he sings the praises of prosperity in sermons called "Thinking for Success" and "Overcoming the Fear of Lack." A megachurch in Houston with forty-seven thousand parishioners is presided over by Joel Osteen, whose best-selling book *Become a Better You* advises that God "created you to live abundantly" and provides counsel on how to succeed.

A generation ago Southern California ministries became forums for free market economic thinking. Gospel teachings there were infused with talk about financial competence as a vital part of a good Christian life: spiritual well-being needed to include financial means put to good use. Evangelical literature included financial news, stories about how to accumulate, investment advice, and analogies likening the church to a sophisticated corporate undertaking. One minister in Mississippi delivered this piece of economic theology that might go down well among many academic economists: "The poor will follow the rich, the rich will follow the rich, but the rich will never follow the poor." A five-million-copy best-seller called *The Prayer of Jabez*, by the preacher Bruce Wilkinson, talked about God rewarding Wall Street portfolios. Founder of the Faith Exchange Fellowship Dan Stratton wrote a book aptly entitled *Divine Provision: Positioning God's Kings for Financial Conquest.* Another author rested his case linking entrepreneurial success to moral worth by alluding to "the God-given prerogatives of pursuing profit."

Love of luxury and wealth has permeated the daily doings and the theology of televangelists for decades now. Missionaries rely on the principal medium of consumer culture, television, to deliver their message. Their tax-exempt multimedia empires are, after all, big business, and they have not been shy about exhibiting its showiest desserts: mansions, private jets, air-conditioned doghouses, you name it. Such extravagances were to be piled up in God's counting room as evidence of capitalism's moral benevolence and its promise of individual freedom: a kind of eschatology of material success, signs of God's grace, free enterprise as a biblical injunction.[11]

Still, something disturbs this spiritual equanimity. Evangelical champions of market society continue to revile the permissiveness and excess encouraged by all the emporiums of popular culture and mass consumption. Jeremiads against material preoccupations still issue from the pulpits of Christian capitalism. Pat Robertson warned that "the law of Satan's Kingdom is Have it now, with a splash. Quick money, quick things, quick success." A Christian yet libertarian economic commentator, Ron Nash argues that "a capitalism that is cut loose from traditional values is a capitalism that is headed for trouble," that is, hedonism. Nash maintains that "capitalism needs Christianity." Likewise, Jerry Falwell observed that "people are living and dying for money," and that left unchecked this would lead to economic collapse, which the minister prophesized might not be entirely a bad thing. Such a calamity might compel a reordering of the economy so that it would be more in line with Christian ethics. He went so far as to cite the book of Leviticus and its invocation of a Jubilee day when all debts would be canceled, wealth would be redistributed, and, in a kind of holy anachronism, Christian capitalism would save civilization.

Yet the conservative evangelical ministry invariably decries economic equality as an inherently unjust form of confiscation. The limousine liberal is today's hydra, that monstrous specter of enraged plebian revolutionaries that once haunted the imagination of the eighteenth-century gentry. R. J. Rushdoory, founder of Christian Reconstruction, alerts his followers that "the socialistic alliance of big business with big government has added itself to big labor, big foundations and a statist education to make up our modern establishment with big churches as the Chaplains of this new order. We are dealing with amoral power today, power which allies itself with power against the weak."

Salvation of the sort that Falwell and others have envisioned means, above all, reversing the "cultural disintegration" inherent in a godless capitalism. Hovering just over the horizon is a modestly provisioned world, not filthy rich, but frugal, devout, and where work is less about wealth than about respectability. Its enemies are legion. Hollywood is exorcized as a breeding ground of impiety. Shopping can verge on demoralizing addiction. In the vernacular of the right, liberalism comes closer to describing a "decadent lifestyle" than a political creed. Speaking to the Democratic National Committee in 1995, Bill Clinton captured the peculiarity of this mythography: "It's a funny world that they're sketching—a world in which Big Bird is an elitist and right-wing media magnates are Populists."

Elitism plus decadence is the cultural primeval soup where limousine liberalism breeds today. Right-wing talk radio host Laura Ingraham explained that "essentially elites are defined not so much by class or wealth as . . . [t]heir core belief that they are superior to WE the People. They know better." Until his death in 2008 Paul Weyrich continued to issue regular alarms that the culture was becoming "an ever-wider sewer," and foresaw "a cultural collapse of historic proportions." Verging on the despondent, the right-wing ideologue lamented an America given over to decadence whose people have "adopted, in large measure, MTV culture." By the end of the millennium Weyrich believed there no longer existed "a moral majority," and that "we have lost the culture war." His pared down desire was for some saving remnant, a monastic retreat by true believers into a sealed-off space, free of TV and Disneyland, where thrift not consumption guided behavior, where enterprise was encouraged but not allowed to grow too big, where children were homeschooled and so immunized against the moral contagion racing through all the institutions of modern society. "Life is not just about getting more stuff," Weyrich argued, nor was economic efficiency the most important virtue even if official society went on and on about it. "We need some sort of quarantine."

Yet the snares and delusions of modern life lie in wait for everybody. Tea Party favorite, Florida senator Marco Rubio, has been perpetually awash in debt, a compulsive purchaser of upscale homes, top-of-the-line Audis, and specialty speed boats. Only money from a benevolent and like-thinking Miami billionaire, Norman Braman, has saved the senator from going under. Still, Rubio never tires of declaiming against the profligacy of big government, the moral swamp of deficit-financed limousine liberalism.[12]

So the old worm still turns beneath the surface of this utopian idyll: Is it Jesus and capitalism or Jesus against capitalism? The gnashing of teeth is almost audible. Temptation is everywhere and wears many faces. This can be insidious. If the play world of mass consumption was the diabolical invention of limousine liberalism, its seductions have proven universal. Indeed, the wily ways of the market are endlessly ingenious and can even minister to the special needs of these reactionary rebels. Clouds of nostalgia hover over the Tea Party movement, which hankers after days gone by. In part, this is because the present and the future seem so anchorless. Along comes consumer capitalism to retrofit the past into saleable nostalgia: retro or vintage clothing, Disneyland, paddle steamboat excursions, resurrected railroad rides to nowhere, three-cornered hats. History for all of us—and most of all, for family capitalism—becomes less a resource than a sedative. It is so easy to slip the traces and fall prey to the magic that limousine liberalism has been concocting for generations.[13]

THE PEOPLE'S CAPITALISM

Property, not the good life, suggests a way out of this dilemma. Evangelical right-wingers have unequivocally endorsed supply side economics (the notion that cutting taxes on businesses and the wealthy will not only generate more investment but in so doing actually increase tax revenues), applauding the gathering in of wealth by the rich in the interests of the general prosperity and viewing that money as a divine gift, a blessing. Pat Robertson called the theory, which most economists have dismissed as bogus and which runs in the face of all previous Christian theology, "the last truly divine theory of money creation." Robertson, Jimmy Swaggart, Jerry Falwell, and others less luminous crafted a ministry that marries the irreconcilable: nineteenth-century morality and twentieth-century consumerism. Independent enterprise is presumed to bridge that divide. In this metaphysics, Jesus is depicted as rather well-to-do and the market as God's workshop. Property serves as vessel of the sacred. So at the height of civil rights agitation in the 1960s, Falwell condemned what was happening as a "terrible violation of human and property rights." Decades later he assured his flock that "the free enterprise system is clearly outlined in the Book of Proverbs."[14]

Evergreen dreams about the American genius for enterprise, self-invention, and second chances reaffirm and bolster biblical injunctions. This is a kind of everyman capitalism that combines resentment of big business with an abiding faith in the business system. Its leveling sensibility when it comes to thumbing its nose at established wealth comports well with its religious egalitarianism, which has no use for church or secular hierarchies. All at once, Christian capitalism seeks to preserve the communalism of the congregation while encouraging forays by enterprising pioneers out onto the economic frontier.

Skating on this line entails closely observing the boundaries separating the self-reliant heroics of family capitalism from its bad twin. J. Vernon McGee, a popular evangelical preacher in California, declared that the free market system was the most "Christian" of any invented, but warned that the "Keynesian" version of economic behavior robbed people of their self-esteem, made them dependent and slaves to debt, and dulled the work ethic. Nonetheless, without the heavy lifting by that Keynesian state over the last two generations— including everything from government-organized and -subsidized research and development on the far frontiers of science and technology to the humdrum provision of power, water, and the means of transportation—born again contemporary family capitalism might never have been born again.[15]

Love for free enterprise, of one form or another, is an American perennial. It goes all the way back to the country's beginnings. That amour has exercised great appeal in more recent times. From the outset it has been part of the popular understructure of conservative resurgence. And it has fueled the broad antipathy felt for limousine liberalism.

Phyllis Schlafly, for example, who came of political age right after World War II working for what would become the American Enterprise Institute, kept her commitment to free market capitalism steadfast. She returned to it as a bedrock faith whether she was on the warpath against subversive "kingmakers" in Washington's upper echelons during the Cold War or she was confronting limousine liberal feminists in the battle to defeat the ERA. In Schlafly's view the real source of women's liberation was the free enterprise system itself, whose native inventiveness produced those technological marvels that emancipated women from the household burdens of yesteryear. Stretched far enough this logic could get silly and end up in a kind of reverse sexism: "It was not the strident demands of the women's libbers that brought high prizes to women's tennis, but the discovery by sports promoters that beautiful female legs gracefully moving around the court made women's tennis a highly marketable television production to delight male audiences." In the end, she was deadly serious that the source of emancipation for both genders was to be found in the free market.[16]

While Schlafly was tangling with bra-burners, a man named Howard Jarvis launched an unlikely tax rebellion in California. Born in Utah in 1903, Jarvis lived a picturesque life even before he became a notorious tribune of middle class rebellion. First a semipro baseball player, then a sparring partner of Jack Dempsey's, he went on to run a newspaper, started a gadget manufacturing enterprise that went under, tried real estate speculation, and finally ended up opening a chain of household appliance factories. A supporter of Nixon, he too tried his hand at electoral politics but failed in his bid to become mayor of Los Angeles. One reason that went nowhere is that the local liberal Republican establishment didn't trust him, especially as he had engaged in some shady fund-raising for Goldwater. Jarvis despised all taxes, especially property taxes that ended up funding social welfare programs. His "Proposition 13," to limit property taxes, actually won (and inspired similar movements in states around the country). It drew much of its strength from homeowners and small businesspeople suffering what was then decried as "bracket creep." Farmers, real estate agents, and middle class professionals flocked to the cause and helped gather a million signatures to put the proposition on the ballot.

The *New York Times* called the tax revolt a "modern Boston Tea Party." The *Times,* which in the eyes of the right-wing opposition was the chief outlet for the limousine liberal viewpoint, was poking fun at the movement and its leader. Liberals called Jarvis a corporate shill. But, at least to begin with, he wasn't. He waged an independent struggle against a prevailing tax structure that was devouring middle class people as inflation vaulted them into higher tax brackets. Major corporations did more than stay away from funding the campaign; instead, Bank of America, Pacific Mutual Insurance, the Southern Pacific Railroad, and Standard Oil, along with the Chamber of Commerce, the AFL, and the League of Women Voters organized and raised money to defeat the antitax uprising. But Jarvis triumphed and for a moment emerged as a people's hero: "You are the people and you will have to take control of the government again or else it is going to control you."[17]

Jerry Falwell's evangelical world and in fact Falwell himself were avid Jarvis supporters. Something was in the air. By 1984 Richard Viguerie was predicting a revolution against the elite establishment, even the emergence of a new populist party born out of the suspicions gathering around "the effete gentlemen of the Northeastern establishment." With some poetic license, this amalgam of Falwell and Viguerie might be called the ideology of Christian democratic capitalism, a marriage of the movement's entrepreneurial populism and its piety.

Clearly its commitment to democracy was contingent and provisional. It shied away from racial inclusion, wanted to shut the borders against birds of passage from abroad, and was hostile to collective forms of democratic practice like collective bargaining. Indeed, precisely because small businesses often live on the edge of commercial extinction, their labor practices are draconian with little regard for the democratic rights or well-being of their employees. Now and then staunch defenders of constitutional liberties, they are at the same time always on guard policing the walls of cultural and moral conformity and expect the iron hand of the state to make people do the right thing.

Its racial and social prejudices notwithstanding, this new populism appeals widely and sometimes with shocking force. The House majority leader, Virginia Republican congressman Eric Cantor, seemed a shoo-in to defeat his opponent in the Republican primary in 2014. He was, of course, supported by the party leadership, the Chamber of Commerce, and those with deep pockets. Cantor was running against David Brat, an obscure economics professor at Randolph Macon College who had virtually no money and no influentials in his corner. But he was backed by the Richmond Tea Party and echoed its complaints that Cantor had become spineless when it came to fighting immigration reform and especially crony capitalism. Brat lambasted the bank bailouts. He called Cantor a stooge for big business and fervently defended the free market. And he made clear that his economic views were also theological ones, that what he was championing was the Protestant work ethic and its salutary moral tutorial.

Brat knew what he was talking about. He had received a master's in divinity from the Princeton Theological Seminary where he wrote a thesis entitled "Human Capital, Religion, and Economic Growth." At a meeting of the Virginia Association of Community Banks, he had delivered a lecture on "The Moral Foundations of Capitalism: From the Great Generation to the Financial Crisis . . . What Went Wrong?" Brat sees himself as a reconstructed Calvinist. He questions whether Christianity could be reconciled with government welfare programs and puzzles over what he calls the relationship between "God and Advanced Mammon."[18]

HISTORY'S TWISTED ARROW

Is the Tea Party then the latest iteration of family capitalism at the barricades? Its preoccupation with fiscal probity and obsession with minimizing its own tax burden and starving the welfare state are certainly suggestive. Surveys demonstrate the presence of many small business owners in party ranks. They tend to be wealthier than average Americans and driven as much by their sense of moral and cultural exile as by their economic circumstances. By the election of 2010, 40 percent of elected Republicans came from the world of small business, and of those newly elected that year, 74 percent hailed from that world. Tea Party partisans in the Boston area see themselves as producers, as productive citizens living in a moral universe—a universe far away from that of the "freeloader," what used to be called back in the Gilded Age the "undeserving poor," especially illegal immigrants presumably living off the government (that is, taxpayers).[19]

Moreover, one need not be in business to get caught up in this romance of business. If most people nowadays work for wages, millions still dream of a business of their own, of a small competence, or even of something far grander that might make them masters of their fate. Our system of neoliberal, flexible capitalism seems to open up that possibility, in some cases to demand it. It converts onetime permanent employees into a precariously positioned mass of "free agents," engaged in a do-or-die adventure in self-re-creation. So too plenty of other dreamers are drawn from the ranks of hard-pressed lower-middle-class and working class people who drive cabs, do work as subcontractors, take care of children, fix cars, paint houses, and live on two credit cards and second mortgages. Many struggling workers imagine escaping hard times through a bootstrap startup and sometimes even manage to do so. This desire is practically a primordial part of the New World genotype. It has always loomed large on the imaginary landscape, present even predating Abraham Lincoln's vision of self-employment as the promised relief from the tedium, dependency, and material deprivations of wage labor.

Tenacious, this entrepreneurial romance also survives in the ranks of the professional middle classes and even within the dense networks of corporate bureaucracy. The manager was once invisible behind the featureless façade of the smoothly functioning organizational machine. Now he or she is encouraged to reconceive himself or herself as a mini venture capitalist, a source of innovation inside his or her specialized realm. The expectation makes him or her not a faceless functionary, but rather a distinctly specialized individual. Management-speak talks of commitment, drive, ambition, leadership, and control— as if managers were miniaturized captains of industry. From the dolorous precincts of the managerial bureaucracy to the hardscrabble streets of the ethnic barrio, from manicured Sunbelt suburban developments to the stressed-out warrens of the self-invented, the dream abides.[20]

10

The Dynasts

L imousine liberal is now an epithet stigmatizing multitudes. When it was born, however, it was an insult directed at a sliver of the rich and well-born, a tiny if powerful circle of patricians who had betrayed their birthright. Possessors of great wealth were not supposed to behave that way. If you drove a limousine (or more likely were driven around in one), it followed that you would naturally line up in defense of the status quo and deploy your economic and political throw-weight to defend or restore configurations of privilege and subordination as well as the moral and ideological justifications they invoked. And as a matter of fact, lately that logic has been on display in the most visible way. Public affairs now resonate to the strenuous efforts by newly minted billionaires to right the wrong done the country by limousine liberalism, to return the homeland to its foundations in free market economics, moral orthodoxy, and the heroics of untrammeled individualism. And so limousine liberalism confronts a rebirth of its original enemy, the enemy that first identified and attacked it decades before Mario Procaccino coined the term.

Observers of right-wing populism have sometimes treated it not as a grassroots movement, but rather as a form of AstroTurf politics invented and paid for by a relative handful of rich businessmen and their think tanks, foundations, and media outlets. Clearly, however, discontent (much of it quite well organized) with both the failures and successes of liberalism, has periodically bubbled to the surface of public life for a long time. The Tea Party is the latest articulation of what is a genuine not confected expression of popular political anger.

Nonetheless, it is also palpably true that powerful business circles have latched onto that upwelling from below and helped it prosper. Why not? The Koch brothers share with Tea Party partisans an aversion to taxes and government regulations, and see eye to eye on other practical matters. Something extramundane is also at work as well. However unalike in their material circumstances, these nouveau riche entrepreneurs are spiritually simpatico with the far more modestly provisioned middling sorts who make up the rank and file of right-wing populism. Business dynasts are living proof of a shared faith. It might be called a triumph of the will, a conviction deeply embedded in the American grain that self-reliance and self-invention are the birthright of the brave and the bold. That credo is offended to the core by limousine liberalism, as much by its hypocrisies as by the way it encourages a dependency on an overweening state.

Money talks loudly in America, too loudly, especially if the integrity of the elementary principles and institutions of democracy are to remain robust. So it is more than reasonable to worry about the extraordinary impact of dynastic fortunes on who gets elected and who doesn't, which laws get passed and which don't, which ideas get considered and which ones are smothered at birth. But this is also true about the outsized influence of the lobbyists working for the faceless corporation. What is distinctively noteworthy about our new dynasts is that they have found common ground on which to stand with their "little man" allies. Hostility to limousine liberalism, to its purported ways of life and beliefs, is the tie that binds, whatever other forms of material self-interest are also at work. Because they loom so large on the landscape, the dynasts embody and help empower a dream that never dies.

OUT OF THE ASHES

Cold facts record that precious few ever emerge as real captains of industry. Whether they start out as middle managers or supplement their blue collar day job with an off-the-books repair business, run a dental clinic and day trade at night, or post their shingle as a consultant while picking up freelance piecework designing software, they are most likely to end up where they started. Nonetheless, captains of industry have indeed established their conspicuous presence in the vanguard of the rebellion against limousine liberalism. Nor is this the first time. Henry Ford's peculiar career as an early crusader against Wall Street's corporate capitalism on behalf of family capitalism should remind us of that fact.

The tumultuous evolution of capitalism has repeatedly offered fresh possibilities to its family variety. And this includes its most grandiose form of the kind embodied by the Koch brothers, Sam Walton, or Sheldon Adelson. Heavyweight funders of Tea Party organizations tend to come from the ranks of newly minted billionaire business clans like the Coors family or the Koch brothers or Robert Mercer, the reclusive Long Island hedge fund billionaire backer of Ted Cruz once described by an associate as an automaton. They imagine themselves outsiders, which in a sense they are.

Nourished especially in the newer economies of the Sunbelt, founders of privately held enterprises in oil, natural gas, real estate, retail and service businesses, and regional finance outside the orbit of eastern corporate capitalism are a different breed than the cosmopolitans of the old order, those blue-blood establishment figures like Averill Harriman or John McCloy. And odd as it may seem, their upbringing and experiences as alpha males fending for themselves on the frontiers of economic derring-do makes them simpatico with legions of "little man" wannabes. Such self-made Napoleons can confront that world like small businesspeople on steroids.[1]

Just because you create (or inherit) a megaton private enterprise does not automatically make you a Tea Party sugar daddy. George Soros, Bill Gates, and Mark Zuckerberg, among others, deploy their financial throw-weight on behalf of causes obnoxious to the radical right. And they feel right at home communing with the bicoastal glitterati and hipsters who induce apoplexy among their heartland counterparts. Nonetheless, the conspicuous, even overbearing presence of our nouveau titans of business, most conspicuously if not exclusively on the right, in the hurly-burly of our political affairs, is striking. It suggests that while damaged and discredited, the institutional legacy of New Deal liberalism not only survives but continues to invite a peculiar and chronic opposition from those who, ironically, have made use of it to race to the top. Moreover, these back-to-the-future champions of the nineteenth century presume that their astonishing ascendancy and outsized wealth entitle them, in some moral sense, to direct and oversee the fate of the country. Such presumption reminds us that family capitalism can metastasize and encourage megalomania. It often has.

Superheroes populate the history of American business going back at least as far the nineteenth century. Then and now they adopt what we might call the imperial position. Titans of industry and finance during the Gilded Age—men like Cornelius Vanderbilt, Jay Gould, John D. Rockefeller, and George Pullman—often assumed that they had the right to supersede the law and tutor the rest of America on how best to order its affairs. They liked to play God. It's a habit that's returned with a vengeance in our own time.

The Koch brothers are only the most visible among a whole tribe of self-made billionaires who imagine themselves architects or master builders of a restorationist America, revamped and rehabilitated. The resurgence of what might be called dynastic capitalism (the megasized enterprise still under the dictate of the founding family), as opposed to the more impersonal managerial capitalism many of us grew up with, is changing the nation's political chemistry.

DREAM AND NIGHTMARE

This, then, is the indigenous romance of American capitalism. The man from nowhere becomes a Napoleon of business, and so a hero, because he confirms a cherished legend: namely, the primordial birthright of those lucky enough to live in the New World and to rise out of obscurity to unimaginable heights. All of this, so the legend tells us, comes through the application of disciplined effort, commercial cunning, and foresight, a take-no-prisoners competitive instinct, and a gambler's sangfroid in the face of the unforgiving riskiness of the marketplace. Master all of that and you deserve to be a master of our universe.

What makes the creation of the titan particularly confounding is that it seems as if it shouldn't be so. Inside the colorless warrens of the counting house and factory workshop, a pedestrian preoccupation with profit and loss might be expected to smother all those instincts we associate with the warrior, the statesman, and the visionary, not to mention the tyrant. As Joseph Schumpeter, the twentieth-century political economist, once observed, "There is surely no trace of any mystic glamour" about the sober-minded bourgeois. He is not likely to "say boo to a goose."

Yet the titan of capitalism overcomes that propensity. As Schumpeter put it, he transforms himself into the sort of man who can "bend a nation to his will," use his "extraordinary physical and nervous energy" to become "a leading man." Something happens through the experience of commercial conquest so intoxicating that it breeds a willful arrogance and a lust for absolute power. Call it the absolutism of self-righteous money.[2]

Sheldon Adelson, Charles and David Koch, Sam Walton, Rupert Murdoch, Linda McMahon, or hedge fund honchos like John Paulson and Robert Mercer all conform in one way or another to this historic profile. Powers to be reckoned with, they presume to know best what we should teach our kids and how we should do it: why and how to defend the borders against alien invasion, revitalize international trade, cure what ails the health care delivery system, create jobs where there are none, rejigger the tax code, balance the national budget, put truculent labor unions in their place, and keep the country on the moral and racial straight and narrow.

All this purported wisdom and self-assurance are homebred. That is to say, these people are first of all family or dynastic capitalists, not the faceless men in suits who climb their way up the greased pole that configures the managerial hierarchies of corporate America. Functionaries at the highest levels of the modern corporation may be just as wealthy, but they are a fungible bunch, whose loyalty to any particular outfit may expire whenever a more attractive package of stock options from another firm comes their way.

In addition, in our age of megamergers and acquisitions, corporations go in and out of existence with remarkable frequency, morphing into a shifting array of abstract acronyms. They are carriers of great power but without an organic attachment to distinct individuals or family lineages or regional loyalties. That's the genetic makeup that leaves them susceptible to the lures of limousine liberalism, to its moral elasticity and pragmatism, to its rubbery willingness to reform, to compromise, to jettison entirely the way things used to be if the winds of change demand it.

Instead dynasts of yesteryear and today have created family businesses or, as in the case of the Koch brothers and Rupert Murdoch, taken over one launched by their fathers to which they are fiercely devoted. They guard their business sanctuaries by keeping them private, wary of becoming dependent on outside capital resources that might interfere with their freedom to do what they please with what they've amassed.

And they think of what they've built up not so much as a pile of cash, but as a patrimony to which they are bound by ties of blood, religion, region, and race. These attachments turn ordinary business into something more transcendent. They represent the tissues of a way of life, even a philosophy of life. Its moral precepts about work, individual freedom, family relations, sexual correctness, meritocracy, equality, and social responsibility are formed out of the same process of self-invention that gave birth to the family business. Habits of methodical self-discipline and the nurturing and prudential stewardship that occasionally turn a modest competency into a propertied goliath encourage the instinct to instruct and command.

There is no Tycoon Party imposing ideological uniformity on a group of billionaires who, by their very nature as übermensch, march to their own drummers and differ on many matters. Some are philanthropically minded, others parsimonious. Some are pious, others are indifferent. Wall Street hedge fund creators may donate to Obama and be card-carrying social liberals on matters of love and marriage, while heartland types like the Koch brothers obviously take another tack politically. But all of them subscribe to one thing: a belief in their own omniscience and irresistible will.

THE GREAT U-TURN

Today's new tycoonery looming over public life might call to mind the legendary robber barons of the country's first Gilded Age. Certainly

Donald Trump's chest-thumping egomania has nothing on the braggadocio of "Jubilee" Jim Fisk, a daredevil speculator in railroads and gold around the time of the Civil War who once said about one of his financial debauches, "Nothing lost save honor." Such recollections might suggest that such figures always exerted a disproportionate and intensely personal influence over our political affairs. However, while there was no doubt a kindred sense of omnipotence detectable during both gilded ages, nineteenth-century business titans were nowhere near as invested in steering the political system, laying out its policies, shaping its ideology. Moreover, these larger-than-life heroes tended to fade from view beneath the onrushing wave of mergers and acquisition around the turn of the twentieth century that created the modern, publicly traded corporation. By and large the political economy of the middle decades of the twentieth century was dominated not by industrial and financial patriarchs but by modern concerns like US Steel, General Motors, and General Electric. Their corporate CEOs were more sensitive to the pressures of multiple constituencies. These included not only workers, but legions of shareholders, customers, suppliers, and local and regional public officials.

Publicly held corporations are, for the most part, "owned" not by a family, dynasty, or even a handful of business partners, but by a vast sea of shareholders. Those "owners" have little if anything to do with running "their" complex companies. This is left to a managerial cadre captained by lavishly rewarded chief executives. Their concerns are inherently political, but not necessarily ideological. They worry about their brand's reputation, have multiple dealings with a broad array of government agencies, look to curry favor with politicians from both parties, and are generally reasonably vigilant about being politically correct when it comes to matters of race, gender, and other socially sensitive issues. Behaving in this way is, after all, a marketing strategy that shows up where it matters most—on the bottom line.

Over the last several decades, however, history has done a U-turn. Old-style private enterprises of enormous size have made a remarkable comeback. Family capitalism has experienced a renaissance. Even giant firms are now often controlled by their owners the way Andrew Carnegie once captained his steelworks or Henry Ford his car company.

Some of these new family firms were once publicly traded corporations that went private thanks to a buyout craze initiated by private equity firms hungry for quick turnaround profits, firms like Mitt Romney's infamous Bain Capital. This might be thought of as entrepreneurial capitalism for the short term, a strictly finance-driven strategy that may now and then rescue an endangered enterprise, but more regularly rewards the private equity outsider.[3]

But giant family-based firms in it for the long haul have also proliferated and flourished in this era of economic turbulence. These are no longer stodgy, technologically antiquated outfits, narrowly dedicated to churning out a single, time-tested product. They are often, in fact, remarkably adept at responding to shifts in the market, often highly diversified in what they make and sell, and—thanks to the expansion of capital markets—enjoy a degree of financial independence not unlike that of their dynastic forebears of the nineteenth century that could rely on internally generated resources to keep free of the banks. Nor are they all small-fry mom and pop operations. One third of the Fortune 500 fall into the category of family-controlled.[4]

Family patriarchs, feet firmly anchored in their business fiefdoms, loom over the twenty-first-century landscape, reminiscent of the heyday of dynastic capitalism during the first Gilded Age. They exercise enormous political influence. They talk loudly and carry big sticks. Their money elects officials, finances their own campaigns for public office, and is reconfiguring our political culture by fertilizing a rain forest of think tanks, journals, and political action committees. A nation that a generation ago largely abandoned its historic resistance to organized wealth and power has allowed this newest version of the robber baron to dominate the public arena to a degree that might have astonished John Jacob Astor, Jay Gould, and Cornelius Vanderbilt.

THE POLITICAL IMPERATIVE

That ancestral generation, living in an era when the state was weak and kept on short rations, didn't need to be as immersed in political affairs. Contacting a kept senator or federal judge when needed was enough. Now, however, the modern regulatory and bureaucratic welfare state has extended its reach so far and wide that it needs to be steered, if not dismantled. Ideological fantasies notwithstanding, there never was a time when the invisible hand of the free market was left to its own devices, even in the golden era of laissez-faire capitalism in the nineteenth century. Even back then the government was relied on to build the infrastructure of a market economy—its roads, canals, wharves, waterworks, and the like—and to provide infant industry with tax exemptions, land grants, subsidies, and protection from foreign competition. But with the rise of the modern corporation as well as the social welfare and regulatory state, those functions increased exponentially. Much of that is essential to ensuring economic and social stability. Even those dynasts most passionate about their commitment to "living free," like Sam Walton was or the Koch brothers were or are, want to make sure governments at every level act on their behalf and don't do things that would injure their interests. They assume the state is here to stay even if trimmed down to size; the problem is guaranteeing that it behaves.

Some of our new tycoons try doing one thing or the other from offstage through a bevy of front organizations and hand-selected candidates for public office. Others dive right into the electoral arena themselves. Linda McMahon, who with her husband created the World Wide Wrestling entertainment empire, is a two-time loser in senate races in Connecticut. Rick Scott, a pharmaceutical entrepreneur, did better, becoming Florida's governor. Such figures, and other triumphalist types like them, claim their rise to business supremacy as their chief credential, often their only credential, when running for office or simply telling those holding office what to do.

Our entrepreneurial maestros come in a remarkable range of sizes and shapes. On style points, "the Donald" looms largest. Like so many nineteenth-century dynasts, his family origins are modest. A German grandfather who arrived here in 1885 was a winemaker, a barber, and a saloonkeeper in California; father Fred became the Henry Ford of homebuilding, helped along by New Deal low-cost housing subsidies. His son went after splashier, flashier enterprises like casinos, luxury resorts, high-end hotels, and domiciles for the 1 percent. In all of this, the family name, splashed on towers of every sort, and the Donald's image—laminated hairdo and all—became his company's chief asset.

Famous for nothing other than being very rich, Trump feels free to pronounce on every conceivable subject of public import, from same-sex marriage and deporting the undocumented to the geopolitics of the Middle East. Periodically, he tosses his hat into the electoral arena, as he did with astonishing impact during 2015. "We need somebody that can take the brand of the United States and make it great again," he announced when joining the sweepstakes for the Republican presidential nomination that year. He invariably and probably with deliberate forethought comports himself like a clown. He even has a game named after himself: *Trump—The Game,* whose play currency bears a likeness of the Donald's face and whose lowest denomination is $10 million. Craving attention so much he's willing to make himself ridiculous, the Donald is his own reality TV show.[5]

Rupert Murdoch, on the other hand, looks and dresses like an accountant and lives mainly in the shadows. Like Trump he inherited a family business. Unlike Trump, his family pedigree was auspicious. His father was Sir Keith, a media magnate from Melbourne, Australia, and Rupert went to Oxford. Now, the family's media influence straddles continents, as Rupert attempts—sometimes with great success—to make or break political careers and steer whole political parties to the right.

News Corporation is a dynastic institution of the modern kind in which Rupert uses relatively little capital and a complex company structure to maintain and vigorously exercise the family's control. Murdoch's empire may, on first glance, seem to conform to American-style managerial corporate capitalism: apparently rootless, cosmopolitan, fixed on the bottom line. In fact, it is tightly tethered to Murdoch's personality and conservative political inclinations and to the rocky dynamics of the Murdoch succession. That is invariably the case with our new breed of dynastic capitalists.[6]

Sheldon Adelson, the CEO of the Las Vegas Sands Corporation and sugar daddy of right-wing political wannabes from city hall to the White House, lacks Murdoch's finesse but shares his convictions and his outsized ambition to command the political arena. He's the eighth richest man in the world but grew up poor as a Ukrainian Jew living in the Dorchester neighborhood of Boston. His father was a cab driver, and his mother ran a knitting shop. He went to trade school to become a court reporter and was a college dropout. He started several small businesses that failed, and he won and lost fortunes. Then he gambled and hit the jackpot, establishing lavish hotels and casinos around the world. When he again lost big-time during the global financial implosion of 2007–2008, he responded the way any nineteenth-century sea-dog capitalist might have: "So I lost $25 billion. I started out with zero. . . . [There is] no such thing as fear, not to any entrepreneur. Concern yes. Fear, no."

A committed Zionist, Adelson was once a Democrat. But he jumped ship over Israel and because he believed the party's economic policies were ruining the country. (He's described Obama's goal as "a socialist-style economy.") He established the Freedom Watch foundation as a counterweight to George Soros's Open Society and to MoveOn.org. Adelson, according to one account, "seeks to dominate politics and public policy through the raw power of money." That means, for instance, that he backed Newt Gingrich in the Republican presidential primaries of 2012 against Mitt Romney, whom he denounced as a "predatory capitalist" (talk about the pot calling the kettle black), and then, not long after, he funneled cash to candidate Romney.[7]

Charles and David Koch are perfect specimens of this new breed of family capitalists on steroids. Koch Industries is a gigantic conglomerate headquartered in the heartland city of Wichita, Kansas. Charles, who really runs the company, lives there. David, the socially and philanthropically minded half of this fraternal duopoly, resides in New York City. Not unlike George "the Duke" Pullman did in creating the model town of Pullman in the late nineteenth century, Charles has converted Wichita into something like a company city, where criticism of Koch Industries is muted at best.

The firm's annual revenue is in the neighborhood of $10 billion, generated by oil refineries, thousands of miles of pipelines, paper towels, Dixie cups, Georgia-Pacific lumber, Lycra, and Stainmaster carpet, among other concerns. It is the second-largest privately owned company in the United States. (Cargill, the international food conglomerate, is first.) The brothers are inordinately wealthy, even for our new tycoonery. Only Warren Buffett and Bill Gates are richer.

While the average businessperson or corporate executive is likely to be pretty nonideological, the Koch brothers are dedicated libertarians. Their free market orthodoxy makes them adamant opponents of all forms of government regulation. Since their companies are among the top ten air polluters in the United States, that aversion to government meddling also comports well with their material interests. Self-interested or not, the Kochs come by their beliefs naturally, so to speak.

Their father, Fred, was the son of a Dutch printer who settled in Texas and started a newspaper. He later became a chemical engineer and invented a better method for converting oil into gasoline. In one of history's little jokes, he was driven out of the industry by the oil giants, who saw him as a threat. Today, Koch Industries is sometimes labeled "the Standard Oil of our time," an irony it's not clear the family would appreciate. After a sojourn in Joseph Stalin's Soviet Union (of all places) helping train oil engineers, Fred returned stateside to set up his own oil refinery business in Wichita. There, he joined the John Birch Society and ranted about the imminent communist takeover of the government. In that connection he was particularly worried that "the colored man looms large in the Communist plan to take over America."

Father Fred raised his sons in the stern regimen of the work ethic and instructed the boys in the libertarian catechism. This left them lifelong foes of the New Deal and every social and economic reform since. That included not only measures like government health insurance or social security, not to mention corporate taxes, but anything connected to the leviathan state. Even the CIA and the FBI are on the Koch chopping block.[8]

FREE MARKETS AND THE ALMIGHTY

Ideological to be sure, the Koch brothers are not, however, known for their religious seriousness, nor do they shy away from displays of omnipotence, what in another context might be deemed hubris. Indeed, humility, Christian humility, especially, and Napoleonic ambition seems an improbable concoction. Yet a circle of suddenly and stupendously wealthy entrepreneurs emerging after World War II engineered the bridge between evangelical proselytizing and the radical right.

So, for example, Lyman Stewart created the Union Oil Company and also the Church of the Open Door, dedicated to denouncing the hopeless secular perfectionism of the New Deal; FDR in his view was a forerunner of the Antichrist. J. Howard Pew, who inherited the Sun Oil Company (Sunoco) business from his father, felt likewise. He joined the anti–New Deal American Liberty League and spent his life warning about the insidious undermining of American freedom. For just that reason the family applauded the breakup of the Standard Oil monopoly by the Supreme Court in 1911.

Pew was raised as a devout Presbyterian. He and his wife lived modestly. His ambitions were more metaphysical and political. He wanted to save America. J. Howard and his siblings set up the Christian Freedom Foundation, itself supported by a dense network of family capitalist firms. He also established the Gordon-Conwell Theological Seminary in Massachusetts, the largest one in the Northeast, and helped create the American Enterprise Institute and the Hoover Institution. After J. Howard's death the family trusts moved far away from the founder's creed and in some instances became branches on the limousine liberal tree. But while he was alive, fusing evangelical theology and conservative political economy was the whole point.[9]

Following in Pew's footsteps other entrepreneurial patriarchs likewise sought to redeem the country. To this day the Bradley Foundation exercises as much or more financial throw-weight in conservative political and cultural circles than many more visible and voluble right-wing institutions. That is due to the pioneering efforts of its founding brothers, Lynde and Harry Lynde Bradley. Both high school dropouts in Milwaukee, they turned a two-man electrical shop into a giant manufacturer of electrical controls. A paternal firm, its employees were enrolled in the company's welfare programs and could participate in a house orchestra, sing in the chorus, and enjoy holiday fetes. Lynde died young in the 1940s. Both brothers were fierce anticommunists, and Harry Lynde was a charter member of the John Birch Society and Goldwater supporter. The foundation was created shortly after Harry Lynde's death in 1965. Since then it has invested in every conceivable right-wing political undertaking from school vouchers to antiunion activities. As one might guess, Scott Walker is a foundation favorite.[10]

George Pepperdine's parents were populists and crusaders for William Jennings Bryan in Kansas. Their son veered rightward. He started a retail auto parts store in Kansas City. Then he moved to Los Angeles, where he contracted tuberculosis. But his business boomed all along the West Coast. He called it the "Western Auto Family," and to work there and be part of the family you needed to be of good character and prove your will to serve. Adamantly antiunion, the "Western Auto Family" nonetheless practiced a kind of welfare capitalism: profit-sharing, stock options, and picnics. Wealthy beyond measure, Pepperdine deployed his resources to perfect a blend of Christianity and capitalism capable of fending off the secularized welfare state. Thus was born Pepperdine College in Los Angeles. Its purpose was to block the takeover of higher education by secular humanism and New Deal liberalism. Opened in 1937, its curriculum emphasized family values, saw them as part of Christ's plan for economic growth, and defended the traditional gender division of labor.[11]

Dynastic conservatism has sometimes taken a generation to mature. Sam Walton, like many of his nineteenth-century analogs, was not a political animal. He just wanted to be left alone to do his thing and deploy his power over the marketplace. So he stayed clear of electoral and party politics, although he implicitly relied on the racial, gender, and political order of the old South, which kept wages low and unions out, to build his business in the Ozarks. After his death in 1992, however, Sam's heirs entered the political arena in a big way.

In other respects Sam Walton conformed to type. He was impressed with himself, noting that "capital isn't scarce; vision is" (although his one-stop shopping concept was already part of the retail industry before he started Walmart). His origins were humble. He was born on a farm in Kingfisher, Oklahoma. His father left farming for a while to become a mortgage broker, which in the Great Depression meant he was a farm repossessor for Metropolitan Life Insurance. Sam did farm chores, then worked his way through college, and started his retail career with a small operation partly funded by his father-in-law.

At every juncture the firm's expansion depended on a network of family relations. Soon enough, his stores blanketed rural and small-town America. Through all the glory years, Sam's day began before dawn as he woke up in the same house he'd lived in for more than thirty years. Then, dressed in clothes from one of his discount stores, off he went to work in his red Ford pickup truck.

Some dynasts are pietistic, and some infuse their business with religion. Sam Walton did a bit of both. In his studiously modest lifestyle, there was also a kind of outward piety. Living without pretension, nose to the grindstone, and methodically building up the family patrimony has for centuries carried a sacerdotal significance, leaving aside any Protestant or other profession of religious faith. But there was professing as well. Though not a fundamentalist, he was a loyal member of the First Presbyterian Church in Bentonville, Arkansas, where he was a "ruling elder" and occasionally taught Sunday school (something he had done as well in college as president of the Burall Bible Class Club).

Christianity played a formative role in his labor relations strategy at Walmart. His employees, or as he dubbed them, his "associates," were drawn from an Ozark world of Christian fraternity, which Walmart management cultivated. "Servant leadership" was a concept designed to encourage workers to undertake their duties to serve the company's customers in the same spirit as Jesus, who saw himself as a "servant leader."

This could work to discourage animosities in the workforce, as well as the dangerous desire to do something about them through unionizing or in some other way that the company's decidedly subpar working conditions and wages might incite. An aura of Christian spiritualism plus company-scripted songs and cheers to instill company loyalty, profit-sharing schemes, and performance bonuses constituted a twentieth-century version of Pullman's town idyll.

All of this remained in place after Sam's passing in 1992. What changed was the decision of his fabulously wealthy relatives to enter the political arena. Walton lobbying operations now cover a broad range of issues, including lowering corporate taxes and getting rid of the estate tax entirely, as his heirs subsidize mainly Republican candidates and causes. Most prominent of all have been the Walton efforts to privatize education through vouchers and by other means, often enough turning public institutions into religiously affiliated schools.[12]

Becoming a modern-day robber baron doesn't automatically mean you go to church regularly or at all, nor does it make you a Tea Party funder. You may even subscribe to social liberalism and subsidize its desires. What is distinctive across party lines is only a sense of omnipotence and omniscience that comes with the territory. Wall Street, for example, has never been known for its piety. But the tycoons who founded the Street's most lucrative hedge funds—men like John Paulson, Paul Tudor Jones II, and Steve Cohen, among others—are also determined to upend the public school system. They are among the country's most powerful proponents of charter schools. Like J. P. Morgan of old, these men grew up in privilege, went to prep schools and the Ivy League, and have zero experience with public education or with the minorities who tend to make up a large proportion of charter school student bodies.

No matter. After all, some of these people make several million dollars a day. What an elixir! They are joined in this educational crusade by fellow business conquistadors of less imposing social backgrounds like Mark Zuckerberg and Bill Gates (Gates, however, although he didn't graduate Harvard, did get raised in a very wealthy family: his grandfather was a bank president, his father a prominent lawyer, and Bill attended an elite private school in Seattle). Zuckerberg has ensured that Facebook will remain a family domain even while "going public." Bill Gates is the most celebrated of a group of techno frontiersmen who—legend would have it—did their pioneering in homely garages, even though the wonders they invented would have been inconceivable without decades of government investment in military-related science and technology. What can't these people do? What don't they know? They are empire builders and liberal with their advice and money when it comes to managing the educational affairs of the nation. They also benefit handsomely from a provision in the tax code passed during the Clinton years that rewards them for investing in "businesses" like charter schools.[13]

Our imperial tycoons are a mixed lot. They range from hip technologists like Zuckerberg to heroic nerds like Gates, but include yesteryear traditionalists like Walton and the Koch brothers. So it is clear that extraordinary success in business is far from a surefire predictor of political allegiance. It is hard to imagine anyone less alike in that regard than the Koch brothers and George Soros. Indeed, the whole point of the original limousine liberal epithet was to highlight the strange phenomenon of wealthy elites championing the dispossessed and the discontented. After all, there have always been limousine conservatives. They were so taken for granted no one bothered to coin the phrase. What today's limousine liberal tycoons share with their more commonplace conservative counterparts is that godlike desire to recreate the world in their own image.

Watching someone play god may amuse us, as the Donald can do in an appalling sort of way. It is, however, a dangerous game with potentially deadly consequences for a democratic way of life already on life support.

Conclusion

The Strange Career of Limousine Liberalism

A re we living in an Alice in Wonderland *Through the Looking-Glass* world? Are Tea Party zealots the right-wing Jacobins of our times? Are the nouveau titans of business who are subsidizing the overthrow of the New Deal Order the subversive elites of the twenty-first century? Should we rechristen limousine liberals as limousine conservatives? After all, today's limousine liberals are defending the laws, institutions, cultural norms, and moral innovations that have governed the country for the past seventy-five years. Is the attempt to dismantle the regulatory and welfare state brick by brick a radical foray into some brave new world? Should we treat the quest by right-wing populists to return bygone social customs and moral conventions back to the way they were before the sixties happened as a kind of retro revolution?

Some might argue that the real agents of radical reform from above are the Koch brothers and their ilk. Like the elite entourage that surrounded Franklin Roosevelt and Lyndon Johnson, they make common cause with beleaguered members of the working and middle classes (if not with the dispossessed and undocumented). Together they mobilize to overthrow an ancient regime that has not only fostered the leviathan state but has poisoned the country's spiritual makeup; dominated its intellectual institutions; run its means of communication, information, and entertainment in the light of its own orthodoxies; and presumed to tutor the unenlightened on the most intimate matters of marriage, child-raising, dress, and deportment. Exercising that degree of global influence over the conduct and purposes of a society is what an establishment does. Dismantling it is what a radical opposition seeks to accomplish.

However appealing that formal analogy may be, it misperceives the nature of limousine liberalism and the movements that have challenged it. Right-wing populism, both as a grassroots rebellion and as a strategic démarche captained by the dynastic heroes of a revived family capitalism, has its feet firmly planted in the past. It is restorationist, not revolutionary. It opens no new roads into the future. It doesn't pretend to. Moreover, its political and moral imagination is profoundly nostalgic and enormously alluring in part for just that reason. What it wants restored never existed, but is instead a fanciful rendering of some self-consoling yesteryear; that is, after all, the seduction of nostalgia.

Limousine liberalism, on the other hand, is the capitalist version of permanent revolution. Naming it *revolution* exaggerates its actual intentions. Nonetheless, it captures something essential about how American society has wrestled with the menace of disorder and even economic and social chaos inherent in free market capitalism. Limousine liberalism was never a myth. Over time those who loathed what it represented did indeed fabricate absurd and scurrilous stories about its conspiratorial machinations and perfidious delinquencies. Those superstitions and tall tales made up the mythical dramaturgy with which to assail something that was on the contrary quite real: a desire on the part of empowered reform-minded elites to redo the way society was organized in order to reclaim social stability in the face of economic collapse as well as class and racial upheaval.

This might be called the American version of Tory socialism. Unlike its British and European cousins, our native variant lacked much in the way of a tradition of noblesse oblige that was common enough abroad, where a residue from centuries of aristocratic rule remained potent. So too, our American Tory socialists were more liberal than socialist. So they were less willing and, given the preeminence of the American economy, also didn't quite see the urgent need to go as far down the road of social welfare reform and even less urgency to socialize sectors of the economy as happened in postwar Europe. Still, they were prepared to leave the past behind rather than try and resurrect it.

So ancient pieties about limited government might continue to color the Democratic Party's annual Jefferson-Jackson Day oratory, but in real life the apparatus of the state grew and grew. It had to. How else to establish a semblance of social harmony in a society subject to periodic economic breakdown and fractured by class, racial, ethnic, regional, and religious suspicions and animosities except by creating a presumably disinterested bureaucratic mediator and referee? The Great Depression proved conclusively that the invisible hand seemed to have lost its magical powers. It became foolhardy to rely on the market to correct itself when it went haywire with frightening regularity. Economic dysfunction produced a chronic state of social unrest, class warfare, and a deep skepticism not only about the viability but about the humanity of capitalism. In the teeth of all that, leading circles of the old order nonetheless stuck by its maxims hoping the storm would pass. But others did not. They chose instead to minister to an ailing capitalism by subjecting it to what they believed to be the rational intervention of the state. They deployed the discoveries of the economic, social, and psychotherapeutic sciences to create a new political or state-supervised capitalism.

Engineering a new order changed the fundamental ground rules of capital accumulation. The skeletal framework of a truly national marketplace had emerged by the turn of the twentieth century. And the modern corporation had formed to service it. It was then that capital accumulation itself came to depend on the intricate interrelationship between the state and the private sector. Indeed, state bureaucracies in many respects imitated what had first emerged to coordinate the complex corporation. Legend might persist in treating the lone inventor and entrepreneur as the romantic genius of economic derring-do, innovation, and growth. But in most instances it took the resources of the multidivisional corporation in league with the fiscal wherewithal, scientific and technical expertise, geographic reach, and administrative coordination of governments at every level to generate and regulate a finely reticulated economic organism.

Modern capitalism recovered from its near terminal crisis of the 1930s by building up the musculature of the rationalizing bureaucracy. This left its mark on much more than country's economic and political institutions. Cultural assumptions about the role of the individual, about the efficacy of religion in civic life, about the nature of liberty and equality, and about the purposes of social organization all were reconceived. Individualism retained its sacred place in the country's folklore. But social engineering as an ethos preferred to think in utilitarian terms about anonymous collectivities. While the nation ritually celebrated its existence "under God," the new order was secular to the bone. Tales of entrepreneurial audacity affirmed that freedom was capitalism's most cherished product. But the actual marketplace was a manipulated arena dominated by oligopolies and agencies of the state. Sovereignty was purportedly vested in the consumer, but his or her "choices" were prefabricated by Madison Avenue technicians of the psyche. The caste system had always rested on notions of inferiority that had once enjoyed some support from the biological sciences. Now science turned its back. Racial equality, rather than the juridical codes of apartheid and informal compacts of white privilege, comported better with the impersonal calculations of the mass market and mass culture. Images of masculine heroism and command continued to entertain multitudes. But the patriarchy that was all but synonymous with nineteenth-century family capitalism lost its grip in the neutered new world of the two-wage-earner home and social work family planning bureaucracy. Democracy was still what the nation sent soldiers to die for, but at home the sinews of actual popular participation in the decisions that determined daily life withered under the watch of state apparatchiks.

Limousine liberalism surfaced as a particularly striking metaphor and epithet (if not the first one) to register the hostility of middling classes to this alarming new social reality. It is the unwanted stepchild of the political capitalism that supplanted its laissez-faire predecessor. Millions have been mobilized by its lush imagery, its self-righteousness, its manly bravado, its devotional commitment to a familial homeland writ large, and its faith in the liberationist metaphysics of the free market. They relish exposing the real and imputed hypocrisies of privileged sophisticates. But in the end, they are reacting both to the successes and the failures of what the modern capitalist order has wrought. Neither suit them yet they are ensnared in both, hence the logic behind the illogical demand that the government keep its hands off Medicare. Consumerism delights but also demoralizes. Racial prejudice lives but in shame. Shrines are erected to the patriarchal family even as it dissolves where it is most worshipped.

Modern liberalism, the liberalism of the New Deal that continued on into the Great Society, once was a populism in its own right. Its ideology and programmatic innovations enlisted the sympathies of the "little man," if sometimes with ambivalence. It has become a hollowed-out vacuum of its earlier self, however. The "little man" finds no home there. The American two-party system makes it especially difficult for such discontent to find forthright political articulation. Often this has been singled out as a great benefit of the country's political genius, functioning as a prophylactic against political polarization, an insurance policy against social instability. Amorphously constituted, the two parties rigorously eschew ideology. Doing this tends to anesthetize opposition. It tempts or coerces movements of discord to sacrifice passion and principle at the altar of the voting booth. The political independence pursued by right-wing insurgents during the Great Depression amounts to pretty definitive evidence that, in the United States at least, attempting to break free of the smothering embrace of the two-party duopoly is a dead end.

This is less the case abroad. There parliamentary arrangements open up space for parties of the middling classes, small business-people, white collar workers, professionals, and others. They, too, have their limousine liberals—Tory socialists in Britain, "champagne socialists" in France—to contend with. These parties of the "little man" mix together serial animosities against immigrants and Euro-banks, against the welfare state and against free trade, against moral laissez-faire yet against centralized authority. The Tea Party is a roughly approximate attempt to do the same in an American context. It is avowedly ideological. Yet it remains within the Republican Party. Strong enough to have shifted that party's center of gravity to the right, even to have lent it more of an ideological edge than the GOP normally feels comfortable conveying, today's "little man" rebels against limousine liberalism walk a fine line.

Elites are always good at organizing on their own behalf. They have the resources. So they make their political will known and respected. But so too have far less advantaged wage laborers managed to mobilize and create a coherent presence in the political universe, at least until the last half century of demobilization and decline. Even the African American mudsills of American life working its cotton fields, surviving in its urban barrios, have despite everything managed to civilize the political order according to their own vision of the right and the just. By and large that has not been the case for the social midsection of American society. Not quite the sack of potatoes to which Marx once likened the political shapelessness of the French peasantry, still the political aspirations and ideological leanings of our society's vast middling strata have remained fuzzy. Limousine liberalism, both as a social reality and animating myth, is a portentous development in part because it breaks that mold.

The social and emotional makeup and political objectives of neither the Tea Party nor its predecessors can be summed up as a single-minded devotion to family capitalism. They were and are as likely to capture the enthusiasm of the small shopkeeper as the patriarchal pride of the dynast, to flatter the dignity of the skilled mechanic while slandering his union, and to denounce big government while depending on it. Still the faith, the ambition, and the anxieties of family capitalism touched them all.

Rebellions against limousine liberalism have been too protean, chaotic, and fed by too many cultural and social and religious subcurrents to be reduced to family capitalism redux. Tea Party partisans scout the landscape for enemies that threaten their way of life or the way of life they imagine once existed and want restored. They are heirs of a long populist tradition indigenous to the American experience and also one not confined to the New World. However, the censure their ancestors once directed at plunderers, Molochs, Judases, plutocrats, and Pharaohs is no longer as inviting an option. Limousine liberals remain in their crosshairs, but the brunt of their fury is aimed rather at the lowly, whom the limousine liberal patronizes.

Many are the lowly and the resented: illegal immigrants perhaps, or the morally dissolute, or those living on the dole, or the racially suspect. After the 2008 market crash, a CNBC market correspondent captured the mean-spiritedness. In an outraged Wall Street state of mind, he declaimed: "This is America. How many of you want to pay for your neighbor's mortgage that has an extra bathroom and can't pay the bills?" Soon enough this piece of Social Darwinism became a recurring feature of Tea Party signage: "Your mortgage is not my problem." All of these "losers" and more may be enlisted in the army captained by limousine liberalism. And to that foe, before all others, Glenn Beck says, "Don't tread on me."[1]

Predicting the future of limousine liberalism—both as fact and fable—is unwise. It won't be decided by the 2016 presidential election. Whether the emotions it has elicited will grow more sour and politically strident, whether instead they will succumb to the tidal currents pulling formations like the Tea Party into the maw of two-party neoliberal consensus, is unknowable. But this in-between and often mysterious world that otherwise exists in plain sight has made its presence felt.

Acknowledgments

This is a history of an epithet: limousine liberal. The potency of that anathema has endured for a half century. When I was writing my previous book *The Age of Acquiescence,* I wondered at this denunciation's extraordinary ability to mobilize people on the right wing of the country's political spectrum. That earlier book contained a chapter about the Tea Party and its antecedents, political movements whose emotional and ideological heat have been in part generated by a hostility to an oddly configured public figure widely pilloried as the limousine liberal. I thought then it might be worth probing the shifting meaning and makeup of this political metaphor more closely to uncover where it came from and why it has lasted so long.

Even before writing that chapter, I had composed an essay called "The Limousine Liberal's Family Tree," which appeared in the *Raritan Review*. I want to thank its editor, Jackson Lears, for allowing me the space to air my first thoughts on this subject and for his editorial advice.

For various reasons I wrote *The Limousine Liberal* more quickly than I have other books. When I finished with a draft, my publisher was eager to have it see the light of day sooner than later. My most discerning critic, my wife, Jill, had read it all along and given me much good advice for which as always I am immensely grateful. But at that point, no one else had read it. So I want to express my special thanks to several friends who dropped everything to read part or all of it very quickly and with no advance notice. I owe a big debt to Josh Freeman, Rochelle Gurstein, and Paul Milkman. In addition, I want to acknowledge here (as well in the notes) how much I have relied on the work of many fellow historians and other scholars who have developed a great body of literature over the past generation that allows people like me to better grasp the complex nature of the conservative ascendancy in American politics. This book would not be possible without their efforts.

Dan Gerstle inspires hope for the future of book publishing. He is a creative, discerning, meticulous, and challenging editor; an intellectual without a pointy head; and a true book lover. I have known Dan awhile, and it is a special pleasure to me that he occupies a position I once held as an editor at the same publishing house I once worked for. Nor is that a coincidence I think. Basic Books remains one of those publishing houses dedicated to increasing the sphere of communication between scholars and the wider reading public. I want to thank project editor Shena Redmond for guiding my manuscript through the production process and Deb Heimann for her careful copyediting. And to publisher Lara Heimert a thanks for welcoming me home.

No book happens without the support of family. My son, Max, and I now talk over our mutual interests in American history and politics, and I learn from him and value his judgment. My daughter, Emma, has grown up to be a remarkably brave and persevering woman, and I try to emulate her will to keep going when things get difficult. We have recently had an addition to the family, my daughter-in-law, Elena, whom we all love. Jill and I feel fortunate to have them all by our side, and I am especially lucky to have Jill.

Notes

Introduction

1. Curtis Klein, "The Era of the Limousine Liberal Is Back," CNSN News.com, June 2, 2014; "Limousine Liberal," Urban Dictionary, accessed October 23, 2015, http://www.urbandictionary.com; Dr. John, "100 Million Reasons Not to Vote for Hillary," *Flopping Aces,* January 6, 2014, http://www.floppingaces.net/2014/01/06/100-million-reasons-not -to-vote-for-hillary/; Charles Krauthammer, "Another View," *Washington Post,* April 19, 2015, http://www.washingtonpost.com/opinions/the -queen-travels-by-van/2015/04/16/4ca7c956-e46c-11e4-b510-962fcfabc 310_story.html; Jennifer Epstein, "Hillary Clinton Begins Courting the Plutocrats," Bloomberg Politics, May 8, 2015, http://www.bloomberg .com/politics/articles/2015-05-08/hillary-clinton-s-big-donor-paradox; David Sirota, "More 2016 Candidates Embrace the Donald Trump Zeitgeist," Truthdig.com, June 24, 2015; "Young Republicans to Protest Sanders Speaking to Arlington Limousine Liberals," *Richmond Sun Times,* July 7, 2015.

2. Rocco DiPippo, "Al Gore and the Limits of Recycling," RealClear Politics, June 2, 2006; Charles Krauthammer, "Limousine Liberal Hypocrisy," *Time,* March 16, 2007; W. James Antle III, "Limousine Liberal: Richard Blumenthal Chases Ambulances All the Way to the Senate," *American Spectator,* May, 2010; Arit John, "Bill de Blasio, the Speeding

Limousine Liberal, Also Jaywalks," The Wire.com, February 24, 2014; Grey Fedora, "Mass Transit and Limousine Liberals," *Daily Kos,* November 24, 2013; Jordan Michael Smith, "Why Do Conservatives Hate Soy Lattes and Striped Pants So Much?" *Politico,* January 9, 2014; Joan Vennochi, "Liberal and a Pickup Truck," *Boston Globe,* September 9, 2012.

3. A. J. Delgado, "Ben Affleck and the Disease of Feel-Good Limousine Liberalism," Mediaite, April 25, 2013; "'Grandstanding Limousine Liberal': Gwyneth Paltrow Vows to Live on SNAP Budget," Twitchy, April 11, 2015, twitchy.com/2015/04/11/grandstanding-limousine-liberal -gwyneth-paltrow-vows-to-live-on-snap-budget; Rich Lowry, "The New Limousine Liberals," townhall.com, February 28, 2003, http://townhall .com/columnists/richlowry/2003/02/28/the_new_limousine_liberals.

4. Krauthammer, "Limousine Liberal Hypocrisy,"; Catherine Rampell, "Limousine Liberalism's Good Works," *Washington Post,* July 7, 2014; Charles Gasparino, "Don't Cry for Wall Street," *New York Post,* February 18, 2014; Daniel Denvir, "Segregation in the Land of Limousine Liberalism," Salon, July 1, 2011, http://www.salon.com/2011/07/01 /denvir_westchester_segregation/; Carlos Lozada, "The Radical Chic of Ta-Nehisi Coates," *Washington Post,* July 16, 2015; Gaius, "Rise of the Limousine Liberals," Blue Crab Boulevard, December 2, 2007.

Chapter 1: In the Beginning Was the Word

1. Godfrey Hodgson, "John V. Lindsay," *The Guardian,* December 20, 2000; Laurence Van Gelder, "Mario Procaccino, 83, Who Lost to Lindsay in 1969, Dies," *New York Times,* December 21, 1995.

2. Mario Procaccino quoted in Vincent J. Cannato, *The Ungovernable City: John Lindsay and His Struggle to Save New York* (New York: Basic Books, 2002), 428, 1–5, 9, 11–12; US Riot Commission, *Report of the National Advisory Commission on Civil Disorders* (New York: Bantam Books, 1968).

3. Jim Sleeper, *The Closest of Strangers: Liberalism and the Politics of Race in New York* (New York: Norton, 1990), 62, 147–148; Joshua B. Freeman, *Working Class New York: Life and Labor Since World War II* (New York: New Press, 2000), 197–198; Cannato, *Ungovernable City.*

4. Freeman, *Working Class New York,* 219, 226; Cannato, *Ungovernable City,* 23, 41, 43, 64, 74, 399, 442; Jack Newfield quoted in Cannato, *Ungovernable City,* 20.

5. *New York Times* quoted in Cannato, *Ungovernable City,* 442; Tom Wolfe, "Radical Chic: The Party at Lenny's," *New York,* June 8, 1970, 5, 19; "False Note on Black Panthers," *New York Times,* January 16, 1970.

6. "New York: The Revolt of the Average Man," *Time,* October 3, 1969; Freeman, *Working Class New York,* 197–198, 211–213, 234, 254.

7. Robert Coles quoted in Cannato, *Ungovernable City,* 393; Whitney Young quoted in Cannato, *Ungovernable City,* 394, 17nL; "New York: The Revolt of the Average Man."

8. "New York: The Revolt of the Average Man"; Lillian Rose, "Procaccino Campaigning," *The New Yorker,* September 27, 1969; Maria C. Lizzi, "My Heart Is as Black as Yours: White Backlash, Racial Identity, and Italian American Stereotypes in New York City's 1969 Mayoral Campaign," *Journal of American Ethnic History* 27 (Spring 2008): 43; Cannato, *Ungovernable City,* 4, 391–392, 404.

9. "New York: The Revolt of the Average Man"; Cannato, *Ungovernable City,* 52, 392, 404, 427, 428; Lizzi, "My Heart Is as Black as Yours"; Joan Walsh, "John Lindsay, Ed Koch, and the End of Liberalism," Salon, February 4, 2013, http://www.salon.com/2013/02/04/john_lindsay_ed _koch_and_the_end_of_liberalism/; Nicholas Pileggi, "The More the Mario," *New York* (magazine), April 14, 1969, 34–37; Freeman, *Working Class New York,* 246.

Chapter 2: Bankers, Bolsheviks, and Jews

1. Ian Millhiser, "Five Conspiracy Theories 2016 Hopeful Ted Cruz Actually Believes," Think Progress, May 1, 2013; Brian Tashman, "Tea Party Movement Is Full of Conspiracy Theories," *Newsweek,* February 8, 2010.

2. T. Jefferson, "American Progressivism," Glenn Beck.com, April 16, 2009, http://www.glennbeck.com/content/articles/article/198/23936/.

3. "Glenn Interviews 'The Creature from Jekyll Island' Author G. Edward Griffin," YouTube, March 25, 2011; Dana Milbank, "Why Glenn Beck Lost It," *Washington Post,* April 6, 2011; "Beck Explains Why the Federal Reserve Is a Complete 'Scam,'" The Blaze, June 22, 2012, http:// www.theblaze.com/stories/2012/06/11/beck-explains-why-the-federal -reserve-is-a-complete-scam/.

4. Jean Strouse, *Morgan: American Financier* (New York: Perennial, 2000), 595; Richard N. Sheldon, "The Pujo Committee on the 'Money

Trust,' 1912–13," in Arthur Schlesinger Jr. and Roger Bruns, eds., *Congress Investigates: A Documented History, 1792–1974* (New York: Chelsea House, 1975), 2251; James Dill quoted by James Livingston, *Origins of the Federal Reserve System: Money, Class, and Corporate Capitalism, 1890–1913* (Ithaca, NY: Cornell University Press, 1986), 31.

5. Steve Fraser, *Every Man a Speculator: A History of Wall Street in American Life* (New York: Harper Collins, 2005), 369; *The International Jew* (Dearborn, MI: The Dearborn Independent, 1922), originally a series of articles published in *The Dearborn Independent* between 1920 and 1922 under the title "The Jewish Question"; Albert Lee, *Henry Ford and the Jews* (New York: Stein and Day, 1980), 7, 8, 14, 16, 45, 47, 49, 59; Leo P. Ribuffo, "Henry Ford and the 'International Jew,'" *American Jewish History* 69, no. 4 (June 1980): 437–477; David L. Lewis, "Henry Ford: Anti-Semitism—Its Repercussions," *Michigan Journal of History* 24 (January 1984): 3–10; Michael N. Dobkowski, *The Tarnished Dream: The Basis of Anti-Semitism* (Westport, CT: Greenwood Press, 1979), 196–200; David H. Bennett, *The Party of Fear: From Nativist Movements to the New American Right in American History* (Chapel Hill: University of North Carolina Press, 1988), 205.

6. Armin Pfal-Traughber, *Der Antisemitisch-anti-freimaurerische Versuch Warungen Mythos in der Weimar Republik und in NS-Staat* (Vienna: Braunmiller, 1933), 39; Adolf Hitler, *Mein Kampf* (New York: Houghton Mifflin, 1943), 639.

7. Robert Murray, *Red Scare: A Study in National Hysteria, 1919–20* (Minneapolis: University of Minnesota Press, 1955); Cameron McWhirter, *Red Summer: The Summer of 1919 and the Awakening of Black America* (New York: Henry Holt, 2011; Emma Goldman, *Living My Life*, 1931 reprint (New York: Arno Press, 1970), 716–717; "Mother Jones Urges Strikers to Violence," *The New York Times*, October 24, 1919; *Chicago Tribune*, October 24, 1919; General Wood quoted in *The American Schoolmaster*, vol. 13, Michigan State Normal College, January 1920; Palmer quoted in "The Postwar Red Scare," Digital History, http://www.digitalhistory.uh.edu/disp_textbook.cfm?smtid=2&psid=3381; Billy Sunday quoted in William E. Leuchtenberg, *The Perils of Prosperity, 1914–32* (Chicago: University of Chicago Press, 1958), 66.

8. William Jennings Bryan quoted in brainy.quote.com, accessed November 16, 2015, http://www.brainyquote.com/quotes/quotes/w/william jen402507.html; *Time*, June 20, 1926; "The Great Trial," *Life*, June 18, June 25, July 2, 1925; William V. Trallinger Jr., *God's Empire: William*

Bell Riley and Midwestern Fundamentalism (Madison: University of Wisconsin Press, 1991); Christopher K. Curtis, "Mississippi's Anti-Evolution Law of 1926," *Journal of Mississippi History* 48 (1986): 15–29; R. Halliburton, "The Adoption of Arkansas' Anti-Evolution Law," *Arkansas Historical Quarterly* 23 (Autumn 1964): 271–283; Edward J. Larson, *Summer for the Gods: The Scopes Trial and America's Continuing Debate over Science and Religion* (New York: Basic Books, 1997).

9. "The Ku Klux Klan," Digital History, http://www.digitalhistory .uh.edu/disp_textbook.cfm?smtID=2&psid=3386; Trevor Griffey, "The Washington State Klan in the 1920s," Seattle Civil Rights and Labor History Project, http://depts.washington.edu/civilr/kkk_history.htm; Bennett, *Party of Fear,* 216–217; David M. Chalmers, *Hooded Americanism: The History of the Ku Klux Klan* (Durham: Duke University Press, 1986).

10. Karl Marx and Friedrich Engels, *Manifesto of the Communist Party* (1848).

Chapter 3: Fear Itself

1. David Greenberg, *Calvin Coolidge: The American Presidents Series: The 30th President, 1923–1929* (New York: Henry Holt, 2006), 153.

2. Franklin Roosevelt quoted in John Brooks, *Once in Golconda: A True Drama of Wall Street, 1920–1938* (New York: Harper and Row, 1969), 156; Franklin Roosevelt quoted in Jordan A. Schwarz, *Liberal: Adolph Berle and the Vision of an American Era* (New York: Free Press, 1987), 108.

3. Franklin Roosevelt quoted in Kevin Phillips, *Wealth and Democracy: A Political History of the American Rich* (New York: Broadway Books, 2002), 71; Franklin Delano Roosevelt, *Looking Forward* (New York: John Day, 1933), 44–45.

4. Ferdinand Lundberg, *America's Sixty Families* (New York: Citadel Press, 1937), 452, 461–463; Nelson W. Aldrich Jr., *Old Money: The Mythology of America's Upper Class* (New York: Knopf, 1988), 234; Leo P. Ribuffo, *The Old Christian Right: The Protestant Far Right from the Great Depression to the Cold War* (Philadelphia: Temple University Press, 1988), 15, 16; Russell Leffingwell quoted in Charles R. Geisst, *Wall Street: From Its Beginnings to the Fall of Enron* (New York: Oxford University Press, 2004), 235–236; Richard Whitney quoted in Brooks, *Once in Golconda,* 143, 220; Robert Winsome, "Wall Street: Reply to the Senate Investigation," *Literary Digest,* July 22, 1933; American Liberty League

quoted in Ferdinand Pecora, *Wall Street Under Oath: The Story of Our Modern Money Changers* (New York: A. McKellen, 1973), 297.

5. William H. Wilson, "How the Chamber of Commerce Viewed the NRA: A Re-examination," *Mid America* (April 1962), 95–108; Gerard Swope, "Reminiscences," Oral History Collection of Columbia University, 20–22; George Frederick, ed., *The Swope Plan: Details, Criticisms, Analysis* (New York: The Business Bourse, 1931), 21–25, 67–68, 80–81.

6. Rexford G. Tugwell, *The Brains Trust* (New York: Viking, 1968), 20; Robert S. McElvaine, *The Great Depression: America, 1929–1941* (New York: Times Books, 1984), 92; Steven Fraser, *Labor Will Rule: Sidney Hillman and the Rise of American Labor* (New York: Free Press, 1991), chapter 10; William J. Barber, *From New Era to New Deal: Herbert Hoover, The Economists, and American Economic Policy, 1921–1933* (New York: Cambridge University Press, 1985), 57; Patrick D. Regan, "The Architects of American National Planning," PhD diss., Ohio State University, 1982, 211–212, 215, 253, 304; Edward Filene to Edgar Rich, February 10, 1928, "Unemployment" file, Edward A. Filene Papers, Credit Union National Association, Madison, Wisconsin; William A. Bremer, *Depression Winters: New York Social Workers and the New Deal* (Princeton, NJ: Princeton University Press, 1984), 54–57.

7. David H. Bennett, *Demagogues in the Depression: American Radicals and the Union Party, 1932–1936* (New Brunswick, NJ: Rutgers University Press, 1969), 118, 124, 125; William Ivy Hair, *The Kingfish and His Realm: The Life and Times of Huey Long* (Baton Rouge: Louisiana State University Press, 1996); T. Harry Williams, *Huey Long* (New York: Knopf, 1970); Colin Gordon, ed., *Major Problems in American History, 1920–1945* (Boston: Houghton Mifflin, 1999), 374–375; Alan Brinkley, *Voices of Protest: Huey Long, Father Coughlin, and the Great Depression* (New York: Knopf, 1982), 40, 41, 71, 117; Hodding Carter, "How Come Huey Long?" *The New Republic*, February 13, 1935, 11–15; Long cited in Christian Roselund, "Remembering Huey Long," *The Brooklyn Rail*, March 6, 2009, and Huey P. Long radio broadcast, January 14, 1935; H. W. Brands, *Traitor to His Class: The Privileged Life and Radical Presidency of Franklin Delano Roosevelt* (New York: Doubleday, 2008), 260.

8. Ribuffo, *Old Christian Right*, 134–135, 138, 142, 144; Bennett, *Demagogues*, 252, 253, Bennett, *Party of Fear*, 246; Seymour Martin Lipset and Ed Raab, *The Politics of Unreason: Right Wing Extremism in America, 1790–1970* (New York: Harper and Row, 1970), 170–171, 182–183; Gerald L. K. Smith quoted in Bennett, *Demagogues*, 11.

9. Bennett, *Demagogues,* 34, 40, 51, 59, 64–65, 192, 230; Bennett, *Party of Fear,* 254; "Roosevelt or Ruin Asserts Radio Priest at Hearing," *Washington Post,* January 17, 1934; Charles E. Coughlin, *Father Charles E. Coughlin's Radio Sermons Complete, October 1930–April 1931* (Baltimore, MD: Know and O'Leary, 1931); Charles E. Coughlin, *Father Coughlin's Radio Discourses, 1931–1932* (Royal Oak, MI: Radio League of the Little Flower, 1932); Charles E. Coughlin, *Money! Questions and Answers* (National Union for Social Justice, 1936); Charles E. Coughlin, "Driving Out the Money Changers," radio broadcast, April 18, 1933.

10. Bennett, *Demagogues,* 40, 51, 60, 62, 78, 230; Charles J. Tull, *Father Coughlin and the New Deal* (Syracuse, NY: Syracuse University Press, 1965), 66–67, 91; Brinkley, *Voices of Protest;* Bennett, *Party of Fear,* 257–259.

11. Bennett, *Demagogues,* 227; Bennett, *Party of Fear,* 263. See also Tull, *Father Coughlin,* 193, 197.

12. Edwin Amenta, *When Movements Matter: The Townsend Plan and the Rise of Social Security* (Princeton, NJ: Princeton University Press, 2006); Bennett, *Demagogues,* 102, 158–159, 164, 166.

13. Bennett, *Demagogues,* 102, 104, 105, 121, 124, 235, 252–253.

14. Tull, *Father Coughlin,* 66–67, 91, 151–152; Brinkley, *Voices of Protest;* Charles E. Coughlin, *Sixteen Radio Lectures, 1938 Series* (self-published, 1938); George Q. Flynn, *American Catholics and the Roosevelt Presidency, 1932–36* (Lexington: University of Kentucky Press, 1968), 203; FDR quoted in Aldrich, *Old Money,* 234; Seymour Martin Lipset, "Three Decades of the Radical Right: Coughlinites, McCarthyites, and Birchers," in Daniel Bell, ed., *The Radical Right* (New York: Anchor Books, 1964).

Chapter 4: All in the Family

1. Richard Hofstadter, *The Paranoid Style in American Politics and Other Essays* (Cambridge, MA: Harvard University Press, 1964).

2. Walter Isaacson and Evan Thomas, *The Wise Men: Six Friends and the World They Made* (New York: Simon and Schuster, 1986), 28–29, 91, 108; Biographical sketches of Winthrop Aldrich, James Forrestal, Averill Harriman, Robert Lovett, Robert Patterson, and Henry Stimson in Susan Ware, ed., *American National Biography* (New York: Oxford University Press, 1999), online version is available at www.anb.org/; David H. Bennett, *Party of Fear: From Nativist Movements to the New American Right*

in American History (Chapel Hill: University of North Carolina Press, 1988), 290; Richard Hofstadter, *The Age of Reform* (New York: Vintage, 1955), 163, 253.

3. Arthur Schlesinger Jr. quoted in Isaacson and Thomas, *The Wise Men*, 29.

4. Daniel Yergin, *Shattered Peace: The Origins of the Cold War and the National Security State* (Boston: Houghton Mifflin, 1978), 306–307.

5. Kai Bird, *The Chairman: John J. McCloy—The Making of an American Establishment* (New York: Simon and Schuster, 1992), 298 and see 108, 110, 131, 230, 233, 273, 285, 288, 291, 297–298; John Judis, *The Paradox of American Democracy: Elites, Special Interests, and the Betrayal of Public Trust* (New York: Pantheon, 2000), 72.

6. Averill Harriman quoted in Eric Hobsbawm, *The Age of Extremes: A History of the World, 1914–1991* (New York: Pantheon, 1994), 273.

7. E. Digby Baltzell, *The Protestant Establishment: Aristocracy and Caste in America* (New York: Random House, 1964), passim.

8. C. Wright Mills, *The Power Elite* (New York: Oxford University Press, 2000), 84, 91–93; Isaacson and Thomas, *Wise Men*, 106, 109; Nelson W. Aldrich, *Old Money: The Mythology of America's Upper Class* (New York: Knopf, 1988), 63, 105; Baltzell, *Protestant Establishment*; Jackson Lears, "The Managerial Revitalization of the Rich," in Steve Fraser and Gary Gerstle, eds., *Ruling America: A History of Wealth and Power in a Democracy* (Cambridge, MA: Harvard University Press, 2005); Henry James quoted in Jane Mulvaugh and Roberto Schezen, *Newport Houses* (New York: Rizzoli, 1989), 9; Thomas Gannon and Richard Cheek, *Newport Mansions: The Gilded Age* (Newport, RI: The Preservation Society of Newport, 1992), 5, 18; Perry Anderson, *The Origins of Postmodernity* (London, UK: Verso, 1998), 62–63, 82.

9. *New York* magazine quoted by Bird, *The Chairman*, 619–620.

10. David M. Oshinsky, *A Conspiracy So Immense: The World of Joe McCarthy* (New York: Macmillan, 1983), 92, 99.

11. Ibid.

12. Senator Taft quoted in Bird, *The Chairman*, 389; Senator McCarthy quoted in Bird, *The Chairman*, 415; Senator McCarthy quoted in Oshinsky, *A Conspiracy*, 108–109; Senator McCarthy quoted in Richard Polenberg, *One Nation Divisible: Class, Race, and Ethnicity in the United States Since 1938* (New York: Viking, 1988), 125; Paul Nitze quoted in Isaacson and Thomas, *Wise Men*, 564; Dean Acheson, *Present at the Creation* (New York: Norton, 1969), chapter 39—"The Attack of the

Primitives Begins," and 366, 369, 370; Senator Taft quoted in Donald T. Critchlow, *Phyllis Schlafly and Grassroots Conservatism: A Woman's Crusade* (Princeton, NJ: Princeton University Press, 2005), 46; Oshinsky, *A Conspiracy*, 261, 289–291, 292; Bennett, *Party of Fear*, 290; Congressional Record, 81st Congress, Second Session, February 20, 1950, 1954–1956.

13. Ribuffo, *Old Christian Right*, 228; Oshinsky, *A Conspiracy*, 323–324.

14. Oshinsky, *A Conspiracy*, 196, 289–291.

15. Bennett, *Party of Fear*, 299.

16. Ibid., 294, 296, 313.

17. Oshinsky, *A Conspiracy*, 210, 243; Lipset, "Three Decades"; Lukacs quoted in Kevin Pask, "Mosaics of American Nationalism," *New Left Review* 88 (July/August 2014); Bell, *The Radical Right*, 16.

18. Critchlow, *Phyllis Schlafly*; Chip Berlet and Matthew Lyons, *Right-Wing Populism in America: Too Close for Comfort* (New York: Guilford Press, 2000), 161, 201, 202; Bell, *The Radical Right*, 4, 24.

19. Lipset, "Three Decades"; Michael Paul Rogin, *The Intellectuals and McCarthy: The Radical Specter* (Cambridge, MA: MIT Press, 1967), 236, 238, 250; Steve Fraser, *Every Man a Speculator: A History of Wall Street in American Life* (New York: Harper Collins, 2005), 521; Donna B. Henriques, *The White Sharks of Wall Street: Thomas Mellon Evans and the Original Corporate Raiders* (New York: Scribner, 2000), 96; Peter Viereck, "The Revolt Against the Elites," in Daniel Bell, ed., *The Radical Right* (New York: Anchor Books, 1964); David Riesman and Nathan Glazer, "The Intellectuals and the Discontented Classes," in Daniel Bell, ed., *The Radical Right* (New York: Anchor Books, 1964); Oshinsky, *A Conspiracy*, 303–305; Franz Schurmann, *The Logic of World Power: An Inquiry into the Origins, Currents, and Contradictions of World Politics* (New York: Pantheon, 1974), 7, 48, 58; "Communists Penetrate Wall Street," *Commercial and Financial Chronicle*, November 6, 1947.

Chapter 5: The Vital Center Trembles

1. Geoffrey Nunberg, *Talking Right: How Conservatives Turned Liberalism into a Tax-Raising, Latte-Drinking, Sushi-Eating, Volvo-Driving, New York Times-Reading, Body-Piercing, Hollywood-Loving, Left-Wing Freak Show* (New York: PublicAffairs, 2007), 41; Donald T. Critchlow,

Phyllis Schlafly and Grassroots Conservatism: A Woman's Crusade (Princeton, NJ: Princeton University Press, 2005), 57.

2. Nunberg, *Talking Right,* 33, 64.

3. William Faulkner quoted in Bruce J. Schulman, *The Seventies: The Great Shift in American Culture, Society, and Politics* (New York: Free Press, 2001), 112; Elizabeth Tandy Shermer, *Sunbelt Capitalism: Phoenix and the Transformation of American Politics* (Philadelphia: University of Pennsylvania Press, 2013); Matthew D. Lassister, *The Silent Majority: Suburban Politics in the Sunbelt South* (Princeton, NJ: Princeton University Press, 2006); Chip Berlet and Matthew N. Lyons, *Right-Wing Populism in America: Too Close for Comfort* (New York: Guilford Press, 2000), 218.

4. Robert Britt Horowitz, *America's Right: Anti-Establishment Conservatism from Goldwater to the Tea Party* (Cambridge, MA: Polity Press, 2013), 50; Phyllis Schlafly, *A Choice Not an Echo* (Alton, IL: Pere Marquette Press, 1964).

5. Darren Dochuk, *From Bible Belt to Sunbelt: Plain-Folk Religion, Grassroots Politics, and the Rise of Evangelical Conservatism* (New York: Norton, 2011), 227, 254.

6. Jack Healy and Michael Paulson, "Vaccine Critics Turn Defensive over Measles," *New York Times,* January 30, 2015; Richard Hofstadter, *The Paranoid Style in American Politics and Other Essays* (Cambridge, MA: Harvard University Press, 1964); Hofstadter quoted in Dominic Sandbrook, *Mad as Hell: The Crisis of the 1970s and the Rise of the Populist Right* (New York: Knopf, 2011), 327; Horowitz, *America's Right,* 50; Shermer, *Sunbelt Capitalism;* Lisa McGirr, *Suburban Warriors: The Origins of the New American Right* (Princeton, NJ: Princeton University Press, 2001); Rick Perlstein, *Before the Storm: Barry Goldwater and the Unmaking of the American Consensus* (New York: Nation Books, 2001), xiv; Anthony Dimaggio, *The Rise of the Tea Party: Political Discontent and Corporate Media in the Age of Obama* (New York: Monthly Review Press, 2011), 99.

7. Schlafly, *A Choice,* 6, 31, 48, 94–95, 103–104; Carol Felsenthal, *The Sweetheart of the Silent Majority: The Biography of Phyllis Schlafly* (New York: Doubleday, 1981), 172.

8. Critchlow, *Phyllis Schlafly,* 5, 60.

9. Felsenthal, *Sweetheart,* 11, 15–16, 18; Critchlow, *Phyllis Schlafly,* 5, 27, 29.

10. "Obituary of John McCloy," *New York Times*, September 10, 1982; Critchlow, *Phyllis Schlafly*, 75, 76; Berlet and Lyons, *Right-Wing Populism*; Perlstein, *Before the Storm*, 5–10, 11, 49, 113, 115, 153.

11. Perlstein, *Before the Storm*, 17–19, 21–22, 23, 30, 124, 150.

12. Ibid., 55, 56, 79, 88, 276, 278–279, 374, 435.

13. Barry M. Goldwater, *Conscience of a Conservative* (Shepherdsville, KY: Victor, 1960); Perlstein, *Before the Storm*, 48–49, 63, 337, 352.

14. McGirr, *Suburban Warriors*, introduction and chapter 1; Dochuk, *Bible Belt*, xxi; Perlstein, *Before the Storm*, 124; Berlet and Lyons, *Right-Wing Populism*, 208, 218; David H. Bennett, *The Party of Fear: From Nativist Movements to the New American Right in American History* (Chapel Hill: University of North Carolina Press, 1988), 319; Alan F. Westin, "The John Birch Society," in Daniel Bell, ed., *The Radical Right* (New York: Anchor Books, 1964); Sandbrook, *Mad as Hell*; Perlstein, *Before the Storm*, 124, 147.

15. Stephen Francoeur, "McCarthyism and the Librarians: Intellectual Freedom Under Fire, 1947–54," MA thesis, Hunter College, 2006.

16. McGirr, *Suburban Warriors*, chapter 3.

Chapter 6: Country and Western Marxism

1. Rick Perlstein, *Before the Storm: Barry Goldwater and the Unmaking of the American Consensus* (New York: Nation Books, 2001), 419; Darren Dochuk, *From Bible Belt to Sunbelt: Plain-Folk Religion, Grassroots Politics, and the Rise of Evangelical Conservatism* (New York: Norton, 2011), 121–123.

2. Bruce J. Schulman, *The Seventies: The Great Shift in American Culture, Society, and Politics* (New York: Free Press, 2001), 200–207; Joseph E. Lowndes, *From the New Deal to the New Right: Race and the Southern Origins of Modern Conservatism* (New Haven, CT: Yale University Press, 2008), 80; George Wallace quoted in Michael Kazin, *The Populist Persuasion: An American History* (New York: Basic Books, 1995), 221; Dan T. Carter, *The Politics of Race: George Wallace, the Origins of the New Conservatism, and the Transformation of American Politics* (New York: Simon and Schuster, 1995), 315–316.

3. George Wallace quoted in Kazin, *Populist Persuasion*, 221; Alan Pell Crawford, *Thunder on the Right: The "New Right" and the Politics of Resentment* (New York: Pantheon, 1980), 1–10, 126; Chip Berlet and

Matthew Lyons, *Right-Wing Populism in America: Too Close for Comfort* (New York: Guilford Press, 2000), 218–222.

4. Eric Hobsbawm, *The Age of Extremes: A History of the World, 1914–1991* (New York: Vintage, 1996), 304; Gregory S. Wilson, "Deindustrialization, Poverty, and Federal Area Redevelopment in the United States, 1945–1965," in Jefferson Cowie and Joseph Heathcott, eds., *Beyond the Ruins: The Meaning of Deindustrialization* (Ithaca, NY: ILR Press, 2003); Dominic Sandbrook, *Mad as Hell: The Crisis of the 1970s and the Rise of the Populist Right* (New York: Knopf, 2011), 32–33.

5. Thomas Sugrue, *The Origins of the Urban Crisis: Race and Inequality in Postwar Detroit* (Princeton, NJ: Princeton University Press, 1996); Sandbrook, *Mad as Hell,* 57, 98.

6. Joshua B. Freeman, *Working Class New York: Life and Labor Since World War II* (New York: New Press, 2000), 197, 198, 212, 218, 219, 234, 235.

7. George Wallace quoted in Lowndes, *From the New Deal to the New Right,* 82; Crawford, *Thunder on the Right.*

8. Lowndes, *From the New Deal to the New Right,* 83, 92, 95, 100, 101; Perlstein, *Before the Storm,* 321, 326, 344; Sandbrook, *Mad as Hell,* 57, 58.

9. Arno Mayer, "The Lower Middle Class as a Historical Problem," *Journal of Modern History* 47 (September 1975): 409–436.

10. Andrea Mitchell, "Me and Frank," *Philly Weekly,* September 7, 2005; "The Nation: Thoughts of Chairman Rizzo," *Time,* October 24, 1977; Joseph Daughen and Peter Binzen, *The Cop Who Would Be King: The Honorable Frank Rizzo* (New York: Little, Brown, 1970); *Philadelphia Daily News,* December 9, 1988; Timothy James Lombardo, "Making Blue-Collar Conservatism: Race, Class, and Politics in Frank Rizzo's Philadelphia," PhD diss., Purdue University, 2013, 21, 175, 198, 199, 220; Italian-American League quoted in Christopher Lasch, *The True and Only Heaven: Progress and Its Critics* (New York: Norton, 1991), 475, 486.

11. Dochuk, *Bible Belt,* 99, 101; Melvin Holli, *The American Mayor: The Best and the Worst Big-City Leaders* (College Park, PA: Pennsylvania State University Press, 1999), 118.

12. Ibid.

13. Ronald P. Formisano, *Boston Against Busing: Race, Class, and Ethnicity in the 1960s and 1970s,* 2nd ed. (Chapel Hill: University of North Carolina Press, 2004), 3, 13, 14, 17; Louise Day Hicks quoted in

J. Anthony Lukas, *Common Ground: A Turbulent Decade in the Lives of Three Families* (New York: Knopf, 1985), 133. See also 136, 153–154, 356, 379–380, 433–434, 482; Schulman, *The Seventies*.

14. Formisano, *Boston Against Busing,* 39–40, 71.

15. Lukas, *Common Ground,* 316.

16. Lukas, *Common Ground,* 259, 452–453; Formisano, *Boston Against Busing,* 2, 15, 17, 50–57, 178, 180, 183.

17. Matthew D. Lassiter, *The Silent Majority: Suburban Politics in the Sunbelt South* (Princeton, NJ: Princeton University Press, 2006), 18, 31nL; George Wallace quoted in Lowndes, *From the New Deal to the New Right,* 95; Formisano, *Boston Against Busing,* 194; Sandbrook, *Mad as Hell,* 57–58.

18. Lukas quoted in Formisano, *Boston Against Busing,* 176.

19. Frances Fox Piven, "How We Once Came to Fight a War on Poverty," *New Labor Forum* 23 (Fall 2014): 20–25; Jim Sleeper, *The Closest of Strangers: Liberalism and the Politics of Race in New York* (New York: Norton, 1990), 62, 147–148.

20. Khruschev Visits the United States, September, 1959, Department of State, Conference Files: Lot 64 D560 CF 1472.

21. Richard D. Kahlenberg, *Tough Liberal: Albert Shanker and the Battles over Schools, Unions, Race, and Democracy* (New York: Columbia University Press, 2007), 67, 72, 83, 86, 116.

22. Richard Harvey Brown, *Culture, Capitalism, and Democracy in the New America* (New Haven, CT: Yale University Press, 2005), 26, 96; Richard Parker, *The Myth of the Middle Class* (New York: Liveright, 1972), 43, 201–202; Michael Novak, *The Rise of the Unmeltable Ethnics: Politics and Culture in the Seventies* (New York: Macmillan, 1972), 7, 16, 142–143; David Brooks, "One Nation, Slightly Divisible," *The Atlantic* (December 2001); Lasch, *True and Only Heaven,* 439, 460.

23. Adolph Reed, "The Strange Career of the Voting Rights Act: Selma in Fact and Fiction," *New Labor Forum* 24 (Spring 2015): 32–41; Wilson, "Deindustrialization, Poverty, and Federal Area Redevelopment"; Donald Critchlow, *Phyllis Schlafly and Grassroots Conservatism: A Woman's Crusade* (Princeton, NJ: Princeton University Press, 2005), 203; Parker, *Myth of the Middle Class,* 201–202, 431.

24. Elizabeth Tandy Shermer, "Indentured Studenthood: The Higher Education Act and the Burden of Student Debt," *New Labor Forum* 24 (Fall 2015); Brown, *Culture, Capitalism, and Democracy,* 26.

25. Freeman, *Working Class New York*, 212, 254; Vincent J. Cannato, *The Ungovernable City: John Lindsay and His Struggle to Save New York* (New York: Basic Books, 2002), 391–392, 399; Thomas Byrne Edsall with Mary D. Edsall, *Chain Reaction: The Impact of Race, Rights, and Taxes on American Politics* (New York: Norton, 1991), 11.

26. Parker, *Myth of the Middle Class*, 12, 43; Brown, *Culture, Capitalism, and Democracy*.

27. Sandbrook, *Mad as Hell*, 109–110; *Newsweek* cited in Sandbrook, *Mad as Hell*, 109–110; Edsall and Edsall, *Chain Reaction*; Lasch, *True and Only Heaven*, 439; Perry Anderson, *The Origins of Postmodernity* (London: Verso, 1998), 62–63; Lukas, *Common Ground*, 506.

28. Jefferson Cowie, *Stayin' Alive: The 1970s and the Last Days of the Working Class* (New York: New Press, 2010), chapters 2, 3, and 6; Parker, *Myth of the Middle Class*, 142–143.

29. Peter Schrag, *The Decline of the WASP* (New York: Simon and Schuster, 1970), 139–140, 166; Lasch, *True and Only Heaven*, 506.

Chapter 7: The Bridge over Troubled Waters

1. Mike Royko quoted in Jefferson Cowie, *Stayin' Alive: The 1970s and the Last Days of the Working Class* (New York: New Press, 2010), 162.

2. Donald T. Critchlow, *Phyllis Schlafly and Grassroots Conservatism: A Woman's Crusade* (Princeton, NJ: Princeton University Press, 2005), 203.

3. Stephen Ambrose, *Nixon*, vol. 1: *The Education of a Politician, 1913–1962* (New York: Simon and Schuster, 1988).

4. Joseph E. Lowndes, *From the New Deal to the New Right: Race and the Southern Origins of Modern Conservatism* (New Haven, CT: Yale University Press, 2008); Matthew D. Lassiter, *The Silent Majority: Suburban Politics in the Sunbelt South* (Princeton, NJ: Princeton University Press, 2006); Daniel Rodgers, *Age of Fracture* (Cambridge, MA: Harvard University Press, 2011), 127.

5. Bruce J. Schulman, *The Seventies: The Great Shift in American Culture, Society, and Politics* (New York: Free Press, 2001), 36–38; Cowie, *Stayin' Alive*, chapter 3.

6. Robert C. Christopher, *Crashing the Gates: The De-Wasping of America's Power Elite* (New York: Simon and Schuster, 1989), 111–112; Schulman, *The Seventies;* Darren Dochuk, *From Bible Belt to Sunbelt:*

Plain-Folk Religion, Grassroots Politics, and the Rise of Evangelical Conservatism (New York: Norton, 2011), 337.

7. Richard Nixon quoted in Robert Collins, *More: The Politics of Economic Growth in Postwar America* (New York: Oxford University Press, 2000), 123; "Obituary of Charles Percy," *New York Times*, September 17, 2011; "Obituary of Elliot Richardson," *New York Times*, January 1, 2008.

8. Christopher Lasch, *The True and Only Heaven: Progress and Its Critics* (New York: Norton, 1991), 510–515; Rodgers, *Age of Fracture*, 83–84; Collins, *More*, 125–130; Alan Crawford, *Thunder on the Right: The "New Right" and the Politics of Resentment* (New York: Pantheon, 1980), 168; Dominic Sandbrook, *Mad as Hell: The Crisis of the 1970s and the Rise of the Populist Right* (New York: Knopf, 2011), 58; Schulman, *The Seventies*, 200–207; "Obituary of Spiro Agnew," *New York Times*, September 18, 1996; George Wallace quoted in Crawford, *Thunder on the Right*, 82, and see also 1–10.

9. "Agnew Blasts Moratorium Day as 'Senseless,'" *Chicago Tribune*, October 29, 1969; Sandbrook, *Mad as Hell*, 57–58; Peter Schrag, *The Decline of the WASP* (New York: Simon and Schuster, 1970), 166, 181–182.

10. Schulman, *The Seventies*, 134, 138; Thomas Byrne Edsall with Mary D. Edsall, *Chain Reaction: The Impact of Race, Rights, and Taxes in American Politics* (New York: Norton, 1990), 10, 23; Lasch, *True and Only Heaven*, 479, 481; Collins, *More*, 155, 159; Eric Hobsbawm, *The Age of Extremes: A History of the World, 1914–1992* (New York: Vintage, 1996), 304, 307; Dale Maharidge, *Journey to Nowhere: The Saga of the New Underclass* (New York: Doubleday, 1985), 22, 34–35; Michael Perleman, "Some Economics of Class," in Michael D. Yates, ed., *More Unequal: Aspects of Class in the United States* (New York: Monthly Review Press, 2007); Lowndes, *From the New Deal to the New Right*, 137; Cowie, *Stayin' Alive*, chapter 5; John Russo and Sherry Lee Linkon, "The Social Costs of De-Industrialization," Center of Working Class Studies, 2008; Robert Brenner, "The Political Economy of Rank and File Rebellion," in Aaron Brenner, Robert Brenner, and Cal Winslow, eds., *Rebel Rank and File: Labor Militancy and Revolt from Below* (New York: Verso, 2010).

11. Edsall and Edsall, *Chain Reaction*, 10–11.

12. Cowie, *Stayin' Alive*, chapter 3; Sandbrook, *Mad as Hell*, 136–137, 331; William Kornblum, *Blue Collar Community* (Chicago, IL: University of Chicago Press, 1974), 209; Roger Shattuck, "The Reddening of

America," *The New York Review of Books,* March 30, 1989; William Deresiewicz, "The Dispossessed," *American Scholar* 75 (Winter 2006); Arno Mayer, "The Lower Middle Class as a Historical Problem," *Journal of Modern History* 47 (September 1975): 409–436.

13. Schulman, *The Seventies,* 114, 120; Doug Marlette, *Faux Bubba: Bill and Hillary Go to Washington* (New York: Times Books, 1993).

14. Lowndes, *From the New Deal to the New Right,* 137; Cowie, *Stayin' Alive,* 114, 122; Carol Felsenthal, "New Right: Strong and Victorious," *Gadsden Times,* December 7–11, 1980; Bruce Webber, "Obituary of Paul Weyrich," *New York Times,* December 12, 2008; Ian Williams, "Burying Conservatism," *The Guardian,* December 19, 2008; David Granin, "Robespierre of the Right," *New Republic,* October 27, 1997; David H. Bennett, *The Party of Fear: From Nativist Movements to the New Right in American History* (Chapel Hill: University of North Carolina Press, 1988), 398–399; Jean Hardisty, *Mobilizing Resentment: Conservative Resurgence from the John Birch Society to the Promise Keepers* (Boston: Beacon Press, 1999), 44.

15. Schulman, *The Seventies,* 37–39; Cowie, *Stayin' Alive,* 134, chapters 4 and 5; Marlette, "Faux Bubba."

16. Damien Cave and Michael Luo, "More of the Rich Run as Populist Outsiders," *New York Times,* July 23, 2010; Jonathan Chait, *The Big Con: The True Story of How Washington Got Hoodwinked and Hijacked by Crackpot Economics* (Boston: Houghton Mifflin, 2008), 120–121, 138.

17. Christopher, *Crashing the Gates,* 52, 55, 111–112.

Chapter 8: The Holy Family

1. Dominic Sandbrook, *Mad as Hell: The Crisis of the 1970s and the Rise of the Populist Right* (New York: Knopf, 2011), 332; William Rusher, Paul Weyrich, and Paul Laxalt quoted in Alan Pell Crawford, *Thunder on the Right: The "New Right" and the Politics of Resentment* (New York: Pantheon, 1980), 168, 213–214, 218–219.

2. Reagan quoted in Darren Dochuk, *From Bible Belt to Sunbelt: Plain-Folk Religion, Grassroots Politics, and the Rise of Evangelical Conservatism* (New York: Norton, 2011), 362; Chip Berlet and Matthew Lyons, *Right-Wing Populism in America: Too Close for Comfort* (New York: Guilford Press, 2000), 201, 202, 222; Billy Graham quoted in Dochuk, *Bible Belt,* 140.

3. Dochuk, *Bible Belt,* 6–13, 52–53, 121–123; Elizabeth Tandy Shermer, *Sunbelt Capitalism: Phoenix and the Transformation of American Politics* (Philadelphia: University of Pennsylvania Press, 2013), 306–307.

4. Dochuk, *Bible Belt,* 119, 130, 202, 268.

5. *The Right Woman* quoted in Crawford, *Thunder on the Right,* 147; Berlet and Lyons, *Right-Wing Populism,* 209–210.

6. Dan Gilgoff, *The Jesus Machine: How James Dobson, Focus on the Family, and Evangelical America Are Winning the Culture War* (New York: St. Martin's Press, 2007), 72; Berlet and Lyons, *Right-Wing Populism,* 209–210; Daniel F. Rodgers, *Age of Fracture* (Cambridge, MA: Harvard University Press, 2011), 169, 171.

7. Bruce J. Schulman, *The Seventies: The Great Shift in American Culture, Society, and Politics* (New York: Free Press, 2001), 92–93; Jefferson Cowie, *Stayin' Alive: The 1970s and the Last Days of the Working Class* (New York: New Press, 2010), 248; Paul Boyer, *When Time Shall Be No More: Prophecy Belief in Modern America Culture* (Cambridge, MA: Harvard University Press, 1992), 3–5; Richard Harvey Brown, *Culture, Capitalism, and Democracy in the New America* (New Haven, CT: Yale University Press, 2005), 127; Berlet and Lyons, *Right-Wing Populism,* 240; Gilgoff, *Jesus Machine,* 79, 95; Michael Lienesch, *Redeeming America: Piety and Politics in the New Christian Right* (Chapel Hill: University of North Carolina Press, 1993), 11.

8. Rodgers, *Age of Fracture,* 169; Brown, *Culture, Capitalism, and Democracy,* 106, 134; Lienesch, *Redeeming America,* 169.

9. Linda Kintz, *Between Jesus and the Market: The Emotions That Matter in Right-Wing America* (Durham, NC: Duke University Press, 1997), chapter 5; Boyer, *When Time Shall Be No More,* 254–255, 263, 265–266; Gilgoff, *Jesus Machine,* 220; Lienesch, *Redeeming America,* 88–93.

10. Christopher Lasch, *The True and Only Heaven: Progress and Its Critics* (New York: Norton, 1991), 455–460; Michael Novak, *The Rise of the Unmeltable Ethnics: Politics and Culture in the Seventies* (New York: Macmillan, 1972), 7, 16, 142–143; David Brooks, "One Nation, Slightly Divisible," *The Atlantic,* December 2001; Patrick Buchanan quoted in Gilgoff, *Jesus Machine,* 97.

11. Thomas Byrne Edsall with Mary D. Edsall, *Chain Reaction: The Impact of Race, Rights, and Taxes on American Politics* (New York: Norton,

1991), 11; Chris Lehmann, *Rich People Things* (New York: OR Books, 2010), 90 and the *New York Times* quoted 29–30; Rodgers, *Age of Fracture,* 169; Ken Auletta, "The Underclass," *The New Yorker,* November 16, 1987; Richard Sennett, *The Corrosion of Character: The Personal Consequences of Work in the New Capitalism* (New York: Norton, 1998); Lienesch, *Redeeming America,* 110; Boyer, *When Time Shall Be No More,* 254–255; Brown, *Culture, Capitalism, and Democracy.*

12. Lasch, *True and Only Heaven;* Rodgers, *Age of Fracture,* 169, 171; Kintz, *Between Jesus and the Market,* chapter 5; Cowie, *Stayin' Alive,* 249; Richard Parker, *The Myth of the Middle Class* (New York: Liveright, 1972), 142–143; Mirra Komarovsky, *Blue Collar Marriage* (New York: Vintage, 1967), 331, 334–335, 340; Brown, *Culture, Capitalism, and Democracy,* 210; David Leonhardt, "The North-South Divide on Two Parent Families," *New York Times,* June 11, 2015, 13.

13. Amber Hollibaugh and Margaret Weiss, "Queer Precarity and the Myth of Gay Affluence," *New Labor Forum* 24 (Fall 2015): 18–27; Berlet and Lyons, *Right-Wing Populism,* 236; Terry Eagleton, *The Illusions of Postmodernity* (London: Verso, 1996), 70.

14. Joseph E. Lowndes, *From the New Deal to the New Right: Race and the Southern Origins of Modern Conservatism* (New Haven, CT: Yale University Press, 2008), 148; Cowie, *Stayin' Alive,* 176–178, and chapter 7; Komarovsky, *Blue Collar Marriage,* 334–335; E. E. LeMasters, *Blue Collar Aristocrats: Lifestyles at a Working-Class Tavern* (Madison: University of Wisconsin Press, 1975), 18–20.

15. Schulman, *The Seventies,* 161, 182; Rodgers, *Age of Fracture,* 171; Brown, *Culture, Capitalism, and Democracy,* 32.

16. Berlet and Lyons, *Right-Wing Populism,* 231, 236; Terry Eagleton, *Illusions,* 70; Joshua B. Freeman, *Working Class New York: Life and Labor Since World War II* (New York: New Press, 2000), 246; Edsall and Edsall, *Chain Reaction,* 10; Stephen Pimpare, "Why No Fire This Time: From the Mass Strike to No Strike," *New Labor Forum* 20 (2011): 17–25; Cowie, *Stayin' Alive,* 249.

17. Carol Felsenthal, *The Sweetheart of the Silent Majority: The Biography of Phyllis Schlafly* (New York: Doubleday, 1981), xiv, xviii, 11, 18, 19, 49, 52–53; Jean Hardisty, *Mobilizing Resentment: Conservative Resurgence from the John Birch Society to the Promise Keepers* (Boston, MA: Beacon Press, 1999), 73; Donald T. Critchlow, *Phyllis Schlafly and Grassroots Conservatism: A Woman's Crusade* (Princeton, NJ: Princeton University Press, 200), 203.

18. Critchlow, *Phyllis Schlafly*, 60, 218, 221, 225, 232; Elizabeth Kolbert, "Firebrand: Phyllis Schlafly and the Conservative Revolution," *The New Yorker*, November 7, 2005, 134.

19. Dochuk, *Bible Belt*, 383; Felsenthal, *Sweetheart*, 73, 112, 159, 277; Critchlow, *Phyllis Schlafly*, 218, 220–221; Michael Sean Winters, *Left at the Altar: How the Democrats Lost the Catholics and How the Catholics Can Save the Democrats* (New York: Basic Books, 2008), 124–125.

Chapter 9: God, Capitalism, and the Tea Party

1. Trip Gabriel, "Rick Santorum Announces Presidential Bid and New Focus on Middle Class," *New York Times*, May 28, 2015.

2. Jonathan Tilove, "Populist Opposites: On Bernie Sanders and Ted Cruz," *Austin Statesman*, May 4, 2015; Elizabeth Williamson, "Ted Cruz Interview: On Obama, the GOP, and Big Business," *Wall Street Journal*, May 20, 2012.

3. Elizabeth Tandy Shermer, *Sunbelt Capitalism: Phoenix and the Transformation of American Politics* (Philadelphia: University of Pennsylvania Press, 2013), 332–333.

4. Thomas Frank, *Pity the Billionaire: The Hard-Times Swindle and the Unlikely Comeback of the Right* (New York: Metropolitan Books, 2012), chapter 6; Jackie Calmes, "Ex-Im Bank Pits Right vs. Far Right," *New York Times*, June 18, 2015; Neil Irwin, "Crony Capitalism, a Fact of Modern Capitalism," *New York Times*, June 19, 2014.

5. Jeremy W. Peters, "After Obama's Immigration Action, a Blast of Energy for the Tea Party," *New York Times*, November 25, 2014; Tilove, "Populist Opposites."

6. Steve Fraser, *Every Man a Speculator: A History of Wall Street in American Life* (New York: Harper Collins, 2005), 538–539; Reagan quoted in Bruce J. Schulman, *The Seventies: The Great Shift in American Culture, Society, and Politics* (New York: Free Press, 2001), 249; Darren Dochuk, *From Bible Belt to Sunbelt: Plain-Folk Religion, Grassroots Politics, and the Rise of Evangelical Conservatism* (New York: Norton, 2011), 268, 391–392.

7. Shermer, *Sunbelt Capitalism*; Schulman, *The Seventies*; F. Bechhofer and B. Elliott, "The Petite Bourgeoisie in Late Capitalism," *Annual Review of Sociology* 11 (1985): 181–207.

8. Bechhofer and Elliott, "The Petite Bourgeoisie"; Scott Shane, "Why Small Business Owners Trust the Tea Party," *The American*, November 17,

2010; Judson Phillips, "The Party of Killing Small Business," *Tea Party Nation Forum,* May 9, 2011; Small Business Administration, "Report 3, The Facts About Small Business, 1999," and "The State of Small Business: A Report of the President, 1997"; Small Business Administration, "Report on Annual Procurement Preferences: Fiscal Year 1999," Office of Government Contracting, April, 4, 2000; David Harvey, *The Conditions of Postmodernity: An Enquiry into the Origins of Cultural Change* (Cambridge, MA: Blackwell, 1990), 192, 194; Richard Parker, *The Myth of the Middle Class* (New York: Liveright, 1972), 43, 201–202; Barry C. Lynn, "Killing the Competition," *Harper's* (February 2012).

9. James Sorowiecki, "Big Is Beautiful," *The New Yorker,* October 31, 2011; Jeffrey R. Cornwall, "Small Business Turns to the Tea Party," *Christian Science Monitor,* June 17, 2010; John McCormick and Lisa Lerer, "Why Business Doesn't Trust the Tea Party," *Bloomberg Business Week,* October 13, 2010; Shane, "Why Small Business Owners Trust the Tea Party"; Mark Naison, "Small Business Nation: Understanding the Social Base of Tea Party America," *NewBlackMan (in Exile),* April 11, 2011; Michael Lemm, "Tea Party Tax Protests . . . The Small Business Person Perspective," Small Business Resources Café, April 4, 2009; Linda Kintz, *Between Jesus and the Market: The Emotions That Matter in Right-Wing America* (Durham, NC: Duke University Press, 1997), chapter 6.

10. Newt Gingrich quoted in Chris Lehmann, "How We Learned to Stop Worrying and Love the Robber Barons," *Mother Jones,* October 18, 2010.

11. Kevin Phillips, *Bad Money: Reckless Finance, Failed Politics, and the Global Crisis of American Capitalism* (New York: Viking, 2008), 92–93; Haynes Johnson, *Sleepwalking Through History: America in the Reagan Years* (New York: Norton, 1991), chapter 16; Richard Harvey Brown, *Culture, Capitalism, and Democracy in the New America* (New Haven, CT: Yale University Press, 2005), 150; Kintz, *Between Jesus and the Market,* 196–197; Michael Lienesch, *Redeeming America: Piety and Politics in the New Christian Right* (Chapel Hill: University of North Carolina Press, 1993), 11, 94, 113.

12. Steve Eder and Michael Barbero, "Marc Rubio's Career Bedeviled by Financial Struggles," *New York Times,* June 9, 2015; Geoffrey Nunberg, *Talking Right: How Conservatives Turned Liberalism into a Tax-Raising, Latte-Drinking, Sushi-Eating, Volvo-Driving, New York Times-Reading, Body-Piercing, Hollywood-Loving, Left-Wing Freak Show* (New York:

PublicAffairs, 2007), 64, 82; Paul M. Weyrich, "Letter to Conservatives," February 16, 1999, https://www.nationalcenter.org/Weyrich299.html; Paul M. Weyrich, "The Next Conservative Economics," World Magazine August 5, 2005, http://www.worldmag.com/2005/08/the_next_conservative _economics; Jerry Falwell quoted in Lienesch, *Redeeming America*, 169.

13. Brown, *Culture, Capitalism, and Democracy.*

14. Johnson, *Sleepwalking*, chapter 16; ; Pat Robertson quoted in David Graeber, *Debt: The First 5,000 Years* (Brooklyn: Melville House, 2011), 376; Jerry Falwell quoted in Dominic Sandbrook, *Mad as Hell: The Crisis of the 1970s and the Rise of the Populist Right* (New York: Knopf, 2011), 355; Falwell quoted in Dan Gilgoff, *The Jesus Machine: How James Dobson, Focus on the Family, and Evangelical America Are Winning the Culture War* (New York: St. Martin's Press, 2008), 2; Lienesch, *Redeeming America*, 11, 94.

15. Dochuk, *Bible Belt*, 16, 52–53, 120–122, 169, 189.

16. Carol Felsenthal, *The Sweetheart of the Silent Majority: The Biography of Phyllis Schlafly* (New York: Doubleday, 1981), 18, 19, 73; Donald T. Critchlow, *Phyllis Schlafly and Grassroots Conservatism: A Woman's Crusade* (Princeton, NJ: Princeton University Press, 2005), 218.

17. Schulman, *The Seventies*, 212; Thomas Byrne Edsall with Mary D. Edsall, *Chain Reaction: The Impact of Race, Rights, and Taxes on American Politics* (New York: Norton, 1991), 1–4; Howard Jarvis quoted in Sandbrook, *Mad as Hell*, 283.

18. Chris Ladd, "How Fundamentalism and Libertarianism Buried the Hatchet," *Houston Chronicle*, October 24, 2011; Dochuk, *Bible Belt*, 375–379, 385; David H. Bennett, *The Party of Fear: From Nativist Movements to the New Right in American History* (Chapel Hill: University of North Carolina Press, 1988), 398–399; Jonathan Martin, "After Primary Upset, G.O.P. Fears Infighting Will Take a Toll," *New York Times*, June 12, 2014; Jennifer Steinhauer, "Once Snubbed, David Brat Turns Tables," *New York Times*, June 12, 2014; Trip Gabriel, "Cantor Forgot Virginia Roots, Voters Contend," *New York Times*, June 12, 2014; Trip Gabriel and Richard Pérez-Peña, "Campus Colleagues, Basketball Teammates, and Now, Political Rivals," *New York Times*, June 13, 2014.

19. Frank, *Pity the Billionaire*, 93–95, 97; Anthony Dimaggio, *The Rise of the Tea Party: Political Discontent and the Corporate Media in the Age of Obama* (New York: Monthly Review Press, 2011); Vanessa Williamson, Theda Skocpol, and John Coggin, "The Tea Party and the

Remaking of Republican Conservatism," *Perspectives on Politics* 9 (March 2011): 25–43.

20. Stanley Deetz, *Democracy in an Age of Corporate Colonization: Developments in Communication and the Politics of Everyday Life* (Albany: State University of New York Press, 1992), 2–5.

Chapter 10: The Dynasts

1. Eric Lichtblau and Alexandra Stevenson, "Behind Cruz Campaign's Striking Start, a Donor of Few Words," *New York Times*, April 4, 2015.

2. Schumpeter quoted in Corey Robin, "Nietzsche's Marginal Children: On Friedrich Hayek," *The Nation*, May 27, 2013.

3. Geoffrey Ingham, *Capitalism: With a New Postscript on the Financial Crisis and Its Aftermath* (London: Polity Press, 2009).

4. Geoffrey Jones and Mary B. Rose, "Family Capitalism," *Business History* 35 (1993): 1–16; Harold James, "Family Values or Crony Capitalism," *Capitalism and Society* 3 (2008).

5. Maggie Haberman and Matt Flegenheimer, "Donald Trump Adds Something Unexpected to His Campaign," *New York Times*, September 16, 2015.

6. *The Economist*, March 17, 2007; "Rupert Murdoch: A Man, A Plan," *The Economist*, August 28, 2003.

7. Connie Bruck, "The Brass Ring: A Multimillionaire's Relentless Quest for Global Influence," *The New Yorker*, June 3, 2008; Robert Frank, "Vegas Tycoon: 'So I Lost $25 Billion'," *Wall Street Journal*, November 22, 2010; "Sheldon Adelson," Wikipedia, accessed November 3, 2015, https://en.wikipedia.org/wiki/Sheldon_Adelson.

8. Jane Mayer, "Covert Operations: The Billionaire Brothers Who Are Waging a War Against Obama," *The New Yorker*, August 3, 2010; Carl Hulse, "In Wichita, Koch Influence Is Revered and Reviled," *New York Times*, June 17, 2014; Fred Koch, "A Businessman Looks at Communism," cited by Peter Drier, *Huffington Post*, August 12, 2013.

9. Evan Sparks, "J. Howard Pew," Philanthropy Roundtable, accessed November 3, 2015, http://www.philanthropyroundtable.org/almanac/hall_of_fame/j._howard_pew.

10. Daniel Bice, Bill Glauber, and Ben Poston, "From Local Roots, Bradley Foundation Builds Conservative Empire," *Milwaukee Journal*

Sentinel, November 19, 2011; Laurie Arendt, "Our Founding Families," GMToday.com, October 4, 2009.

11. Darren Dochuk, *From Bible Belt to Sunbelt: Plain-Folk Religion, Grassroots Politics, and the Rise of Evangelical Conservatism* (New York: Norton, 2011), 67–73.

12. Yahya Hussain, "Capital Isn't Scarce, Vision Is—Sam Walton," *The Financial Daily,* September 29, 2008; Nelson Lichtenstein, *The Retail Revolution: How Wal-Mart Created a Brave New World of Business* (New York: Metropolitan Books, 2010); Bethany Moreton, *To Serve God and Wal-Mart: The Making of Christian Free Enterprise* (Cambridge, MA: Harvard University Press, 2010); Mike Schuster, "Religious CEOs: Wal-Mart Founder, Sam Walton," Minyanville, May 19, 2010.

13. Valerie Strauss, "Why Hedge Funds Love Charter Schools," *Washington Post,* June 4, 2014; Diane Ravitch, "Bill Moyers Explains Why Hedge Fund Managers Love Charters," Diane Ravitch's blog, May 21, 2014.

Conclusion: The Strange Career of Limousine Liberalism

1. CNBC quoted in Chris Lehmann, "How We Learned to Stop Worrying and Love the Robber Barons," *Mother Jones,* October 18, 2010.

Index

Wood, Leonard, 38
Wood, Robert E., 101, 113–114
Wood River Oil and Refining
    Company, 119–120
workers, insurgencies erupting
    among, 60
    See also labor movement
working class stereotype, 171
"working people" category, elasticity
    of, 137
Works Progress Administration, 75
World Bank, 81, 186
World War I, 33, 81, 82, 83, 84,
    85, 97

World War II, 78, 80, 81, 82, 83, 84,
    85, 91, 99, 113, 115, 117, 132,
    151, 180, 233

Yorty, Sam, 139, 180
Young, John, 112
Young, Robert, 101
Young, Whitney, 17
Young Republicans, 3
Youngstown Sheet and Tube, 120, 169

Zinke, Ryan, 23
Zuckerberg, Mark, 202–203, 223,
    236, 237

Credit: Jill Andresky Fraser

Steve Fraser is the author of *The Age of Acquiescence, Every Man a Speculator, Wall Street,* and *Labor Will Rule,* which won the Philip Taft Award for the best book in labor history. He also is the co-editor of *The Rise and Fall of the New Deal Order, 1930–1980,* and *Ruling America: A History of Wealth and Power in a Democracy.* His work has appeared in the *Los Angeles Times,* the *New York Times, The Nation, The American Prospect, Raritan,* and the *London Review of Books.* He has written for the website tomdispatch.com, and his work has appeared on the Huffington Post, Salon, Truthout, and Alternet, among others. He lives in New York City.